Political Thoughts and Polemics

Political Thoughts
and Polemics

BERNARD CRICK

EDINBURGH UNIVERSITY PRESS

© Bernard Crick 1990

Edinburgh University Press
22 George Square, Edinburgh

Set in Itek Times Roman
by Jetset Typesetters, Aberdeen, and
printed in Great Britain by
Redwood Burn Limited, ,
Trowbridge, Wilts

British Library Cataloguing
   in Publication Data
Crick, Bernard, *1929–*
   Political thoughts and polemics.
   1. Great Britain. Politics
   I. Title
   320.941

ISBN 0 7486 0120 1
      0 7486 0145 7 pbk

Contents

Preface

I enjoy writing essays more than books, for reasons I explained in the Preface to *Essays on Politics and Literature* (Edinburgh University Press, 1989), a companion volume to this. Since politics, both as thinking about it and practising it, is an activity (as Hannah Arendt's writings taught me), it follows that an appropriate form of expression to portray such an activity must allow a writer to be flexible, speculative as well as informative, while sceptical about ever being definitive or able to settle an argument conclusively.

Students of politics need to find out and to set down objectively and honestly the facts of a case, and in the past I've done my share of that; but the essayist is more interested in what cases we should take up. Essays may use and exploit monographs but they are not essentially concerned (if there are three logical divisions) with *what is the case* but rather with *what is thought to be the case* and with *what ought to be the case.* Essays can range from amusing gossip, through wise analysis and learned speculation to topical polemic; but they always invite the reader's reaction. The object is to arouse, stimulate and provoke, neither to convert nor to saturate with pontifical fact. Learned essays are somewhat out of fashion, alas. A glance at the pages of the *English Historical Review* or of *The British Journal of Political Science* will show one that either research or close textual analysis is king. The answer to all important human problems (of which faint glimmers occasionally penetrate such dark pages) is apparently more research (if funded from outside). So thinking has to take place elsewhere and opportunistically, on any occasion one can find or make; as well as printed books there are seminars, book reviews, letters to the press, informal discussions, conversations, broadcasting and journalism. Of course, if one wishes to be serious and to heard outside the walls, one really must try not to be boring.

In my last years in service at Birkbeck College, a marvellous place because it is all part-time mature students, merry as well as earnest and who can mix learning with experience, I renamed my Political

Philosophy seminar 'Political Speculation'. Most accepted the invitation, though a few felt defrauded when expected to do most of the thinking themselves, and so sat back and waited to be taught what to think, like Mr. Kenneth Baker's ideal sixth form employment fodder; or they asked for their money back. Sometimes my nerve did crack if faced with prolonged loud silence. But as a student just after the War at University College London I had attended, if somewhat accidentally, Freddie Ayer's seminar. I was supposed to be studying Economics, but how could Pamela possibly have a lover who was not a philosopher? "What *is* philosophy?" you ask, I find that a very odd question. Meaningless, surely? Philosophy is, well philosophy is philosophising.' His philosophising was a total activity but had no preconceived conclusions, and one discovered the rules only by playing it. To my mind both Politics and politics are like that. It is no accident that Montaigne, the sceptical and discursive father of the essay, was a card-carrying '*Politique*'. Political thinkers are committed to relevance but seldom at their best when offering confident or unqualified answers.

Nonetheless there are essays and essays; so I have divided these into 'Thoughts' (longer – mostly learned) and 'Polemics' (shorter –mostly popular). In 'Thoughts' I have republished most of my longer pieces since my *Political Theory and Practice* collection (Allen Lane, the Penguin Press, 1973) and in 'Polemics' a small selection of shorter pieces from weeklies or newspapers. But the distinction between thoughts and polemics is not absolute. If most of 'Thoughts' are learned or academic, they are all written to be accessible to colleagues in other disciplines or to graduates who continue to think after release from the three or four year term. (Note that the University of Buckingham offers cut rates.) A 'university' should be a creative sharing not a departmentalisation of learning and thinking. And I hope that none of my 'Polemics' are without thought. I more often, I admit, polemicize against something than for something, or rather, if I am not lacking in positive judgements, I think it right to be more confident in negative judgements than in positive ones. 'The Character of a Moderate (Socialist)' could begin 'Polemics' rather than end 'Thoughts'. And 'An Englishman Considers His Passport', written for an Irish audience, is in some manner a popular version of the two heavy pieces on sovereignty and on consent in relation to the Northern Ireland question, and so could be among the 'Polemics', but for its length.

The 'Polemics' are all, in fact, journalism, which I not merely enjoy but hold the private view that journalism is too important to be left to journalists. All honour to those few columnists in British newspapers who regularly intend and succeed in making their readers think, rather than simply informing or amusing; but they are, indeed, a small band with the air among themselves of making, like Leonidas's hoplites or the Seven Samurai, an heroic, professional, gay and desperate last stand against barbarians. Most of these 'Polemics' came from a fortnightly column I used to write in *The Scotsman* (in the space once filled by my late friend, John Mackintosh, MP). I confess to enjoying this writing more than anything I have done since the *In Defence of Politics* of over twenty-five years ago. (For an actor must have a sense of audience to give of his best, which is difficult with books that sell to a silent and scattered three thousand; and if one can't act, one shouldn't teach.) I would choose some topical theme specifically as a peg on which to hang a lay sermon or moral reflection turning on the definition, or alternative contested definitions, of some abstract concept of political or moral philosophy. Fortunately the editor of the time failed either to notice this didactic sub-text or to deconstruct it. He dismissed me not, as far as I know, for trying to force his readers to think (there is, after all, a Scottish tradition of commonsense philosophy) but simply for refusing to write during the strike of *The Scotsman* journalists in 1986. To be given the Order of the Boot by the Thompson Organization and its minions is, in some ways, an honour. But I was saddened by the NUJ journalists who passionately asked me to join them but who then forgot about me when they went back defeated but on a non-recrimination agreement. But it was their livelihood, only my pocket-money, pleasure and pulpit. And yet somehow I don't think that free politics is possible, as both Aristotle and Kant argued, without friendship and mutual trust.

In other words, I take the popularisation of political thinking seriously. There is something paradoxical and self-defeating when the reflective, analytical and speculative tradition of Western political thought avoids public engagement and shelters too exclusively amid the internalised dialogues of the ivory tower. The philistines might not have got into the gates of the universities if some of us had sallied out more often and counter-attacked. Something happens to men when they become Vice-Chancellors (perhaps we should try some women; some women now show more civic courage). I've nothing against the market place in its place, except when it tries to occupy everywhere.

I should explain that throughout I have made no attempt at updating. In essays context must remain part of the meaning, for better or for worse; in any case, the point of each of the 'Polemics' is perennial even when the pegs begin to crumble like memory. And I should add that the bibliography of my writings on socialism is, indeed, confusing since I've kept on, because of the polemical element in them, redoing them in different forms. The one reprinted here, 'The Character of a Moderate (Socialist)', was the main source of what then became 'A Footnote to Rally Fellow Socialists', the appendix to the second Penguin edition in 1983 of my *In Defence of Politics*. This grew into *Socialist Values and Time* (Fabian Tract 495), then shrank into the last chapter of my *Socialism* (Open University Press, 1987). And some of the ideas were finally recycled in a pamphlet I wrote with David Blunkett, MP, *Labour's Aims and Values: An Unofficial Statement* (Spokesman Press, 1988). This was an hopeless premptive strike against the almost inevitable wind, waffle, evasiveness, banality, historical ignorance and sheer thoughtlessness of the then impending official version. (I speak only for myself, of course). Also I apologise that in some of the essays not merely the same critique of sovereignty recurs but some of the same references; that's the way of essays. Oliver Wendell Holmes Jnr. once wrote to Harold Laski that he believed it a waste of a good phrase to use it only once. And besides, I'm obsessed with the issue: 'sovereignty' is the perfect example of an abstract and contentious concept which has an almost tyrannical despotism over politicians who pride themselves on not having an abstract thought in their heads, I mean who believe that it is possible and desirable to be (as Michael Oakeshott once mocked) 'purely practical'.

Lastly I state my great pleasure at now being published by the Edinburgh University Press, especially since Scotland has, since 1984, become both my adopted home, country even, and my main stimulant for now trying to concentrate my studies on the relations of the nations of these islands. Pluralism to me is not just a political theory but a cultural value. The low standard of political debate at Westminster, considering the importance of the issues, the lack of any reasoning in political argument other than appeal to self-interest or assertion of 'sincerity', all this has something to do at least (as I try to explain) with the declining understanding by English politicians of the nature of the United Kingdom and its different nations. There is suddenly a remarkable revival of constitutional debate; but it nearly all (like the Charter 88 movement and the Campaign for a Scottish Assembly) comes from outside Parliament, and when it filters in it is, as yet, tainted with the appearance of short-term tactical opportunism rather than long-term fundamental thinking.

BRC
Edinburgh, January 1989

Acknowledgements

For permission to reproduce here material that has previously appeared in their journals, I thank the editors of *Government & Opposition, The Irish Review, The New Statesman and Society, The Political Quarterly, The Guardian, Tribune, The Scotsman* and *Social Research*. I similarly thank the following publishers: the Oxford University Press, Frank Cass, the Falmer Press, Macmillan, Macmillan and Gill (Dublin), Tavistock Press, Routledge, Sweet & Maxwell, and the Department of Extramural and Continuing Education at Leeds. In compiling many of these essays I was helped greatly while at Birkbeck College by Audrey Coppard. And I thank Iris Walkland for helping me with the proofs, once again.

I would not so much dedicate this book to my son, Tom — that sounds so formal — as hope that, as an erstwhile student of politics, he will enjoy it. My next book, to be called *Three Insoluble Problems*, owes a great deal to him as we talked while on political safari in South Africa.

Foreword

Bernard Crick's most characteristic impulse, almost an itch, is to break out, a refusal to be comfortably boxed in as a traditional academic.

He moves out from the practice of political science as a university discipline to various parts of the non-academic literary world. Being a cousin in spirit of Orwell, he was a natural choice to write the Life, and brought it off very well indeed – knowing all the time that some of the stuffier people in professional literary studies would argue that he should have kept off the grass, or would patronise the success they had to recognise. In his literary tastes he is exceptionally well-read and wide-ranging. One good test of a left-winger's literary judgement is the way he squares up to the novel. Bernard Crick has the sort of free, undogmatic spirit which can recognise and value the 'bourgeois novel' as the greatest literary form Europe has produced.

A related side of him is an actor, or an actor-manager, or a producer or a dramatic critic – manqué in all those cases; a man of the theatre of some sort, certainly. His theatre reviews, available in the companion volume, exhibit an unusual, multi-sided exuberance and perceptiveness, and we are the poorer for having so few.

He moves out also from the enclosed scholarly life to the world of political action; at all levels, the provincial, the Northern Irish, the Scottish even more than the fashionably metropolitan.

And he determinably breaks away from all the private languages – some of it professional jargon – so that he can try to reach the intelligent lay-reader. He likes writing for such people and writes well for them; he is a natural stylist of the demotic, unbuttoned kind; much like Orwell.

This is also why he determined long ago to give as much weight to teaching as to scholarship, why he took evening classes with adults when most of his colleagues didn't, and why he chose to work at Birkbeck, to our shame the only university institution in this country devoted entirely to part-time students.

Bernard Crick, in his high and warm commonsense, his pragmatism, his 'rather truculent' scepticism, is a very British type of socialist; a liberal socialist for whom the state's first duty is to make us free, not to try to make us virtuous according to its own model. In all this he is not wayward or out to make a show. He is cheerfully but seriously irreverent, a voice very much native to these islands.

RICHARD HOGGART

Thoughts

One

Education and the Polity

As printed in Gordon Roderick and Michael Stephens (eds), *Higher Education For All* (Falmer Press, Lewes: 1979). An earlier version appeared in *The Journal of Higher Education.*

In times such as these some might think that it is their duty, or mine, to defend the sacred walls of education against the evil encroachments of politics. Freedom must always be defended, whether intellectual or practical, especially against bureaucratic routine and particularly against some of its friends who would store it all up for the future, but not wish others to practice it now. Spheres like 'education' and 'politics' are, however, less easily distinguishable than most people imagine; definitions do not make or change social relationships; and empirically these two spheres are not autonomous, not even in principle.

So forgive me if this is not a rhetorical, public defence of the idea of education against the practices of politics, but rather, for a domestic occasion,[1] some home truths or impertinent questions. For education is a hypocrite if she pretends to be a vestal virgin when she so often embraces her ravishers. I agree with the Marxists that all educational systems reflect and seek to perpetuate the values and customs of governing elites. I only do not agree with them that all elites are based solely or even always primarily upon economic exploitation and class oppression: or if I agree with them for the sake of argument (and with Professor Hayek, incidentally) that 'in the last analysis' the economic motive is dominant, yet I would still not agree that all elites are equally malign and would indeed modestly argue that some elites, by virtue of the ideologies or ideal images that they hold of human activity, are remarkably better than others. To say that education reflects the values of the political and social order is, to my mind, a truism, something true for all societies, not a dramatic and specific unmasking of bourgeois-capitalist society. And whether on hearing such an utterance we shudder or nod depends on what the values of the order in question are, and we cannot presume, except from the dogmatism of both Marx and Talcott Parsons, that these values are necessarily systematic and unified. A plurality of values is more often typical of human societies.

So, far from defending the idea of education against the practice of

3

coarse politics, I want to ask you to speculate with me about what the practices of education would be like if they followed the ideal of politics.

This is an enterprise that will sound strange or shocking to the modern liberal, but would have seemed natural to the Greek and Roman republicans. What sort of education would we have, in other words, if we pursued more openly, honestly and consistently the idea of politics that we already possess in the Western tradition? Some of the Greeks had, after all, an ideal that, whatever happened to it in practice, however much negation of it, betrayal or falling short, has none the less dominated the imagination of the world: the ideal of politics as being the public activities of free and equal men, the positive actions that constitute a state or polity composed of citizens. To be a free man was to have the right to participate and actually to participate, something quite unlike the modern liberal notion that liberty is being left alone from interference by the state. And it is this negative liberalism that becomes advanced as if axiomatic in every trite defence of academic freedom (by which people often seem to mean 'autonomy', which is impossible). As Hannah Arendt constantly argued, those who see civil liberties as withdrawal from politics should not be puzzled when they are then ignored and exploited.[2] If this idea of making decisions politically seems trite, then contrast it to the more common ideas of leaving government to priests, warlords, technical experts, yogis or commissars, or in a word, to others.

The political tradition

The platitudinous, the obvious and the simple are often difficult to grasp. If we go badly wrong, we go wrong in our initial assumptions, less often in the technicalities of the entailments. So let me remind us what the political tradition is about. Free-ranging speculation about what can be done through politics and the belief that man is at his best when active in a public arena, this appears to be no older than the fifth century Greeks. Plato was the first man we know who drew a clear distinction between what is in fact *law* and what is in reason *just,* and then Plato went on to argue that men could construct either an ideal state (as in his dialogue, *The Republic)* or at least a very much better one, a rational compromise between the ideal and the real (as in his dialogue, *The Laws).* The contrast is vivid between the speculative Greeks, recognising a variety of forms of government-and-society and believing that men could actually choose, if they fitted actions to words, which to have; and the otherwise almost universal acceptance in the ancient world of rulers and regimes as being an ordained part of divine order or in the modern world of objective necessity. But to Plato political freedom as creativity was to be limited only to those few who were capable of undergoing what one might call 'total education' culminating in a change of consciousness, the few shepherds of so very many sheep.

Aristotle first introduces wider, though still not complete, notions that human freedom is integral to justice and the business of good government. In his *Politics* he made three basic assertions – each of which I will apply as a critique of present educational arrangements. First, he asserted that man is naturally a political animal. This embraces all that we might mean by saying that man is a social animal, but also something more: political man can act upon his environment in concert with his fellow men, not simply react. He actually said that 'the man who can live outside the *polis* is either a beast or a god', for to be self-sufficient was not to be fully human. Perhaps he was thinking of his great pupil Alexander who, in breaking from the political relationship, could find no other title to claim to rule diverse cultures than that of being a god.

His second assertion is that society is composed of a diversity of elements. He says that his teacher Plato made the great mistake of thinking that a state without a single standard of righteousness is both unjust and unstable. Aristotle argues, on the contrary, against any attempt to apply a single standard – as tyrants and despots do. 'There is a point', he says, 'at which a *polis* by advancing in unity, will cease to be a *polis*: there is another point, short of that, at which it may still remain a *polis*, but will none the less come near to losing its essence, and will thus be a worse *polis*. It is as if you were to turn [musical] harmony into mere unison, or to reduce a theme to a single beat.'

His third assertion is that 'mixed government' is the best. For he thought that a true polity was neither monarchy, aristocracy nor democracy alone (which he treated as pure types), but a creative blending of elements. To call it a 'creative tension' would not be too far off, something between Plato's idea of dialectic as the method of philosophic argument and Hegel's idea of dialectic as the process of history, 'Democracy' to Aristotle is to be preferred to monarchy or aristocracy, if that is the only practical choice; but better than the rule of the *demos* alone (the mob, the poor and the ignorant) is a deliberate mixture of consent and power, the 'many electing the few', he says. The only possible justification for monarchy or rule by one man is, he says, when this man is perfectly wise and perfectly good – a theoretical possibility; but since to the Greeks a perfectly good man would therefore become a god, the case is rather unlikely, as distinct from Tyrants apeing gods. The only possible justification for aristocracy is wisdom and skill, but in practice the best if put into office without rotation and with the checks of democratic power degenerate into an exploitative plutocracy, the rule of the rich. The only possible justification for democracy or rule of numbers is equality, but such a justification by itself is to Aristotle fallacious: 'the belief that because men are equal in some things, they are equal in all'. So it is better by far to tie the skill of the few to the need to get the consent of the majority, hence to controls by the majority; and if the few can carry the majority with them, then the state is far more powerful than a simple autocracy which keeps its people subdued. Much of Roman political thought and practice was just a footnote to this basic point: *auctoritas in Senatum, potestas in populum* – 'always remember', as it were, 'that if skill and knowledge are in the Senate, power is with the common people'. And Machiavelli was to see, in this same tradition, that states who could make their inhabitants citizens, could then trust them with arms and thus find, with skill and civic patriotism combined, a power and a flexibility far greater than that of princes, dependent as they were on cowed men or hired mercenaries. Gramsci was simply to see the skilled worker as the industrial equivalent of Machiavelli's, Danton's or Jefferson's citizen-in-arms.

Moreover Aristotle argued that the fundamental way of changing a society from one type to another was through *paedeia* or education. We come close. Granted that with Aristotle, as Louis MacNeice remembered when he taught classics as humanism at Bedford College, 'lastly we remember the slaves'. For Aristotle justified slavery as creating the leisure which was needed both for learning and for citizenship, so some see the very source as tainted or as a proof that politics is only the subtlest method of class exploitation. But Aristotle also said that we will have slavery until we have the machines of Prometheus to work for us. As now we do. For the first time in human history there is the possibility, by political activity, of educational attainment and welfare for all. It is our neglect of will and of reason if we do not make better use of the machines. We should no more blame the inherent structure of society than we should blame the stars.

With the possibility of education for all, moreover, even Aristotle's caution about democracy can vanish: any distinction between polity as mixed government and a truly educated democracy would wither away. Aristotle's criterion for political justice could be applied to everyone, not just to an elite of citizens: 'ruling and being ruled in turn'. The distinction between polity and democracy would vanish so long as democracy itself operated in a political manner, recognising and respecting differences of values, striving to enhance human freedom and human knowledge, not simply to create, in Tocqueville's heavy words, 'a tyranny of the majority'.

Three broad inferences

It is the sin of the academic to be so long in getting to the point. Now three broad inferences for what education would be like had it emerged from a tradition of political thinking rather than from a Christian scholastic tradition of those who know condescending to preach the truth to those fit to be saved or fit to join the clerisy. And after that, some half-a-dozen points of contemporary policy.

From Aristotle's first concept that man is a political animal, it would follow very clearly that there should be more self-government at every level of education. In the government of schools and polytechnics and F E colleges, the collegiate form should be the norm rather than both the ideal and the exception. In schools and polytechnics particularly, the power of the head teacher or director in relation to his colleagues is one of the best anti-political examples for which any autocrat or bureaucrat could possibly wish. A school, for instance, may actually teach civics – if the head teacher wishes – and if not, not. Even in universities and colleges of universities, one may loyally question whether such headships need be so permanent, whether they could not alternate, or power be far more rationally and functionally divided. After all, it is a civil servant and not a politician who is the permanent head of departments of government; and he, if the politicians are worth their salt, carries out policy, not formulates it.

What complicates the call for more self-government in education is that it is not clear what we should mean even by education as an institution. It would be ridiculously solipsistic and formal for us to think of colleges and schools as exhausting and monopolising education. Are not books and libraries, newspapers, radio and television, and even the behaviour and speeches of public men part of education? And the family? We are currently invited to debate the educational effect of schools and colleges, and to look for the proper role of parent, pupil and teacher participation in school government. But not, for instance, to have second thoughts about commercial advertising on television, which every teacher knows is among the most anti-educational institutions of contemporary society. And we are not asked to consider how every type of educator should be involved: not just teachers, parents, politicians and officials, but journalists, librarians and publishers too. The debate may prove rather narrow. We do not live in isolated hutches. Rather we live in a great big interconnecting, and rather grubby, warm warren. 'Only connect', indeed.

From Aristotle's second concept that society is composed of a diversity of elements, it should follow that we should educate for diversity and not for consensus. Civilisation 'as we know it' is not going to fall apart if schools do not teach good manners, good English, the tables, morals, docility and the British Constitution; rather it may be the case that even more alienation and resentment may occur among young people if schools try to carry the alarm clock back along such worn-out paths. An education for diversity would stress problems and critical method rather than offering authoritative solutions. And it would allow for the fact that freedom means acting spontaneously, not in some pre-determined manner, so that the student must be allowed time to ask the awkward and even irrelevant question, not simply the one that helps the orderly progression of a lesson. And it would let pupils and students make genuine choices at every age and at every level, both in cultural and vocational studies, only insisting that both are always present. The experience of choosing is a greater human value than memorising blocks of assessable facts faster.

From Aristotle's third concept that the best form of government is mixed government, it would follow that much of the great debate about what parts of education shall be cultural, which vocational or productive and which 'political' or concerned with maintaining or changing the social system, that much of this debate is, in absolute terms, needless and meaningless. We need all three. Any society is necessarily involved in all three. If there is to be a common core, it must contain all three. But by looking at it politically, we might get the proportion better – as I will now try to do.

Policy and time

Hannah Arendt points out that political activity is something that must be carried out continuously.[3] In that respect it is rather like labour to earn food, fuel and clothing to stay alive: for most people there is little possibility of capital accumulation, so once we stop, the thing comes to an end. Whereas with a book or a work of art or a building, there is a sense in which it can be finished and yet remain, even if it is forgotten or rediscovered or if its meaning or significance changes. Education, like politics is not an activity in this sense. So it is odd, indeed, in a society wealthy enough (despite our present difficulties) to make choices, that we appear to have chosen to lump an incredible amount of education, most of it compulsory, in the first two decades. And then it all comes to a stop. Well, not all, but expenditure on extramural, adult education and continuing education is very small indeed compared to that on secondary education. Indeed is very small, I am bound to add, compared to university and polytechnic expenditure. If the budget is fixed, the resources should be spread far more widely through different kinds of institutions and throughout life.

Here at Birkbeck we have every right to blow our own trumpet a little more boldly and loudly. We should not just say that we are offering the chance of a conventional university education to older people who missed out straight from school or who want to try again, to change course, or to refresh and refuel. We should say that we are doing something intrinsically better than the straight-from-school institutions. For many of the problems of the relationship of education to industry, many of the problems of pure as against applied, or culture as against technology, or of the intellectual as against the vocational, seem so much less pressing and so much more easy to resolve in practical ways when one is teaching and learning with people who have already been out and about in industrial society, in the world of work, post-experience rather than post-school.

I don't say that evening part-time study is always the best solution. Sandwich courses can work well. And there is room for a greater variety of experiment and experience in both, and indeed for more full-time study for mature students on the Coleg Harlech and Ruskin models; and for institutions of higher education to play a larger and a more responsible role in this, not just to offer cut-down segments of conventional single honours degrees. If we were able to stop and think, we might see that it does not help the values of a political civilisation to pitch so many straight from school into three years of higher education. Even from the narrow self-interest of the traditionally academic university, it would help if they had grown up a bit or knew what they wanted. I have sympathy with the draconian views of the Swedish TUC who recently passed a resolution that no one should receive a university grant who had not first done two years of useful work in, or service for, society.

When the Robbins Report said that it was going to make a purely quantitative claim and was not concerned (ever so liberal) to say what should be taught, it in fact exhibited all that is worst in liberal economics: a pretence that large allocations of resources can be made without raising political and qualitative questions. When so many came up, we in the universities should have taught them differently, offered a much more deliberate mixture of intellectual and vocational subjects in a more general syllabus and abandoned the traditional single honours degree, at least until the taught or seminar M.A. level. Indeed, it was always an odd and self-interested argument to believe that a single honours degree, whether in arts or in engineering, was particularly likely to produce a well-rounded, cultured and effective person. Scholars should not have carried on so stubbornly and successfully repeating the Lord God's first great mistake: creating mankind in his own image. Robbins' statistical proof that ever so many more could benefit from a traditional higher education than was once supposed, should have been seen as also proving that even more among less favoured mortals could cope with lesser offerings, even shorter offerings of the same standard, at very different stages of life, not just in late adolescence or in the arrested adolescence that our famous new universities seem to have so successfully created in their youth-camp isolation.

To tell the truth, and tell it at a nasty time as cuts rain down upon us, universities were over-expanded in the 1950s and 1960s. The university educated elites acted recklessly and selfishly. They ignored adult, continuing and post-experience education, and the youth and community services, as being socially below the salt and economically irrelevant; and they left teacher training in proud but stagnant

municipal isolation, instead of integrating it fully with higher education. Our rulers in peace exhibited, as Shaw remarked in the context of
war, jobbery, snobbery and incompetence. I am against the present
cuts because of their motives and arbitrariness of application, but I do
favour a massive re-allocation of resources within the whole education
sector which university teachers would do well to support, not
resist.

Political thinking, even on the humblest level, such as 'what sort of
policies should the Labour Party have had?', would make one
surprised that the London Birkbeck model, that is a full-time staff
wholly devoted to mature and predominantly part-time students, was
not applied to the other great conurbations; and that some of the mis-
begotten polytechnics, instead of copying conventional universities at
lower cost and with even more autocratic, bureaucratic government,
should not have been turned – could not even now be turned – into
Birkbeck-like institutions. The television access of the Open University has great virtues in open space, I mean for people trying to study
outside the major centres of population. But the advantages of regular
face-to-face teaching would seem obvious. Yet directed home-study
has advantages and attractions to many; and certainly the innovations
of the Open University in curricula construction have, by way of
contrast, exposed the gentlemanly amateurism and the unreflective
traditionalism with which so many university courses are strung
together. If I claim that the Birkbeck model is, for the needs of most
students, though not all students, a better one to follow than expanding
Open University, I certainly admit that we here have been all too
conservative in curricular innovation, looking over our shoulders at
what the straight-from-school undergraduate colleges of London
University will think of us, rather than considering the special needs of
and possibilities for teaching of and learning from mature citizen-
students. The way most of us – not all – have clung wherever possible to
single honours degrees following three A levels seems a particularly
bad case of putting disciplinary preservation orders before the cultural
and educational interests of many if not most mature students.

Time presses, otherwise a fairly obvious and by now well-known
argument about time could be developed at the other end of the
spectrum. Is it right or wise to keep fifteen and sixteen year olds full
time in school against their will, often with few visible results, except
increased alienation (one does not need to be Ivan Illich to be a little
worried here). It is fairly natural – dare I say this in a university?
– for some people to want to work, in the ordinary sense of that
word. The dilemma would be less if governments had followed the
logic of the Industrial Training Acts of the late 1940s and had extended
– throughout all industry, commerce, administration and the professions – some spasmodic or even continuous day-release for
education throughout working life.

Mobility

The political tradition in its ideal form, however bureaucratised some republics and political parties become in practice, places great stress on mobility, adaptability, alternation of office, ruling and being ruled in turn. Universities however, long before some trade unions became nearly so powerful, have long established security of tenure for working life on criteria, which, once a person is appointed at all, are remarkably easy and routine to fulfil. In this they have followed in the footsteps of the great British civil service reforms of the 1850s and 1860s, establishing job security, incremental salaries and pensions. In the civil service this was done in the name of political neutrality. In the universities, it was done in the name of scholarship – or if signs of scholarship are utterly lacking, then it is said, *ipso facto*, that a man is a good teacher and his good teaching would be disturbed – will businessmen, lawyers and doctors please note? – by any occupational insecurity, not, as the economists would teach us, stimulated.

What in fact happens is that very many people stay put in one place all their life, or at the best will make no more than one move. Take into account also the small size of the average department (a group who soon know each other's viewpoints inside-out, and are bored stiff with each other), and a stranger might be forgiven for thinking that a man would need almost superhuman powers of self-renewal not to lapse, by middle age, into a pedantic and bureaucratic parody of his younger self. Is this good for teaching? Is this good for scholarship?

Are the abuses to which contracts shorter than life could give rise greater or lesser than the risks of inertia? I am not sure, but the question needs raising urgently. Or if we insist on taking for granted the same occupational security as the pace-setters of the higher civil service (even if we as yet lack their inflation-proof and non-contributory pensions), could we resist a public and political demand that we should be treated as a Service and circulated from time to time? or perhaps not be promoted or allowed to pass the efficiency bar unless at least a third of one's service had been elsewhere? If we want security, then mobility should be institutionalised. I can think of some stagnant pools called colleges where.... No names, no pack-drill.

Consider that when tenure until sixty-five was given to the new Home Civil Service, life span was much as it is now, though life expectancy much less. Fewer people would have survived until sixty-five and, in any case, most higher civil servants or new university professors would have retired long before to look after the family property. Now we are all bureaucrats, hanging on to the last, few gentlemen. 'Sit on your arse for forty years and hang your hat on a pension', as Louis MacNeice sang.

Obviously I am raising a wider question about the fructifying effects of occupational mobility between education, administration, the professions and industry, not simply for individuals but for the economy. But I could linger on a narrower question simply for education. Should not ways be found by which we all teach in schools for a while, some also in further education, fewer in higher education; but none in one kind of institution for all their working life? And should not sabbatical entitlement be universal – why just in higher education? If it was compulsory and pension funded, it could apply to industry as well. Mobility should lead us towards versatility, which was a great cultural ideal in pre-industrial republics before division of labour became an ossified dogma rather than a partial necessity. And greater mobility would create much more mutual aid and understanding between education, government and industry.

Space

The Greeks stressed that politics was a public activity and that a freeman does not live in isolation, he must emerge from the private shadows of the home and of the workshop into the public sunlight of the market place. And in terms of cultural and social history, both high culture and political and social reform are associated with great cities, which have assembly places where different classes, creeds, functions, families, crafts and age-groups mingle and meet. Even the misogynist Thomas Hobbes says that: 'Leisure is the mother of Philosophy; and Commonwealth, the mother of Peace, and Leisure: where first were great and flourishing Cities, there was first the study of Philosophy'. And yet – am I passing from the sublime to the ridiculous? – we created at vast expense new universities with names of famous cities, but all, without exception, completely self-contained and mostly far outside the city walls! Why? The obvious alternative would be to have expanded the then quite small civic universities which were all, with two possible exceptions, firmly embedded in cities. I suspect an Oxbridge bias against industrial cities and industrial Britain exercised, moreover, by civil servants with the mentality of commuter-belt pseudo-gentry. Who can look at Kent, Warwick, Essex, Brighton, York and Lancaster without seeing the fagged out end of the garden suburb movement? No wonder many of them have been such disturbed places. What collective lunacy or architectural arrogance ever thought of putting three thousand young people straight from school out in the fields together, as if learning and life can be divorced from the culture, both high and low, of cities? In some ways these buildings were worse than garden suburbs, for they represent an idea of a university as a refuge from the world of productivity, partly monastic in origins and partly arising from Matthew Arnold-like scorn for the common culture and for the new technologies that fed him and his pupils. The new universities should have been, as some of the polytechnics tried to be, spearheads of inner-city renewal.

Anyway, I am sure that citizenship has something to do with living in cities; and so has a broad, not a narrowly liberal, education.

The common core: knowledge

Skirmishing. Now to the hardest point. If we wish to preserve and extend a political culture, a civilised one which is also productive, what kind of education should we have?

Bertrand de Jouvenal has well said that education has a dual purpose: 'to make man's labour more productive, and his leisure more fruitful. And the greater the gains in one direction, the more necessary is progress in the other'. But after saying that, he argued convincingly against any assumptions that education for efficiency and education for improvement are radically distinct, that 'to give both is twice as much trouble and takes twice as much time'. For he doubted that 'the time presently spent on education is well spent.'[4]

My political assumption is that education should serve industry quite as much as it serves learning and culture. But that our general educational institutions, like schools and colleges, will do this best not by training for specific jobs or by keeping up the cant that the liberally educated man can turn his mind and hands to anything – he plainly can't – rather than by defining an essential common core; by leaving plenty of time for choice of other subjects or part-time jobs; and by encouraging a greater versatility and practicality.

For the two main components of the common core in secondary education, I will again follow De Jouvenal:

> 'Would anyone doubt that the art of correct expression (litera-ture) and the art of rigorous reasoning (mathematics) are basic both to business and to culture? I would contend that the acquisition of these two skills is by far the most important part of education.'[5]

These are the two forms of knowledge (and they are also transferable skills) which are essential, and from which everything else can follow. But everything else does not have to follow all at once, certainly not in secondary school. So it would defeat the idea of a core curriculum if everything else that we have at the moment simply piled in afterwards. For room must be left for individual project work, and crafts which, together with some education for political literacy, would constitute an education for practicality – so lacking in our formal culture at the moment. Let me notionally say that these three – literature, mathematics and practicality – could each take a fifth of the time-table; then the remaining time must be a time for genuine options, an education in choice, and options must include the possibility of jobs, jobs around the school for the youngest, jobs in local shops, factories, offices or services and voluntary work for the older pupils. If deschool-ing would probably be disastrous, yet some relaxation of compulsion is needed when it so plainly does not work for the less motivated and is not necessary for the motivated.

Could the common core of knowledge be as small as literature and mathematics? Most of what we learn in school, in history, geography, physics, chemistry, biology or geology – I am quoting de Jouvenal again (I would not dare say this myself) – is simply forgotten as soon as it has been assessed and can be retrieved in public libraries when wanted. A massively simple point. What we need to know is where to find these things out in books and other sources of information when we need them and when we are interested. There is so much factual, purely to be memorised, lumber in the curriculum, only there for assessment. In most subjects in university, students could begin from scratch, indeed perhaps do better than now, if a high standard of critical literacy and of numeracy came up from the schools. 'My subject is, of course, different'; but unless it is English or Mathematics, I doubt it. To dare to name names, History and Geography are surely the greatest offenders in schools, remorselessly insatiable for yet another period and yet another area to be covered – remembered up to the exam and then forgotten. Whereas what historians and geographers say they want in higher studies is critical method. I hastily say that I am not arguing for no History or Geography in schools (for most History is, in fact, treated exactly as if it were literature), but to have them and the others among the options, with tutor-teachers who concentrate on helping pupils to find out for themselves when and if they want to, in school or public library and elsewhere. And if they don't want to, so what? Will the pupils be less cultured, less effective, less decent as human beings? I cannot see the remotest reason why.

The political viewpoint would support de Jouvenal in his basic contention that we do not need to choose, to put it in other words, between the scientific, the cultural and the vocational. We must keep them separate. They each have their own logic and their own justifications. We should not try to produce thin pretentious syntheses, but we should lay them each side by side both in curricula and in institutions. For as with the need for mobility, so much of the hopes for mutual understanding and respect between these different activities depend not upon the formal curriculum at all, but on students of different areas rubbing shoulders in the corridors, canteens and common-rooms of polyglot institutions, where everyone must do a bit of each.

De Jouvenal, however, does not go quite far enough. True, he sees the need for a third leg to his stool – what he calls 'the art of checking factual statements', of weighing evidence, of finding alternative sources, a kind of education in practical scepticism.[6] I would agree and see this largely in terms of individual or small group project work, how to discover and check things in a critical spirit. But I would include in this practical information about welfare rights and employment and filling in forms as well as intellectual discovery. Indeed many comprehensive schools do this kind of practical finding out very well already, calling it Social Studies, but usually for the least able; whereas the more able also need it, if they are to be practically minded. Indeed it is odd that the very successful 'play and discovery' methods of primary education are not applied to options throughout secondary and even higher education (sometimes a long research essay, occasionally projects). There is a good deal of evidence that formal learning and retention of it is actually enhanced by developing such skills. But I think that this third leg of de Jouvenal's needs extending more radically to be allied with political literacy and with crafts as part of a practical education.

The smallest component of this third leg, though an important one, is political literacy. It needs doing because politicians and the media provide so little on politics, economic and social problems that is genuinely educational. A little of it will go a long way, simply to teach and to discover together what the main issues and problems of contemporary society are thought to be, to examine different viewpoints on them in an empathetic way and above all, once again, to help pupils to use alternative sources of information in a critical way. Much of political literacy can be acquired from the proper running (rarely as at present) of a school itself, above all observing the relationship of head teachers to their staff; but some knowledge of national and local issues is necessary. But I see this as a very simple thing, not needing the disciplines of Politics, Economics and Sociology, all of which, to my mind, would have no place as such except as 'do it yourself' options in a school system reformed to correspond to the principles of polity.

Far more important for this third leg, however (important in the sense of demanding far more time), is to remedy the neglect of basic practicalities. Things worth studying for their own sake must, indeed, be studied for their own sake, hence without compulsion, beginning with some instances at school and having the choice of all disciplines in higher and continuing education. But there cannot be, without great harm, a permanent divorce between culture and industry. The solution, however, is not to teach technology, or particular local trades in schools, but is to nurture a technological spirit and competence in practical ways.

The common core: practicality

By practicality I simply mean that an educated man should be able to tackle most of the small technical problems that he meets in everyday life. Consider woodwork and handicraft. These are tiny gestures in that direction, usually for the 'less able', usually skimped for the more academically able when faced with the over-loaded disciplinary timetable, skimped for those very people who may need it most, if one thinks of the technological illiteracy of our political and administrative elites. Practicality and technological awareness is not to be taught directly then, but may start with woodwork and metal work, progress to repairing bicycles, motor-bikes and routine servicing and minor repairs to cars; the repair of common domestic electrical apparatus; painting and decorating, where arts and crafts and chemistry may be said to touch; the whole range of how to use well the new and culturally most interesting 'do it yourself shops'; how to record music and perhaps something about the music; repairing and making of clothes; cooking and knowledge of sources of dietetic and consumer information; and typing even. These should be as natural a part of the curriculum as physical and health education, and should be done irrespective of sex. Think of those male ninnies in administration and universities who cannot type a draft themselves – perhaps a memorandum on efficiency, wasting the time of a skilled secretary; or proud beauty who cannot mend a fuse or inflate a tyre.

This all should be part of a common education for a new common-man. The basic experience of making and repairing things is surely the first stage in making us all productivity-minded, without in any way impairing intellectuality and culture. [7] A person who cannot use his mind reflectively or creatively, who cannot use his hands and who cannot take action politically, this person should be thought of as less than a full and educated person – the Greeks would have said, not fit to be a citizen.

In conclusion

What in fact do we have? We have a highly bureaucratised and centralised system of education both in schools and universities, nominally under local control, but in fact with little significant diversity of practice – except the great divide of the state and the private section of education. Even in the private sector, there is an astounding sameness and lack of experiment. Both school systems are dominated by ideas of disciplinary attainments; little has been done to foster practical and political skills and sociability. A purely office-holding, job preserving bureaucratic assumption that all disciplines are equal hinders both concentration and cutting down. And until we cut down both the profusion of subjects and the time-scales of secondary education, we cannot take away the stigma of unwanted compulsion from most people's education and begin to spread resources more evenly through life. There is such a wasteful over-concentration of resources on the early years and on immediate post-school university and polytechnic, and far too little for post-experience learning at every conceivable level.

Instead of the absurd distinction of the binary policy, we should indeed have developed – even though it is an ugly word – multi-universities. The vocational and the cultural and the scientific should there have, not merged, but simply rubbed shoulders. Each student to do a little of each at least, but mostly to rub shoulders with different kinds of specialists. By limiting universities, or by universities limiting themselves to the scientific and the cultural in the pattern of Humboldt's conventional disciplines, universities are in danger of becoming as sterile and as irrelevant as a parliament that limited its debates to constitutional matters, ignoring the economy, production and culture; indeed worse, they are like a parliament that thinks that politics should only be practised in a parliamentary context, that sees any extra-parliamentary politics or stirrings for self-government in other fields as a threat to parliamentary democracy. Parliamentarians seem to suggest that all extra-parliamentary politics is necessarily anti-parliamentary; and universities often seem to say that any encouragement of culture and learning except through themselves is a threat. On the contrary, we need more democracy in the workshop, in the office and in the school or college; and we need more centres and devices of higher learning, other than the – at times – awful formality and laboriousness of universities and polytechnics.

The polytechnic/university distinction has been mainly one of costs. But if we cannot afford such multi-purpose agglomerations as I suggest, then we should spread the costs more fairly through time, recurrent and continuing, and look again at the greatest under-used asset we have: the free public library system. Rather than the last new university, I would have liked to have seen a new breed of tutor-librarians in each major public library to help people with self-study, and two or three small-sized meeting rooms in each library where WEA and extra-mural activities can take place. And why not self-administering neighbourhood centres of this kind, like the heavily-named 'Culture and Leisure Houses' which already exist in some German Social Democratic cities and in Israel?

Not to flinch at the post, we should also consider whether money would not be better spent on the Arts Council grants, considering their pathetically small funding, compared to these fifty or so universities, each doing much the same kind of thing to so many who are only there for the ride or because they got three A levels, or would get more out of the ride if they took it all, or even part of it, much later.

I have not really tried to apply deschooling doctrines, of however mild a kind, to universities. I am only trying to remind us that we do not monopolise culture and learning, and that in the interests of the whole polity we should not try to do so. Consider what threat it would be to literature if every novelist and poet could become a writer in residence or a university lecturer. And social and political speculation have almost entirely lost their public voice now that they are social sciences and are commonly written in a jargon that you have to go to college to understand. Scientists should not be shy of their contacts with industry, if they can go back and forth; and they are, alas, sometimes right to be less than fully enthusiastic about teaching 'a normal load', if research is the thing. But we cannot justify the expense of research and pure scholarship in so very many different centres. Research is not a right of individuals, but a cultural need whose proper allocation of resources can only be settled justly in a political way, by political justice.

Ideological postscript

What I have to say about the relationship of politics to education has been coloured by the fact that I am a moderate, but a moderate socialist, not a moderate of the middle or the muddle of the whole political spectrum; and moderate, indeed, not as to ends, but only as to means.[8] Moreover if one is an idealist, in the sense of wishing to work to realise the spirit of enlightenment and the great slogans of the French Revolution, whose business is not yet finished, however often frustrated or perverted, 'Liberty, Equality, Fraternity', then one must proceed carefully, deliberately and with determination and on a long time-scale. 'The man who striveth for the mastery', said Paul, 'is temperate in all things'. If he is serious, that is, and not just trendy, theatrical, pharisaical, using doctrine as a way of isolating him or herself from the world rather than genuinely seeking to transform it through time, instead of through visions of – to quote Dylan Thomas on the crucifixion – 'the mountain minute, time's nerve in vinegar' as if revolution like the crucifixion will qualitatively transform all human history and the possibilities of human nature.

For part of why I have spoken in a moderate perspective by some lights, however radical it would appear to conventional liberals, is because I believe we should think in a long time-scale. Most of my fellow social scientists exaggerate the uniqueness of the capitalist-industrial world. The idea of free citizenship has deeper and enduring roots in our culture; it is to be used, not transcended. And used much more. Too many socialists, indeed, seem to reject industrialism and all concern with production rather than try to socialise it; they reject it either in the shamefully vague Marxist accounts of a classless society, or in the far more precise, but specifically anti-industrial, anarchist or Communard tradition of small groups and small groups only.

Heaven knows that it is not wise to destroy anything until there is something better to put in its place. But if we are to have a better civilisation than we enjoy at the present, which is not a difficult thought, it can only come through deliberate political means, by argument, persuasion, policy and legislation, not through coercion or mystical qualitative events like revolution or conversion. And it will come, in part, through education.[9]

Notes

1 This is a revised version of an inaugural lecture to the chair of
   politics at Birkbeck College, University of London, delivered on
   January 20 1977.

2 See Hannah Arendt's *The Human Condition* (Cambridge
   University Press, Cambridge: 1958), *On Revolution* (Faber &
   Faber, London: 1963) and *On Violence* (Allen Lane, London:
   1970) especially.

3 Hannah Arendt, *The Human Condition,* Part II, *passim.*

4 Bertrand de Jouvenal, 'Toward a Political Theory of Education'
   in *Humanistic Education and Western Civilisation: Essays for Robert
   M. Hutchins,* edited by Arthur A Cohen, (New York 1964) p. 67.

5 *Ibid*, p. 68.

6 *Ibid*, p. 69.

7 When George Orwell thought, in his *The Lion and the Unicorn*
   (first published 1941, reprinted 1962), that a social revolution was
   taking place as a consequence of the war, he said that 'Most of its
   directing brains will come from the new indeterminate class of
   skilled workers, technical experts, airmen, scientists, architects
   and journalists, the people who feel at home in the radio and
   ferro- concrete age' (pp. 85–6). Orwell saw no inconsistency in
   valuing both literary culture and common culture.

8 See my 'The Character of a Moderate (Socialist)', *The Political
   Quarterly,* Vol 47, No 1, January 1976, and below p. 158 ff.

9 Reading this in 1990, over ten years later, I am grimly aware how
   Thatcherite my ideas on tenure, mobility, 'practicality' and
   relative levels of funding will sound – or else dangerous hostages
   to fortune. But I am unrepentant, indeed think I was prescient
   and right. Something had to be done. The universities should
   have reformed themselves in the 1970s (when they were still
   dragging their feet with Parliament about financial accountability,
   even). The Labour Government could have looked at all sectors
   of education together and pushed the universities (albeit in a
   more political, compromising and consultative way) into a far
   greater commitment to continuing education and curricular
   reform, and (unlike now) to a benign result.

Two

Are the Universities Teaching the Right People.

* The Twelfth Mansbridge Memorial Lecture of the Department of Adult and Continuing Education, University of Leeds, 1983.

When twenty years ago the Robbins Report went off, the whole university line got out of its trenches and moved forward, like after the great landmine at Ypres in 1916, a few hundred yards before getting stuck in the mud and digging in again. Some there were who rubbed their hands with prophetic joy at that 'untapped pool of ability' about to be run off; others, like the young Kingsley Amis, the Nietzsche of Radio Two, proclaimed that 'More Means Worse'; while I, sensing an opportunity for precocious fame, tried unsuccessfully to launch a counter-slogan, 'Beware! More Means the Same!' I was right. Now a generation later I wish, in memory of Albert Mansbridge and in praise of the Adult Education movement, to return to the attack.

So much of the potter's clay has now turned to dust in our hands. The social hopes have proved self-defeating: to take only one graphic figure from E.G. Edward's recent book, *Higher Education for Everyone* (a truly noble polemic),[1] by the end of the 1970s the rate of entry to university of sons of senior professional families had risen to eighty per cent of their total sons in the age group, whereas for the daughters of unskilled workers, entry was one hundred times lower. The proportion of children coming from the homes of manual workers actually fell during the decade from twenty-nine to twenty-three per cent and from children of parents with professional technical jobs rose from twenty-eight per cent to thirty-seven per cent. It is the same story as with effective 'take-up' in all the social services: those who are better prepared can take better advantage of facilities available. The educational changes have been less than expected. There was a lot of talk about the new universities doing new things, just as there was to be about polytechnics serving a unique civic and community function. Some of us still remember the new Vice-Chancellors like Sloman and Fulton going round everywhere giving talks about 'the new spirit' of Sussex or Essex, so that we actually believed, indeed they must have actually believed when they were resting from their tours at home, that new things were actually happening on the ground. Don't you believe it. By and large, now the dust has settled, the kinds of things that British universities teach, who they teach, and how they teach, are remarkably unchanged, or certainly show more continuity with the past than some of us had hoped and others had feared twenty years ago. For all their different rules and regulations, specialities, sites, architects and eccentric inhabitants, at the end of a generation one British university (always excepting Oxford and Cambridge) looks, as was once said of British gentlemen, 'damnably like any other'. Some changes, I admit: subjects can be more often combined with one another; syllabuses do get changed occasionally and explained to the students more often; but I suspect that these were concessions made to the student unrest of the late 1960s rather than any direct consequence of the Robbins Report.

Even the effectiveness of the Robbins Report itself can be doubted. Which was cause and which effect? 'Who the rider, who the horse?' Just as Sir Peter Medawar has demonstrated that atmosphere and river pollution began to decline significantly before the famous Clean Air and Anti-Pollution Acts were passed, so Edwards and others have shown that effective demand and increase in numbers began around 1956, seven years before Robbins. But expansion, of course, might not have continued at the rate it did until two years ago if greater facilities and funding had not been forthcoming; but often these great reforming Commissions and Reports do not so much identify social needs as arise from them. What proves this point is that the timing and degree of university expansion were remarkably similar in all Western industrial societies: demand called forth supply.

Such a consideration may be our main hope as I now consider the main failing of British universities themselves and of public policy towards them. Five years ago in my inaugural lecture at Birkbeck on 'Education and the Polity' [reprinted above] I ventured to remark that:

> The university-educated elites acted recklessly and selfishly. They ignored adult, continuing and post-experience education, and the youth and community services, as being socially below the salt and economically irrelevant; and they left teacher training in proud but stagnant municipal isolation, instead of integrating it fully with higher education. Our rulers exhibited in peace, as Shaw remarked in the context of war, 'jobbery, snobbery and incompetence'.

And I added that though I was not a sadist, and was not in favour of cutting and bleeding at random (and the cuts of five years ago were only a mild forecast of today's), I did favour a massive reallocation of resources within the whole educational system from immediate post-school full-time degree work into a relatively greater concentration on part-time, continuing and mature study, both for certification and because people want it.

To allocate costs is difficult, but just consider numbers. In the ten years from 1967 to 1977 total numbers of full-time students enrolling on first degree courses at universities and polytechnics in England and Wales rose from 21,600 to 79,400 and on part-time first degree courses from 2300 to 6800. But as a proportion of the total, the part-time numbers had actually fallen from 9.6 per cent to 7.9 per cent.[2] Of course, you will say, I am ignoring the Open University. By the year 1979–80 there were 69,000 students registered for OU undergraduate degree courses – a remarkable achievement. But unhappily the existence of the OU has enabled the university sector largely to ignore both the demand for part-time degrees and for the careful curriculum planning and innovation demanded by the distance learning of the OU. An unexpected effect of the existence and numerical success of the OU has been to defeat or delay any consideration in the universities of their responsibility for offering advanced education to the whole population. And do the OU's customers necessarily want distance teaching? That is one survey that will never get funded by the OU, nor by the universities neither. Some may, but some may not. I happen to teach at the one institution in the traditional university sector, Birkbeck College, that is wholly devoted to teaching advanced courses, still overwhelmingly degree work, to part-time evening students. I know what our students think about the relative merits of distance and face-to-face teaching – so long as they can hold out against the running down of London Transport and the pyrrhic victories of community politics in denying London, when there was cash to be had, a modern road system. I am profoundly puzzled as to why there seems not to be a similar demand in all the great conurbations. I am sure there is one, but for the supply to arise that would reveal the demand one would have to tread on something very sacred and tender to the staff of civic and new universities: the right to work a normal nine to five job (I'll give them all the credit I can, so I stick by nine to five). The one good thing I can say of the Oxford dons is that most of them, even if as a product of the ludicrously short teaching term, are fully willing to meet students in the evenings.

It seems very silly and simple, but all that I want to argue for, with all the profound social implications involved, could be met if, during term time, universities in conurbations were willing to work a two to nine timetable, and to teach all courses and options on alternate years in the afternoon and then in the evening. In that way, the urban universities and polytechnics could share their rich assets with the whole population, not concentrate on being a finishing school for the 18 plus cadre. Indeed, why should the two systems, OU and full-time degree provision be so separate? The OU has provided an admirable national system of curriculum construction and assessment; but could not universities and polytechnics take on much of the actual teaching, where and when people can come in? To a surprising extent the polytechnics, though they have been far more venturesome in providing sandwich courses, a valuable mixture of work experience and education, also do less than is commonly supposed, both in part-time degree work and non-degree part -time advanced courses generally: they have indeed, with honourable exceptions, mainly followed the path set by the civic universities. Local politicians may imagine that they are or should be great centres of adult community education at all levels, but the real interests of the polys are, like the universities, dominated by their success in attracting full-time degree students straight from school; and most of the polytechnic directors actually wish for a more fully national system of funding. This wish may be a sad tribute to many LEAs, I'm not sure; but it seems to me that there is a great loss as well as narrow gain in this aspiration, a loss of local roots – such as the civic universities once accepted and enjoyed before the post-war centralization of funding by the UGC. I fear that at the best the centrist yearnings of the polys may lead 'out of the frying pan and into the fire', or at the worst yet another case of a lady from Riga. I've certainly become a great convert to local government in the past few years, for all its inadequacies and inequities. If local political power means variations of standards and provisions, so does liberty.

Something more profound about the matter of England lies here, and I say 'England' deliberately, for the case is rather different in Scotland and Wales. We suffer from centralism in many ways in this country. Most of what is worst in England is the culture of the Home Counties and what is best is found in provincial values and variations. In some ways since the War the prestige of the Home Counties has suffered. I am not suggesting a uniform process. Although I speak it, as something expensively acquired by my father's investment in my future, yet standard English no longer has its old dominance. That is one of the few things one can unequivocally admire in both the BBC and in Sir Harold Wilson. But before that, it was the young northern playwrights and then the radio and television popular dramas and comedy shows. Compare and contrast with pre-war, or if your memories are as old as mine, the solitary eminence of one wartime radio announcer, Wilfred Pickles. Now I am not a mad Leavisite, nor a gentlemanly romantic suffering from a dialectic infusion of Byron and the Beatles. I stand humbly in a very long and respectable tradition of political thought, stemming from the Greeks, progressing through Machiavelli, Rousseau, Burke, Tocqueville, and one half of the socialist tradition: that which stresses the importance for both human freedom and creativity of subsidiary groups, participative local loyalties and face-to-face societies. In Hardy, Meredith, Bennett, Gissing even, and in score of lesser twentieth-century novelists (but not forgetting Lawrence and even a nod to Orwell's novels), we find the central theme of roots, of going away and the uprooting, the difficulty of leading a moral life in, quite literally, London – a metropolitan and non-civic, almost an anti-civic culture. The comprehensible community lies at the heart of both political justice and of common morality. And yet we find, quite simply, every university aspiring successfully (except Glasgow, Edinburgh and Queen's, Belfast to a lesser degree) to be fully national in their student profile. I do not think that this is wholly good.

Now the answer is not to keep the young at home artificially. For the young do want to wander, to try (to mix two great metaphors) their own wings without our roots. The real answer is part of a more general problem: the major folly of not spreading, whatever our resources, education provision more fully throughout life and in less rigid packets, and the minor folly of the obsession with certification shared by both universities and polytechnics – the three-year honours degree above all else, certainly above study for its own sake; 'keeping up standards' is it, or 'the measurable production line'?

Why should there be so much concentration on full-time straight-from-school, and that so unbroken and strictly sequential? Let me tell you two true stories which had a great effect on my thinking and education. The one is about unbroken study and the other about the dangers of eighteen plus.

The unbroken study story. There was a girl called Helen. She had worked hard and been worked hard at school. She came to see me at the end of her second year to say she would like 'a year off', she was feeling tired and stale. She thought she would go to France, *au pair*, consolidate her French, get a bit of reading done and come back the following year. It seemed a good idea to me. But most of my colleagues got very excited. The regulations did not allow it, they spoke of 'continuous study'. 'Then we'll move a special regulation', I said. 'What if they are all to do it?', said the admissions tutor (an unlikely hypothesis for a social scientist to believe). 'A bit unfair on the others', said backbone of the department (evidently moved by the sporting spirit, as if it was a horserace). 'She'll probably not come back and the rate-payers' money down the drain', said another ('That's her own damned business', said I). Eventually the university doctor certified my diagnosis that she was on the edge of a nervous breakdown, which was solemnly accepted by the Faculty. But I felt angry that two good men and a good woman had had to perjure themselves because the system was so foolishly rigid.

The 18+ story. There was a man called Alan who came as a mature student from the Steel Industry and got a First in Economics and Politics. He used to teach some of the classes after my first-year lectures. He asked me once, over a glass, if he could 'say something to you straight'. I was impatient or upset that he thought he couldn't. He wanted to say I was the best lecturer he had ever heard – well, apart from Royden Harrison, Michael Barrett Brown, Michael Foot, and a half-dozen miners' and steelworkers' leaders. 'Come on, what do you really want to say?', 'That you're a bloody good first-year lecturer, but it makes me sometimes ashamed to think that you have to, meta-phorically speaking, stand on yer 'ead and take your trousers off to interest that bloody lot in bloody subject. What the fuck are they here for if they are not interested in the bloody subject'.

Quite seriously, that is what set me on the path to Birkbeck.

You will think that I have forgotten where I am orating, in an extra-mural department, a very active and distinguished one. Not so, for I hold the embarrassing view that so-called extra-mural activity (which some think Latin for 'below the salt', and others think means 'salt of the earth') should be the central activity of universities and polytechnics – not a peripheral one, at times almost a fig leaf. Any segment of what universities and polytechnics choose to offer should be available to anyone who wishes to take it, if minimally qualified at degree *level*, but not necessarily wanting to take anything like the whole package that might then constitute a degree, or various other forms of certification either along the way or as ends in themselves. And since university teachers have, it has to be said, amidst all the follies and worries of the past two years, a very favourable kind of contract and job situation compared to anyone except higher civil servants (who quite simply have the power to look after themselves at our expense), they could well be required by contract to teach at any level (a fair test of knowing one's subject and how to teach). Should an extramural department be, on my argument, the largest teaching department in any university, or simply a small administrative unit in the Registrar's office with control of so many hours of staff time and the role of publicizing what exists already and organizing other courses for which there is a demand?

It could be either. I would like to blur the distinction between extra- and intramural. A few of my colleagues are truly incapable of coming down to earth. But more create that appearance by idleness, unreliability, abstruseness, and eccentricity to avoid any elementary teaching (like some insects who render themselves noxious in taste to avoid being eaten). But quite as important as flexibility on levels is flexibility on timing. Why should it all be done in one spurt? Why should not my Helen have had a year off, just as much as wouldn't *everyone* be happier if my Alan had had his way and the straight-from-school had had to do a little work first, if they could find any, or had to do a bit of growing up on their own before they landed us with all the problems of living away from home for the first time that used to take

up about one-third of my time when I was a kindly young professor at
Sheffield rather than an angry old man.

I am truly angry at the rigidity of my colleagues and appalled at how
the whole university system acts as if it had a right to the funding levels
of the 1960s and 1970s, to be used at its own discretion for its own
traditional purposes, rather than having a duty, indeed an interest, to
serve the people of Britain as a whole. My colleagues should at least
have some curiosity as to why they have lost political and public
support, perhaps even some self-interest to build up such confidence
again by work at local roots and levels. Part of the reason why the
universities have lost their popularity may be that they have actually
lost part-time students to other sectors, let alone that they have failed to
diversify their efforts with some sensible response to social changes. I
use 'social changes', incidentally, not as a piece of pseudo-social
scientific rhetoric, but in quite specific dimensions: increased leisure,
increased life-span, increased occupational mobility, and increased
need both for retraining and restimulating — all these should shift the
emphasis from full-time post-eighteen to continuing adult education.

Now, of course, little of what I am saying is original. Even the
Robbins Report had urged the provision of more evening courses for
first degrees and 'the establishment by some universities of correspondence courses' – which foreshadowed the Open University, which in
turn let the universities off the hook and allowed them to lurch back to
their old introverted, pseudo-Oxbridge ways. The Russell Report on
Adult Education of 1973 argued for a substantial shift of university
resources and activity towards extra-mural and this was supported by
a subsequent House of Commons Select Committee. The only trouble
is that precisely nothing has been done about either of these noble
objectives. So one keeps on preaching; not even Birkbeck is willing to
stick its neck out against the rest of the university system: it passively
thanks God for small mercies.

Let me make all this more concrete by offering a commentary on the
seven principal recommendations of a recent unofficial report entitled
Part Time Degree Level Study in the United Kingdom, commonly known
as the Tight Report, after its research officer and draughtsman.[3]

> *There needs to be a shift of resources towards the provision of part-time
> study opportunities, an area in which provision is notably lacking. If
> access for adults were to be improved by this means students would be
> more able to enter the higher education system at different stages in life
> rather than having to opt in immediately after leaving school.*

I find it difficult to imagine why my university colleagues seem to
believe that even all qualified human beings should rationally wish to
have three years sweet labour and then next to nothing for the rest of
life. Obviously we need, as the Labour Party now vainly argues, an

educational entitlement that can be cashed at any time, backed up by sabbatical entitlement as part of normal contracts of employment throughout industry and commerce, let alone education.

I used to find it difficult to imagine why my colleagues seemed to believe that higher education must consist of a three-year continuous course which is debased if taken in segments or taken in a mixture of full-time, part-time and even distance modes – as the otherwise anglophile New Zealanders freely allow, out of sheer common-sense, pragmatism and economy. As far as I could discover there never was any great debate in New Zealand about relaxing the sacred principle of all horses on the course at the same time covering the same distance, to be cleared off before the next set of horses line up. The revulsion of most British academics to the New Zealand system is hard to explain on rational grounds. The answer may lie historically in the proximity of the University of Cambridge to Newmarket Heath – it is the sporting spirit. The tutors are trainers.

We see both economic and social advantages in the encouragement of part-time study. Part-time students can remain economically active while studying, and can more easily retrain at critical points in their careers. Mature students have a better knowledge of working life, are able to make more deliberate and considered choices about their educational needs, and are often more able ... to make useful contributions to their courses. For higher education institutions, there are clear advantages in establishing stronger links with the surrounding community.

If some of those words seem to repeat what has already been said in this lecture, it may be because I helped to write them – long before the research had been completed. Every piece of applied research needs some initial sense of direction. Steering Committees must steer.

Notice that the words I wrote tried hard to fudge the often over-sharp distinction between vocational and non-vocational. Compare the language of the Secretary of State's consultative document *Higher Education in England Outside the Universities: Policy, Funding and Management* (July 1981):

In the 1972 White Paper, 'Framework for Expansion', it was noted that 'the continuously changing relationship between higher education and subsequent employment should be reflected in the institutions and in individual choices.' (Para 171). This is still true and is particularly reflected amongst other things in the non-university sectors' emphasis on vocational education, as shown by its provision of, for example, professional and technological resources. This sector's ability to offer such courses part-time and to serve the needs of individuals and industrial concerns locally and regionally is another hallmark of the sector.

There may well be an *emphasis* in the non-university sector on vocational, but it is far from exclusive. And it is derogatory to the individual's own assessment of his or her needs to imply that this provision will only be forthcoming if narrowly vocational – as if adults are to be YOPs[4] for life. All too often we end up, as Laski said of the British army, in a constant state of readiness to fight the last war. There is a lot of evidence suggesting that a vocationally-educated person is less flexible, even if reprogrammed or retrained, than a well-educated person. And personally, as I have argued elsewhere, I believe that we all need both: *techne* and *paedia*, skills and culture from the earliest age onwards.

> *All institutions of higher education should be encouraged to make more of their existing . . . full-time courses available to part-time students, whether for credit or not.*

I am not arguing against provision by extra-mural departments of special courses, I am only arguing that ordinary university lecture courses could perfectly well be opened up to larger numbers – 'whether for credit or not'. All credits, if tied to courses, could be applied for or not, so that registering at a university would not then always require an immediate decision of whether to go for a degree or diploma or not.

> *Institutions of higher education should be encouraged by education authorities and their validating bodies to develop, perhaps in collaboration with others, a range of daytime and evening courses designed for part-time undergraduates.*

This is where the timetable is important. In a conurbation like Birmingham, for instance, why should not one of the two polys, or one of the two universities, shift to a two-to-nine timetable, or even, like Birkbeck, entirely to evening provision? 'Should be encouraged . . .' indeed! I am afraid it needs carrots *and* sticks. Sweet reason rarely cuts into deeply-entrenched habits and prejudice.

> *We recognise the importance of the Open University in the provision of part-time degree opportunities, and feel that its experience serves to indicate the need for much further expansion of this kind of provision, using both face-to-face and distance teaching methods. In many less densely populated areas a mixture of these modes of provision, perhaps involving short intensive periods of full-time study, may be the most appropriate means of offering part-time study opportunities.*

Again the argument is for a mixed mode rather than for a rigid rivalry.

> *There should be greater provision of short preparatory courses, designed to introduce and prepare adults for degree level study. University extra-mural departments and local adult education centres have a particular role to play here. Entry to degree level courses should be based on a broader assessment of students' capacities and experience rather than on qualifications as such.*
>
> *The work of the university extra-mural departments in the provision*

of longer part-time courses, particularly those leading to awards, deserves greater recognition and development. Students successfully undertaking such courses should be able to transfer with credit to other higher level course . . .

I have no wish to over-emphasize degree work or certification, but sometimes even if extra-mural students do not want to go for a degree, certification provides a sensible objective, can lead to an easier self-imposed discipline, more positive involvement in study, not just sitting back and listening. It isn't always better than the telly, and as I have said I can see a different role for extra-mural departments: to become the publicizing, counselling service and the course-provider that specializes in part-time advanced work generally – whether degree or not, whether the student has yet decided to progress on or not by taking more of the same courses. However the fees must be reasonable in relation to the gross inequity that the straight-from-schools get paid for and the part-timers do all their own paying; and the universities must be positively required to make their staff participate as a normal part of the day's educational work. I have spent so long on the Tight Report because, although nominally concerned with degree work only, it does show a way to bring the universities down not from their high horse, but from their narrow hobby horse, and to reintegrate them into a wider and more critical adult public world. I am not against the post-school generation coming up to university. I dislike the cuts. But minimally, I wish they would all – as some of them now do for themselves – take a year off first, whether to get on to Mr Tebbitt's magic bicycle and look for a job, or to hitch-hike towards a source of light in Nepal. Straight from school, they are too used to a clear but concentrated imposed provision. Older, they would have to think for themselves a bit. These are the values I find in mature and adult students. One cannot teach people to think for themselves except by letting them think for themselves. The mature students are both more grateful and a damn sight more intelligently critical. They vote with their feet, for instance, if one cannot teach or is boring them. They worry more about those things and less about whether one banks with Barclays or thinks the students' union should or should not provide free coaches to political rallies.

Universities maintain learning and free study; as a kind of side product they teach. But they should think again about the mixture of who they teach. In terms of learning and free study it is impossible to justify the scale of university provision and the number of universities in this country: that can only be done in terms of teaching. I think that true communities are both primarily local and also a mixture of the ages, not a deliberate separation. Some of my values might sound like those of an old-fashioned self-help Tory and some of them like a democratic, community-conscious Socialist. So be it. The most amazing thing for a student of politics is to realize that both the main political parties are sceptical of existing university policy, both profess to favour self-help and the mature student; but neither – with all the curious crusades that the present Secretary of State[5] does become involved in – appears to do much about it. Perhaps the universities should do something for themselves while there is still time, but I admit that I do not think the chances for voluntarism are high.

Notes

1. E.G. Edwards, *Higher Education for Everyone* (Spokesman Press. Nottingham: 1982).
2. Malcolm Tight, ed, *Part-Time Degree Level Study in the United Kingdom* (Advisory Council for Adult and Continuing Education, Leicester, 1982), being the report of a working party set up jointly by the Advisory Council . . . the Baring Foundation, Birkbeck College, Goldsmiths' College, the Guild of St. George, and London University Department of Extra-Mural Studies.
3 *Ibid.*
4. The former Youth Opportunity Programme. For a while "YOP" became an ironic synonym for Yahoo, though these modern Yahoos were to be given a minimum of work, training and corn to prevent them attacking the Houyhnhnms.
5. Then Sir Keith Joseph, MP.

Three

The British Way of Political Studies

From *Government and Opposition,* Summer/Autumn 1980, a special
number to mark its 20th anniversary. Contributors were asked to give
"their personal view of the subject". I did.

One has to be careful on these occasions. There is so much accident
about it. Personally, as a late developer at school, I did not have
matriculation Latin but if I had I would have read History at Oxford.
Instead I began in Economics at London University, at University
College, by the way, not LSE — I had not heard of either, but LSE
looked like the office blocks of Croydon in which my father worked in
insurance and UCL looked like a university, as I had seen them in the
cinema. But I moved out of Economics when my tutor at the beginning
of the third year gave me a very high mark on an essay on 'Value
Theory', but said: 'Get out. I advise you to get out. You plainly don't
believe in the subject. You will be a brilliant critic of it if you go on. But
you don't believe that economic theory is anything else but an analytical card-castle. If you go on, you'll end up by hating your subject,
hating yourself, and feeling like I do that you've wasted your life,' I said
that as I was taking Finals that summer, it was a little late to switch.
'Nonsense', Alfred Stonier replied, 'not if you really want to get out of
Economics. You are going along to LSE for Laski's lectures for
subsidiary. Government's easy, just reading books. Switch to that till
you're clear what to do.'

I am still not wholly clear, but I admire the basic human courage of
always being able to rationalize an accident. Ontology has its uses.
Moving to the level of rationalization, trying to answer the self-
examination question set by the chairperson of the Board, I have an
odd feeling that I have come back to where I started thirty years ago. I
would have been a post-graduate student of Laski's but he died the year
I graduated in 1950. I was quite clear then that Politics was part of
politics. Well, not entirely so. I did have a strict Logical Positivist girl-
friend and embarked for about a year on the quest for a Science of
Politics that was to be based on Psychology, though whether Behavioural or Freudian I could never quite decide (for most of Ayer's circle
at that time were behaviourists undergoing analysis). My thesis title
was actually registered as 'The Method and Scope of Political Science:

31

the problem of the integration of empirical social research into the study of politics'. But I attended Popper's lectures and seminars, and 'Psychologism' reeled and my notions of scientific method opened up; and all the while the ghost of Laski kept needling. I was embarrassed at his philosophical thinness, but accepted that, even if there was no 'science of politics', there was some separation, beyond taste and prudence, between the study and the practice of politics. I don't take the ideological position (though that in fact was what I argued when my thesis became *The American Science of Politics*) that political studies are simply an instrumental part of the superstructure or, in some sense, derive from circumstances; rather I take the view that the study of politics is a critical activity which necessarily has implications for practice. There is no neutrality, only relative critical dispassion and reasonable objectivity: we can, with experience, knowledge and a conscious effort, give a fair, in the sense of a recognizable, account of doctrines we dislike. There is good and bad political judgement.

Much later I was to argue that toleration is a two-dimensional concept: how we limit our reactions, either out of principle or prudence, to things of which we disapprove. This seems to me fundamental both for political practice and for intellectual inquiry, that we are *capable* of such restraints (which does not mean that we should always be restrained); but that we move in a world of conscious approvals or disapprovals seems to me the only guarantee against triviality. There is still so much triviality in the social sciences, though less, I fancy, in the last few years than in the 1950s and 1960s.

This is to anticipate. My point is that reading at LSE as a post-graduate student in 1950–52 I knew nothing about what political studies were like elsewhere, all this was a decade before the great expansion; but that before leaving for four years in North America I had already grown sceptical of 'the science of politics', and the idea was in my head of studying why it was so plausible in American conditions. (George Catlin was to tell me some years later that my thesis was *wrong*, the science of politics was not American because he had published his *Science of Politics* before leaving for America in 1928.) I must have read some Mannheim which immediately made me want to study an important idea in its social setting, not to go on talking about the possibility of so doing. But Mannheim's notion of the sociology of knowledge was not reductionist: simply an interesting matter to see *the degree* to which ideas are conditioned (never caused or determined) by circumstances and social institutions. Or perhaps I was reading Mannheim in a Popperian way, just as I can now, after years of virtual abstinence, read some Marx in this conditional spirit: the degree to which social stratification places requirements on knowledge. But I can never accept that philosophy, indeed politics, does not have a final autonomy. We can study for its own sake; some ideas do precede and outlive historical contexts, though they are always coloured by them; I am convinced by Arendt's contention that Aristotle's teleological argument, much like modern utilitarianism, is a harmful abridgement, narrowing of the classic political tradition, a tradition that actually valued political action for its own sake, even when unsuccessful. Certainly we should keep on asking critically 'action for what?' (to expose the trouble with so much of the participation kick, whether among Liberals or Bennites), but action is prior to discovering any sense of direction: political action is not irrational unless it has a guaranteed sense of direction or systematic framework (here I find both Marxists and Hayekians wrong). Some political action is, in Oakeshott's senses, administering and keeping afloat, but also, which he cannot seem to concede, some is experimental, simply stirring the pot to see what happens. It is good if one can, but one does not have to say 'what should be done' as a condition for criticizing nonsense, triviality or refusing to take one-way tickets on a train with closed blinds.

This is still to anticipate. The actual state of political studies in the 1950s was obsessed not so much with the Faustian question, whether knowledge can lead to power (which is, I think, what Orwell was really satirizing – through James Burnham – in *Nineteen Eighty-Four*; but that's not recognized as political thought), but with more mundane question of the right balance to strike in the syllabus between ideas and institutions. To make matters worse 'ideas' were generally taught (even by Laski) so-called historically (in fact simply descriptions in chronological order) and institutions were also done descriptively, what I used to call, when the dead horse was still alive (though sightings are still occasionally reported), 'best British blinkered empiricism' (no names, no pack-drill).

This is what made Harvard in the mid-fifties seem very exciting to me: Carl Friedrich (whose work admittedly varied in its quality) at his best, say in the early editions of his *Constitutionalism and Government*, had an easy integration of the two. This I had not encountered before, simple though it now sounds. It was a more social-anthropological approach to politics: institutions were patterns of ideas. Or, put it another way, Friedrich, in his way, and Sam Beer, in a more consciously Weberian manner, asked what general concepts we formed that enabled us to define the distinctiveness and function of institutions. They also saw institutions as both carriers of ideas and as influenced by them. And other people reached the same position independently, say Raymond Aron or Masao Maruyama in Japan (though Weber lay behind them all); but I simply report that this conceptualization was relatively novel when I began teaching back in Britain and at LSE in 1957. At the time I feared, hearing a growing talk about 'a profession', that the American empiricist methods would penetrate deeply. In fact I think that this Weberian strain (even upon people who never read Weber) has had more influence, not by argument about method, but by the example of good studies. American visitors began to produce serious studies of British institutions which would include their politics, their social setting and which were self conscious about the investigators' own presuppositions. I think of Harry Eckstein's book on the politics of the BMA; this must have been a model for many of the later studies of pressure groups and parties. They came to call it 'the political culture approach'. I'm not sure that this was ever really very tightly defined, but better that it wasn't: it avoided the rigidities of the Easton and the Almond school and all that mysterious talk about 'process' that at one time in the later 1950s seemed likely to obfuscate us all, particularly in that strange period of university expansion when our supply of postgraduates was actually inadequate, and anyone who had been anywhere in the States was not even lucky to get a job.

Behaviourism only really dominated Essex and then Strathclyde, most of the other new departments hedged their bets and lazily or wisely added a behaviourist or so to political ideas and institutions men. Some area specialists appeared, but so often alone that they had to adopt an integrative political culture approach almost from necessity. Consider the difference between the rather formal Almond and Verba functional headings of the first edition of Richard Rose's *Politics in England* (Parliament appeared in a chapter on 'Communications') and the far more genuinely integrated revised edition, *Politics in England Today*. There the main themes of actual British politics were the organizing principles of the book, while the former's somewhat artificially imposed conceptual framework detumesced into occasional suggestiveness. By the time of his fine study of Northern Ireland, *Governing Without Consensus*, he was himself, as it were, fully socialized into British politics.

Politics, as a subject of study, has not been alone in its expansion in the last twenty-five years. Hardly had the handful of pre- and post-war chairs in Politics begun to increase and multiply with university expansion, moving away from older subsidiary subject dependencies on History and Economics, when Sociology appeared as a challenge. It was a challenge both intellectually, tending to a definite view of 'politics' as an inherently subsidiary or derivative activity, and a challenge in terms of student numbers and hence resources. But Politics and Sociology both benefited from the looser degree structures typical of the new universities and the polytechnics (even if it was only the poor bloody students who were supposed to integrate, few of the people who were teaching them did or could). And some alliances were struck: the intellectual formulation of 'political sociology'.

Faced in the early 1960s by a double challenge from Sociology, the belief of both Marx and Parsons that politics is but a derivative, even an irrational factor, and the beliefs of the Sunday papers that it was not so much Marxist as 'with it', like the new universities and the mini-skirt, some students of politics reacted by trying to make 'Political Sociology' the very centre of things. Political theorists were politely told that they could keep their old 'History of Political Thought from Plato to . . .' course so long as they proved themselves *genuine* political theorists by providing tighter theoretical constructs for empirical verification (or very often there was not even an hypothesis to verify, or to falsify *vide* Popper, but simply an area to research or a private field to graze in with a new S.S.R.C. grant). Some advertisements actually appeared in the press for 'empirical theorists'. A few political theorists actually climbed onto such procrustean beds voluntarily. They either bled to death or emigrated. I reacted to all this, in curricular terms, by lecturing on the history of political systems, which I claimed could actually be found embedded in traditional political thought but suppressed by the philosophers.

However some people, both old-stagers who had had to teach right across the ideas and institutions syllabuses of small departments and new specialists in sub-fields, made a virtue of not being an integrated discipline, like Economics and Anthropology, but of being simply a range of conventionally related problems which demand the making and crossing of bridges all the time, both in research and teaching, between History, Philosophy, Economics, Sociology and experience of public service. For there were always the good old fellows who had no fancy thoughts about the epistemological problems of theory and practice, but who simply assumed that if you lived in London or Oxford (or in Sir Denis Brogan's case could get away from Cambridge), you simply talked to civil servants and Cabinet Ministers, as in the good old days of the war, and sat hard on committees; and if you were not in London or Oxford, there was always Town Hall even before the short-lived pleasures of the Regional Planning Boards. The silent majority never felt worried about or jealous of the scientific status of Economics or Psychology.

The range of studies that fell within the expanding departments of Politics was remarkable. There could be, growingly was, both a 'History of Political Ideas' and 'Political Philosophy'. 'British Central Government', 'Parties and Pressure Groups' and 'Public Administration' and/or Local Government' tended to form the staple or common-core, even when given trendy labels. 'Comparative Government' was universal, but ranged from 'Some Modern Foreign Governments' to 'Political Systems': sometimes it became, indeed, the behaviourist preserve, since it was often hard to get the older men to give up the British Government core courses. It was an unlikely event when one of the old guard, like Victor Wiseman, Leeds Labour Party, Study of

Parliament Group and public administration, became converted to behaviourism on a trip to America and built a department on those lines, more or less, for a while, at Exeter. Area studies became more interesting: something that one could call 'comparative historical political sociology', that had not been seen since Tocqueville, began to penetrate. Sometimes methodological preoccupations predominated and imposed jargon drowned the demotic voices. But some of this work was very readable and interesting.

One area declined, constitutional theory. Partly it declined because it was too identified with constitutional law as a branch of the study of institutions, held to be too narrow. Most of the books on the Constitution cited, for instance, in the thoughtful bibliography to Max Beloff and Gillian Peele's recent *The Government of the United Kingdom* (1980) are very old books, certainly pre-dating the demise of British world power, the symptomatic institutional reforms of the post-1964 decade and the worsening industrial crisis and the breakdown of consensus of the last decade. Even Geoffrey Marshall's *Constitutional Theory* (1971), which they call the best introduction to constitutional theory, and which indeed is a very good book, seems strangely dated with its lack of any discussion of Northern Ireland or Scotland or of the tri-partite hypothesis (or what Keith Middlemas in his *Politics of Industrial Society* now calls 'the corporatist bias' of the modern British system of government). But there are now some signs of a revival of constitutional speculation, fed in part by a revival of serious juris-prudence, but also by political events. Some kind of genuine constitutional thought got into the government's speculative White Paper (more a Green 'un) on *the Government of Northern Ireland* of November 1979, that hasn't been seen in or near the machine of government for a long time, certainly was totally lacking in the drafting of the appalling Scotland Bill. It would be nice to think that this influence came from political scientists, but that is very doubtful: more likely that some lawyers are having to think about political issues rather seriously (not just John Griffith), for whatever reasons.

So from the 1950s and through the 1960s there was no possible general characterization of British political studies, except to say 'tolerant eclecticism'. On the whole it was tolerant: Manchester and Glasgow both seemed to have a bit of everything in the best sense. There were some things that LSE and Oxford would never have, mainly those that Essex and Strathclyde seemed to have in abund-ance, and vice versa. Some might say, too much tolerance. For a while in the mid and late '60s some of the students seemed to say this. But compared to Sociology, there were relatively few Marxists in Politics departments. Among the students, a dual honours Politics and Sociol-ogy course could be quite lively; but single honours Politics tended to be almost disappointingly law-abiding. I confess that at Sheffield I enjoyed the time of the troubles (so mild, of course, compared to German, American, French and Italian experiences).

What did grow out of the troubles of the late '60s, I believe, was a remarkable revival of political thought. This was partly a misapprehension. Political Thought courses often or usually did not contain what students hoped to find, either discussion of the great issues of principle or of the truth of the great theoretical explanations of political, economic and social behaviour. But there were some things even in the old courses that seemed less trivial and parochial to the serious radical students than much of Brit. Gov. or Comp. Pol. And as these courses grew, so did appointments (in those last happy days of intellectual supply and demand). Many young and more radical political theorists emerged, but the 'pure men', whether of the Oakeshott brand or of what I used to call the Peter Laslett but now the Quentin Skinner school, also got many more option-takers. Even Philosophers, perhaps even Ernest Gellner would admit, seemed marginally but noticeably more interested in social problems by the end of the 1970s than they were in the '50s or '60s. Indeed fewer people seem interested in the history of political ideas, though among the few there is some extraordinary scholarship; and more are interested in the application of concepts to contemporary political and moral problems. We may see a genuine revival of political speculation, even among academics (often novelists and poets have carried the great tradition of republican speculativeness more effectively than dons since the professionalization of learning). Will political theorists and institutionalists together, one wonders, have anything to contribute to discussions about industrial democracy – beyond a depressive and descriptive realism? They *should*. There are occasions for inventing institutions.

Some behaviourists claimed to have rediscovered 'values' when challenged from below, but they mainly thought either of a new subject for research or thought in manipulative vein. I remember hearing a Prince of behaviourists publicly 'confess', he said (at some length at an international conference) that he had once tried to exclude values. But now he saw that political science should serve democratic values. And he argued that a centre for policy studies should be set up in every state of the Union, of the world indeed, so that when the democratically elected people would decide on 'value-oriented policy objectives', political scientists could then determine how to achieve 'the legitimately designated goal'. Occasionally one says it, and I whimsically did: that I saw no virtue in moving so quickly from being a eunuch into being a whore. Such arguments seem to me to betray both democracy and learning. I hope the future does not go that way.

Actually I am not very concerned to prophesy or to project trends. One no longer has to be so pseudo-scientific. One can argue the merit of what one would like to see, and only consult trends to demonstrate

the possibility. There must always be more possibilities than probabilities, and probabilities in fluid political circumstances need a
great deal of forcing. 'The ethically desirable must be the sociologically
possible', but that is the order of it.

The central problem of politics (both the study and the practice) is
that of justice – the adjective 'social' is not needed unless anyone could
think that I am talking about jurisprudence. Rawls does not merely
make an argument about 'justice', he asserts the centrality of the
concept. How people are treated and how they react is conditioned by
their economic interests; but finally what is acceptable depends upon
thinking that the process that leads to the result is just. It seems to me
almost axiomatic, for example, that an incomes policy that is simply
concerned to limit wages as a temporary reaction to inflation is bound
to be regarded as arbitrary, unless general principles or processes,
accepted as just, for determining rewards can be established. Equally
to believe in a free market seems simply to try to substitute a myth of
fatality for the familiar freedom of political action, which is a freedom
to act upon nature, not to accept anything, except death, as inevitable.
Popular politics is not aberrant in refusing to accept that unemployment and poverty are necessary, permanent parts of the human
conditions: it is humane and sensible.

The study of politics must at least expose the oddity of those who
complain, for instance, at the *intrusion* of political factors into
economics, education or private life. Its very existence, its setting in a
tradition of political action, must assert that depoliticization is impossible. Talk of good or bad politics, of purely political factors being
carried too far, but to talk of a state not intervening on principle in
matters that affect all society, this is an absurdity. The study-practice of
Politics cannot, indeed, discover or collectively endorse single correct
policies: but it is bound to the view that political factors in general are
natural, not something to be eradicated. It is not committed to a belief
in planning, even in the benign old public administrative Fabian
Town and Country Planning way (no Marxism that), but it is committed to the view that political intervention into anything cannot be
excluded in principle and can sometimes be justified. But in a political
situation there are always different routes, worth arguing about,
towards even an agreed goal.

I see a complete symmetry between the common view that genuine
political studies are only possible in what we call, in broad terms
(however incomplete these freedoms), free societies, and the less common view that free societies are only possible where there is some
independent study-and-criticism of rulers and politicians. This may
seem scary talk to some. But independent study and criticism has in
fact been much practised by, as it were, the main-line tradition of the
duller parts of British political studies, the institutions men who sit on

committees or who give occasional advice. This is at a rather low and instrumental level. And some of the advice may be bad as well as good. But it is essentially the same activity as a philosopher asking questions of principle about the limits of *tolerance* (which is in fact the Williams Report) or an historian, like Dr Middlemas in his recent *Politics of Industrial Society*, showing that an old system of management and accommodation has broken down and trying to indicate (always less successfully, necessarily so) possible responses. I stress the plural. If he had or insinuates only one response, this strictly speaking is ideology, not politics. We may speak of the best response, in our opinion and for these reasons etc., but never that it is the only response.

What is at issue is not whether we conceptualize our study in terms of science, philosophy, history or policy. For even if we say 'science', we can mean pure or we can mean applied; and if we say 'philosophy', we can mean the aesthetic or we can mean practical reason – in neither case is the theory and practice debate resolved, except by definition. What is at issue is the integrity and sound judgement of the scholar. We cannot avoid relationships with practice, and I believe should not. But we owe practical politics and public policy our good judgement, our critical judgement (particularly towards our own side), not our endorsements. I do not find Orwell paradoxical when he says both that the writer should take sides *and* that he cannot ever be a 'loyal member' of a political party. Speaking of writers he said: 'The more one is conscious of one's political bias, the more chance one has of acting politically without sacrificing one's aesthetic and intellectual integrity'. So, too, for writing about society, it is no different, we have no special status. We can be partisan and yet give a fair picture of opponents and fair warnings to our own people, that it is unlikely to work or even take a mistaken direction. But we can simply be partisan, an easy and self-indulgent thing to do. Gellner's view like Orwell's is essentially dualistic, *Spectacles and Predicaments* he calls his latest essays: we are necessarily both observers and involved in the game. How else can it be? Theory and doctrine (as I have argued in my *Political Theory and Practice*) are different articulations for different purposes, but they are not logically separable: every theory has underlying values and every doctrine claims to be empirically realizable. Nonetheless political studies ebb and flow in their stress. When I began the story the best men, whether in scientific or philosophical vein, aspired to purity and the duller ones to practice; now the positions seem to be reversing themselves. And I find, personally, that dialogue on public policy becomes more fruitful, not less, between different political camps.

I think that political studies in the coming decade will get drawn more closely in nearly every aspect into political practice, into an indirect but vital relevance, not a blind partisanship in response to the growing crisis of our economy and polity. But that is not the only possible response.[1] Ivory towers have thick walls and some people (among them, incidentally, both Marxists and pluralists) prefer to be eunuchs or voyeurs.

Notes

1. Another response for another anniversary set of home-truths was to examine the principles that should apply to political education in schools and the lack of interest in this, either intellectual or practical, shown by most Politics departments in universities and polytechnics. See my 'Chalk-Dust, Punch-Card and the Polity' in F.F. Ridley, ed., *Studies in Politics: essays to mark the 25th anniversary of the Political Studies Association* (Clarendon Press, Oxford: Oxford, 1975), pp. 43-60.

Four

On Rereading *The Origins of Totalitarianism*

* From *Social Research*, Spring 1977

So many quibble at the word and so few will look at the thing itself. To understand a concept, it is necessary to consider it in its context; but to judge its usefulness for general theory is not simply to reduce a concept to a particular context. *The Origins of Totalitarianism* is, in many ways, Hannah Arendt's greatest achievement, but the one most misunderstood. This first major political work, 'is also the one for which she is most widely known and has been both highly praised and much criticised', as Margaret Canovan wrote in her thoughtful introduction to Arendt's ideas.[1]

She wrote it in 1949 and it was published in 1951, exactly a year later in each case than Orwell's *Nineteen Eighty-Four*, written in much the same mood, also a warning not a prophecy, but to which she oddly never refers in much-revised (indeed overrevised) later editions. The preface to the first edition began: 'Two World Wars in one generation, separated by an uninterrupted chain of local wars and revolutions, followed by no peace treaty for the vanquished and no respite for the victor, have ended in the anticipation of a third World War between the two remaining world powers.'[2] And to force herself and her readers to see that she was writing with relevance for humanity and not professionally for political scientists, she put as a legend over all a quotation from her old Heidelberg teacher, Karl Jaspers: *'Weder dem Vergangenen anheim fallen noch dem Zukünftigen. Es kommt darauf an, ganz gegenwärtig zu sein.'* ('To give in neither to the past nor to the future. What matters is to be entirely present.')

However, it is as crude as it is stupid, therefore, to treat the origins of the whole concept as either wartime propaganda or as a device of the cold war – as does, for instance, the entry under 'Totalitarianism' written by Herbert J. Spiro in the *International Encyclopedia of the Social Sciences* of 1968:

> The word, which first gained currency through anti-Nazi propaganda during World War II, later became an anti-Communist slogan in the cold war. Its utility for propaganda purposes has tended to obscure whatever utility it may have had for systematic

analysis ... As the social sciences develop more discriminating concepts of comparison ... and as, hopefully, the more glaring differences between the major parties to the cold war begin to wither away, use of the term 'totalitarianism' may also become less frequent. If these expectations are borne out, then a third encyclopedia of the social sciences, like the first one, will not list 'totalitarianism.'

It is an almost Orwellian thought that the offensive word will simply be removed from the vocabulary of a political science of such dubious predictive value. But what is intellectually disreputable is that Spiro can ignore the evidence, either because it does not suit his thesis or possibly simply through ignorance, that the term was current before the Second World War. From about 1936, very much a product of the behaviour of the Communist Party in the Spanish Civil War, several well-known, or to become well-known, political writers or literary intellectuals began to take over Mussolini's unrealistic and bombastic term, if applied to Italian Fascism, and to apply it to something that they saw independently of each other and at first found hard to believe. They saw with unwelcome horror that there were astonishing similarities between the style, the structure of thought, and the key institutions of the Nazis and the Russian Communists. Borkenau, Gide, Koestler, Malraux, Orwell, and Silone all saw this.[3] Even some political scientists began to discuss it heavily, earnestly, and professionally.[4] The concept used in this sense was, certainly, that of a minority, but they made it a commonplace nonetheless, long before the cold war. Some people, however, still do not want to face the past. I am sure that Arendt would have liked what Orwell wrote in an introduction to *Animal Farm* which he never used: 'Liberty is telling people what they do not want to hear.'[5] Or else people think that totalitarianism was not an assault on humanity that failed, but is simply a concept with which professional games of classification can be played. Since so many political scientists have used or 'defined' it so idiosyncratically and often overschematically, it can be declared meaningless. Political science will then, like economics presumably, confine itself to concepts that can be defined precisely and used to build quantifiable models, thus escaping from the mess of the real world.[6]

A Peculiar Explanation

To begin in such a way is, of course, partly defensive. For I think Arendt was a great thinker although she certainly never wrote in a way either familiar to or pleasing to social scientists — much the same as Orwell, even though he was on a lower philosophical plane and far closer to immediate practice than she. He was saved from banality by not having gone to university; and she was saved from the internalizing routines of the social scientists by writing her great book on her own, coming back into the university only when mature, famous, and independent. On the other hand, she herself was either less than generous or not perceptive about the pre-war fashioners of the concept. In fact, she spent no time in the first edition justifying the term at all. She simply accepted its existence, both as a worthwhile concept and as a phenomenon of our times, and got down straight away to her peculiar explanation of its origins. She did not make the claim to be the first to use the concept analytically, even if perhaps one may infer such a claim from her ignoring literary progenitors. For otherwise she used literary sources well when she wished to establish the *plausibility* of the concept. Only in the second and later editions did she become self-conscious about the concept, responding both to criticism of the whole concept and to a sudden plethora of rival characterizations and models.[7] But she could never believe that scholars living in freedom could be so insensitive as to claim that something historically unique and world-shaking had not been attempted.

I said 'her peculiar *explanation*' of its origins. Strictly speaking, there is no explanation of the origins of totalitarianism. Indeed, she did not believe from her general philosophical position that there could be any unique and necessary line of development toward what occurred. This is where the 'model-builders', with their pretence at causality, go astray in reading her, or rather with their very abstracted notion of causality. Things occur because of antecedent 'causes' – events, conditions, and beliefs – but they need not occur. To find the causes of a phenomenon is not, strictly speaking, to explain it but simply to understand it better. Above all, it is to understand why a secular ambition to transform society totally became plausible. Became plausible, that is, to bands of resolute, determined, and yet to a large extent lucky fanatics and adventurers ('armed bohemians', she said once) when conditions were ripe; and conditions were ripe not in terms of these men preparing for, still less making, the revolution, but in terms of the breakdown of the previous social order. The breakdown, she argued, was of something far more fundamental than any one form of social order. The breakdown was of all settled expectations, of any possibility of ordinary people seeing the world as reasonable and predictable.

So with Arendt, it is necessary to distinguish sharply between her account of the growth of the ideology of Nazism and her account of the breakdown of traditional bourgeois values and expectations. There can be a true historical account of each of these, but it is only the ideologist himself who claims either that he (or even his opponents, getting trapped into accepting his concepts) caused the breakdown, or that he foretold its character and could always prove that when it came it would uniquely and necessarily benefit him. Strictly speaking, the two accounts have no logical connection. But what is to be explained, then, is not the necessary preconditions of the rise of Nazism and of

Stalinism respectively, but how these two groups ever picked up, long before they came to power or power came to them, the astonishing concept that they held 'the key to history' and possessed a total and comprehensive explanation and prophecy of *everything*, not simply of political phenomena – what she calls simply 'ideologies'.[8]

This accounts for her seeming arbitrariness, both to the generalizing social scientist and to the nominalist historian, in moving from one event to another and one country to another, leaving her critics giddy and gasping that there is no connection between the Dreyfus Affair and the imperialism of Cecil Rhodes, or between either Britain and France and German Nazism, nor between racialist Pan-Slavism and Stalin. But that seems to her (though it would have helped to have said so more clearly) not the point. The point is simply (if such a word can be used of such a person – occasionally) to establish the existence and plausibility of ideologies (in her special sense).

In fact, her methodology is not at all unlike that of Tocqueville. In the first chapter of his *Souvenirs*, Tocqueville says that he detests equally those literary men remote from public affairs who produce vast, abstract, and all-embracing iron laws and first causes of human history and those politicians and men of affairs who believe that everything is, on the contrary, just a matter of pulling strings or of accident. He believes, he says, that both are equally mistaken. Nothing can happen without antecedent social conditions changing and giving an opportunity, but nothing actually happens without the actions of men; and many different sorts of actions and inactions can occur in changing social conditions, some better, some worse, some good, some evil, some successful and some unsuccessful – 'although I firmly believe that chance does nothing that has not been prepared beforehand'.[9] So she sets out the broad 'causes' and *also* the particular conditions that led to the breakdown of traditional expectations of government in Germany, whether authoritarian or republican; but her main effort goes into demonstrating the intense if terrible plausibility of Nazism.

This explains the much criticized lopsidedness of the book: three hundred pages on anti-Semitism and then imperialism (neither on the face of it very relevant to Stalin's Communism) before a hundred and fifty pages on totalitarianism, on the character and working of totalitarian society, which suddenly embrace both the Soviet Union and Germany. In the second edition, in the famous epilogue 'Reflections on the Hungarian Revolution', she first admits hope that a totalitarian regime can, once established, be destroyed from within, not simply, as happened to Hitler, from without; and she first clearly links the short-lived workers' councils of Budapest to the soviets that Lenin first stirred up and then suppressed, to the Commune of Paris, to Proudhon rather than Marx as the great *social* theorist, and to the historical fame and some of the actual practices of fifth-century Athens – themes to become very important, the anarchist twist to her conservatism (a marriage, as it were, of Tocqueville and Proudhon), in *The Human Condition* and in *On Revolution*. She concentrates on Germany surely because, though without sufficient explanation, few people would then, perhaps even now, concede that the Nazis had a full-blown ideology, irrational in its power to comprehend the real world but rational in terms of a broad internal consistency. For two arguments are going on in parallel. Many who deny that the Nazis ever had an ideology or that it was important, such as A.J.P. Taylor in his accounts of the origins of the Second World War or Bertold Brecht caricaturing Hitler as a mere gangster in politics, cheerfully concede or firmly claim that Communism is an ideology – in something very close to Arendt's sense of 'a key to history'.[10] This Arendt has to refute, but not merely in terms of showing the origins of Nazism but of showing how a racialism with exterminatory inferences (beyond *mere* racial prejudice, like *mere* anti-Semitism) could emerge even in a relatively benign imperialism, like the British, the French, or the Belgian. See what can happen, she is saying, in unprecedented and dehumanizing circumstances; she is talking about a new kind of human imagination, as when Cecil Rhodes 'dreamed in centuries and thought in continents' and 'would annex the planets if I could';[11] or as when ordinary Frenchmen during the Dreyfus Affair became convinced that there was an international Jewish conspiracy aimed both at the Church and at the safety of the Republic.

Arendt certainly knew more about Germany than about the Soviet Union. But this does not explain the strategy of the book. The first point for her to settle was that the Nazis had such an ideology and that it had precedents elsewhere. Only then could the parallel argument be developed, that the Soviet Communist ideology once in power (and it needs less or no explanation of what it is) behaved remarkably similarly in its mode of government to that of the Nazis. Certainly when compared to any previous 'mere' autocratic regimes or military dictatorships, they had, as the times had, much in common. And she never said anything as foolish as that they were the same way, as death on the road can be by different kinds of vehicles, not necessarily by the same kind. However, the modern age was not simply characterized by technology, by new instruments of power; it was characterized by a new mode of thought, a new way of perceiving things, which she called ideological.

If the book does seem unbalanced in the space it gives to Germany, perhaps this is a fault, but to see it as a gross fault would be to misconceive the whole purpose and strategy of the book. It would be rather like, having been able to grasp that Tocqueville's *Democracy in America* is really meant to be about the whole of Western European civilisation, to then say that he should have given equal and explicit space to France and to England. He assumed that his readers knew more about them already, whereas America was both unfamiliar and represented a projection of the European future. But the second volume is completely generalized, about democracy in general or, rather, about the general character of the social effects of holding a democratic doctrine – like the last section of Arendt's *Origins*.

Ideological Superstition

In other words, Arendt is the most rational of the revolt against reason theorists. Small wonder that those who still cannot grasp the enormity of the events, the scale and the utter economic irrationality both of the camps and of the purges, either accuse her of making abstract models or, as a leading British political philosopher says in his table-talk, of 'metaphysical free association'. She does move from one thing to another, but she is not trying to write either a complete history or to give a complete causal explanation of why Nazism and Stalinism arose precisely in the form they did (that she would hold, in light of her views on freedom and on action, to be anyway impossible). She is rather an historical sociologist, trying to show why certain crazy ideas could become plausible. She deals in the rationality of the irrational, something that empiricists are often ill-equipped (both frightened and incompetent) to touch.

> While the totalitarian regimes are thus resolutely and cynically emptying the world of the only thing that makes sense to the utilitarian expectations of common sense, they impose upon it at the same time a kind of supersense which the ideologies actually always meant when they pretended to have found the key to history or the solution to the riddles of the universe. Over and above the senselessness of totalitarian society is enthroned the ridiculous supersense of its ideological superstition. Ideologies are harmless, uncritical and arbitrary opinions only as long as they are not believed in seriously. Once their claim to total validity is taken literally they become the nuclei of logical systems in which, as in the systems of paranoiacs, everything follows comprehensibly and even compulsorily once the first premise is accepted. The insanity of such systems lies not only in their first premise but in the very logicality with which they are constructed. The curious logicality of all isms, their simple-minded trust in the salvation value of stubborn devotion without regard for specific, varying factors, already harbors the first germs of totalitarian contempt for reality and factuality.[12]

Again like Tocqueville and Hegel, she starts from the shattering effect of the French Revolution. Even amid injustice, there was a clarity about social relationships in the old regime, she asserts, Once masses of people became detached from clear class allegiances, they became not class-conscious workers but rather classless and massified, open to superstitions but now political superstitions more than religious, available for mobilization. Her famous distinction between the mentality of 'the mob' and of 'the mass' emerges: the 'mob' the active and aggressive residue of classes, the ready followers of political adventurers; the masses inert and hopeless, until stirred in times of desperation.

The specific desperation that created the immediate conditions for ideologists to gain mass support was, Arendt argues, the experience of the First World War — mass slaughter — followed almost immediately by mass unemployment and inflation. She talks of war and mass unemployment as being like 'two demons' who completely refuted and destroyed the rationality of liberal political and economic expectations.[13] The statelessness of so many people thrust out of nation-states seemed suddenly to create a condition even before the camps, but in some ways a foretaste of the camps, in which all 'normal' human rights seemed to be removed from human beings if they were not securely citizens of a state. The man without a political homeland became a man without rights: the whole message and understanding of the Enlightenment reversed. Even within nation-states, men came to be declared not merely not citizens but anticitizens, corruptive of the society, if they were, in one instance, of the wrong social class and, in the other instance, of the wrong race.

For racialism as a principle of allegiance cut right through nations. It was no longer enough to be, as most Jews in Germany were before and during the First World War, 'a good German': to be a citizen and to have rights one had to be an Aryan, or what the party said was an Aryan. And imperialism, in seeking 'the expansion of political power without the foundation of a body politic', needed not merely a justification such as racialism (for 'improvement' would doom the imperialists eventually to hand over or to share power) but also needed an excuse to treat mere subjects, seen as never fit for citizenship, as less than men. Precedents were set, as in the Congo and South Africa, as to what could be done when rulers were liberated from the normal constraints of politics. Arendt is almost obsessed to convince her readers that racialism is an authentic ideology, something to be taken seriously as an original and irreducible mental force, however factually wrong, however irrational. It cannot be reduced to economic circumstances, even though these can exacerbate it:

> ... an ideology differs from a simple opinion in that claims to possess either the key to history, or the solution for all the 'riddles of the universe,' or the intimate knowledge of the hidden universal laws which are supposed to govern nature and man. Few ideologies have won enough prominence to survive the hard

competitive struggle of persuasion, and only two have come out on top and essentially defeated all others; the ideology which interprets history as an economic struggle of classes, and the other that interprets history as an economic struggle of races.[14] This is simple, but surely convincing. To call this kind of thing 'ideology' need not be to deny that the word is well used in other contexts. This is not *the true* meaning of ideology.[15] But it is one possible meaning which cannot reasonably be denied and which functions, in many ways, like a secular religion.[16] Perhaps she is incautious in always talking about 'ideology' as a comprehensive world view, seeking transformation, engendering terror out of its very irrationality and out of its hostility to the spontaneity and unpredictability of free human actions.[17] It may well be, as I have argued elsewhere, that the notion that ideas are products of circumstances (be circumstances conceived as biological or economic) dangerously inclines towards a contempt for human freedom, to a belief that justice can be obtained only by reforming circumstances by force rather than by reasoning and acting among men. But not everyone who speaks the language of causation in fact means what he says. Usually these causal statements of 'necessity' and 'determination' are scientific rhetoric for more conditional assertions: circumstances *condition* ideas, ideas are *not unaffected* by circumstances – relative statements and negative formulations can make the study of *how much* ideas are 'products' of circumstances almost innocent of any totalitarian implications (while not making 'ideology' so empty as to mean simply that all ideas about politics imply practice, as Martin Seliger has recently argued at length[18]).

However, Arendt is simply not concerned with the debate about usages of ideology. She is concerned simply to establish that ideologies, in her sense, have existed and have done uniquely terrible things. But done them by the opportunity of wielding power, not by any special prescience in knowing how to or ability in actually overthrowing conventional society.

An Element of Accident

Here we are close to the two great confusions in the whole debate about 'totalitarianism'. Accounts of how they came to power and of what they did when they were in power are often confused, and, as I have already argued, they are not logically related. And accounts of what they intended to do when in power and of what they actually did are often confused; or rather (where I find Arendt herself is confusing) their actions were not as systematic as the ideologies would lead us to suppose. Both Hitler and Stalin were selective, but grimly selective: not selective by the normal political mechanisms that engender compromise, but selective by fanatical pursuit of what they thought to be the most important parts of the ideology.[19] So to claim that there was, indeed that there ever could be, a fully and literally totalitarian system of government is to claim too much. But to use a theoretical or logical refutation of this rhetorical claim to deny the uniqueness of the two regimes, particularly the massive horror and uniqueness of the Nazi extermination camps and of Stalin's purges, this is to miss the point and to trivialize 'the burden of our times' (which was the morally apt, if uninformative, title of the first English edition of *Origins*).

Let an historian prefer Bracher's, Bullock's, or even A.J.P. Taylor's account of how Hitler came to power to Arendt's. But this still does not meet her main point. What did Hitler do when he came to power? Hitler was (in part) a clever nationalist politician (*vide* Taylor), he was also (in part) a cunning demagogue who pursued a 'tactic of legality', saying one thing to the party and another to the public (*vide* Bullock); but neither seems to give an adequate account either of what happened when Hitler came to power or of his motives.[20]

Strictly speaking, the historian is on firmer ground to claim that Arendt gives no clear explanation of how the Nazis came to power. She virtually says so herself: 'There is an abyss between men of brilliant and facile conceptions and men of brutal deeds and active bestiality which no intellectual explanation is able to bridge.'[21] Nazism and Marxism might have been as futile as Freemasonry and Single Tax had conditions not proved ripe. There is an element of terrible accident about – not 'it all', for something terrible would have happened amid such breakdown – but what actually happened. The formation of ideologies can be described. The breakdown of old systems can be described. And what then happens can be described. But there are no inevitable connections between them. Arendt never implies that there are. Her critics have either not read her closely or else are just using other formulations of the origins and conditions of totalitarianism, often crude, rigid, and deterministic, as sticks to beat both her and the concept. Or often they are angered, even if not Marxist, by the comparison: of course Marxism is nothing at all like Nazism, has no totalitarian qualities, and is, of course, a much more comprehensive and total view of human history than was ever Nazism, and it happens either to be true or to be the only ideology scientific enough for liberal tolerance or respect.

An appearance of determinism could be given to Arendt's argument because, quite naturally, she concentrates on an account of the growth in the nineteenth century of those elements of thought that became important in Nazism in the twentieth century; and she gives all too few glimpses of the nonstarters and the less successful ideologies of the *salon* and of the gutter. She is, quite properly, writing history backwards: she selects what is relevant to understanding the mentality of the Nazis and of the Communists under Stalin; and she is not writing a general account of nineteenth-century extreme political sects. She should have said this more explicitly, or a few examples of the 'also rans' would have shown the historian that she was not arguing a direct causal connection between the thought of Gobineau and the deeds of Hitler or between the thought of Marx and the deeds of Stalin, but only showing how it was, given power, that they were able and eager to think in world-transforming terms rather than – like traditional autocrats – in power-preserving and power-enjoying terms. One example from elsewhere:

> What have these Saints achieved? In the midst of a free people, they have founded a despotic power. In a land which repudiates state religions, they have placed their church above human laws. Among a society of Anglo-Saxons, they have introduced some of the ideas, many of the practices of red Indian tribes, of Utes, Shoshones and Snakes ... Putting under their feet both the laws of science and the lessons of history, they preach the duty of going back in the spirit and in the name, to that priestly and paternal form of government which existed in Syria four thousand years ago; casting from them, as so much waste, the things which all other white men have learned to regard as the most precious conquests of time and thought – personal freedom, family life, change of rulers, concurrence in laws, equality before the judge, liberty of writing and voting. They cast aside these conquests of time and thought in favor of Asiatic obedience to a man without birth, without education, whom they have chosen to regard as God's own vicar on the earth.
>
> With them to do any piece of work is a righteous act; to be a toiling and producing man is to be in a state of grace.
>
> What need is there to dwell on the political value of such a note?[22]

Indeed this intelligent English traveller, watching in 1866 a large wagon train of converts from South Wales pouring down into Salt Lake city, worried himself profoundly, for a moment, at what might happen if Mormonism were to increase its appeal to the poor (the white poor, anyway) everywhere. Forgive this digression. The Mormons were not serious starters in the twentieth-century totalitarian stakes – though perhaps more due to their lingering cultural realism when faced by an ultimatum from the U.S. Senate or the U.S. cavalry-on-the-move than by self-willed political constraints. But this traveller saw in them something of the logic of plausibility of what Arendt was to call totalitarian ideology. That is the main point that Arendt sought to establish.

If criticized for being digressive, she might have done better to be more digressive and seemingly 'irrelevant' to the plain tale of development from Gobineau to Hitler that so many mistakenly expect, as in those absurd and terrible old attempts to jazz up or give a kind of pornographic interest to political thought by titles like ... *From Luther to Hitler* (usually, with almost wicked ignorance and superficiality, via Hegel).[23] She should have shown more instances of new lights that failed. For she is sustaining the claim that ideologies (in her sense) arose at all, not that the two that won out and came to power themselves explain how they came to power, nor even that the movements associated with them created the revolutionary situations. When in power they made history, but not until then.

What She Has Said

Certainly there are many questionable judgements, irrelevancies, mistakes, and eccentricities in Arendt's analysis.[24] Her prefaces establish the sense of the problem, to comprehend how the attempt at totalitarian government was possible, but say nothing helpful to the reader faced with a work so large, so unusual, so diverse, so outside the Anglo-American scholarly tradition, about her presuppositions. The student reader is, I find, awed, bewildered, and enthralled all at once. But bewildered more than a bit, like all of us on first reading, because her premises and preconceptions are not made clear, at least not in the prefaces or in any one place in the text. They become clear in her later books. *The Human Condition* (1958) makes clear her assumptions about the political, human freedom, and the capacity for action. *On Revolution* (1963) makes clear her assumptions about the possibilities of deliberate social change. *Eichmann in Jerusalem* (1963), while a *livre d'occasion*, extends her account of freedom in relation to totalitarian power and exemplifies what freedom should be in practice, particularly in the lack of a political tradition. And in the shortest and clearest of her works, *On Violence*, she answers those who preach the necessity of, or who would even make a cult of, violence; but more fundamentally she makes clear her views on the nature of power and of authority.

If these books are read as each taking up a theme that emerges in *The Origins of Totalitarianism,* but is left unresolved or insufficiently clarified, then we see her writings in true perspective and as constituting a whole.

I think that what she has said is something like this: 'Power corresponds to the human ability not just to act but to act in concert.' So it is never the property of an individual: an individual must persuade others to follow or obey. Violence, 'which is distinguished by its instrumental character', cannot be wielded by one person to create more than a momentary power among very few people. So violence reaches its height in the breakdown of power rather than through power. Acting in concert means some minimal respect for human freedom, even if only of an elite. But since the time of the Greeks in the fifth century, an ideal and a memory has always been living with us: of men treating each other as equals in a public realm of argument and debate, politics. So to her, politics and freedom are virtually the same thing. Freedom is 'the ability to begin' action which is not necessary or predetermined and whose consequences cannot be predicted. Basically it arises from the double aspect of humanity: nothing more like one man than another, but each man absolutely individual. Freedom is not, as liberals began to maintain, being left undisturbed by power, particularly the power of the state: on the contrary, freedom is the mutual exercise of power. Governments which try to suppress public politics are actually weaker than political regimes, unless they go to inhuman and (while they last) irreversible lengths of terror. It is this negativism of liberalism which rendered it so weak both in preventing total war, mass unemployment, and inflation, and in dealing with the ideological terrorists who could take advantage of the revolutionary conditions. Ordinary people lost the capacity for action and despaired of being able to influence things at all.

Minorities, like the Jews, at first thought it enough to be emancipated from formal restraints; it took them long to realize that the price of freedom-from-restraint is not just eternal vigilance but constant activity. The breakdown of liberalism explained the sudden plausibility to masses of people of the ideologists' belief, not in human action but in world-changing, qualitative transformation. The unity of ideology, however, contradicts the facts of human nature: it can grasp the commonness but not the individuality of men. So terror is piled upon terror to convince people that freedom of action for individuals is impossible but that 'everything is possible' to the party. *Eichmann in Jerusalem* (whether historically right or wrong – was there more Jewish resistance than she believed?) is at least a terrible parable about what can happen when the totalitarian assumptions of inevitability are accepted even by the victims. Here her pagan, humanistic, existentialist ethics become quite clear: to be human is to act freely, even if effective resistance is impossible. When prudence and compromise break down or are impossible, compliance and hopeless resignation only feed the irrational belief of the new oppressors that some objective necessity, not man, rules. Thus the *need* for the extermination, not just concentration camps, as she sees it, to degrade people before they were killed anyway; something as economically and governmentally irrelevant as Stalin's purges, in order to prove to the elite and their followers that individuals cannot sustain themselves outside social relationships of a specific kind. And hence the need even for hopeless resistance to such things and for her grim reminder (which comes right to the edge of what one human being may ever say to another) of Cicero's dictum that a free man, if captured in war and taken into slavery hopelessly, irredeemably, and with no chance of escape, *should* commit suicide: the last free action possible to prevent degradation.

Slightly crazy to think that one can compress all of Arendt into a nutshell of even a long paragraph. For she is such a profound wide-ranging writer, and at times both richly and irritatingly digressive. Each of her books, except *On Violence*, could have been so much shorter. The essential theory is clear, and to add so many examples was to create the appearance of writing history and to attract simple and obvious empiricist objections. But I offer a summary, however abstract, poor, or unbalanced, simply to establish the point that her works should be looked at as a consistent world view in which the later books establish and sometimes modify the premises about the human condition underlying her greatest, but most pell-mell and least philosophical work, *The Origins of Totalitarianism.*

Arendt sees the continuities as well as the discontinuities more clearly than Marx between the consciousness and conditions of the ancient and the modern worlds. If her sociology of the modern state is far less developed than Marx's, yet she sees that it is easily possible – both in liberal and in Marxist economic theory – to exaggerate the unique effects of industrialization. The struggle is not between capitalism and communism, it is between the political or republican tradition and its totalitarian caricatures. If we are ever to establish the republic for all, she implies, it will be through drawing on yet transcending the past, not repudiating it utterly. Yet, of course, the most likely alternative now seems, from all her works and all the events that came after the first publication of *The Origins of Totalitarianism*, that we fear so much the perversion of the political tradition that was totalitarianism, that we do not dare try for the republic, so we stay with or lapse into the banal evils (and the banal welfare goods) of autocracies, open or concealed, better or worse. (The nastiest and most plausible prophecy may now not be that we will reach '1984' but that we will continue much as we so shoddily and inadequately are – without even fear of something far worse that could scare us into action for something far better; and with all conventional wisdom saying, so impressive to the young, 'run no risks.') Certainly her message is not that of a J.S. Talmon who, after his studies of the origins of totalitarianism, to guard against the abuse of politics lapses, though an Israeli, into a kind of Burkean and elitist conservatism. If totalitarianism showed that 'anything is possible', good government as common citizenship and social justice is still, to her, among those possibilities. This became more and more clear in her later writings.

Rereading her, I am convinced that even yet her stature has been underestimated. There is a view of political and social man just as comprehensive as those of Hobbes, Hegel, Mill, and Marx; and, to my mind, one far more flattering to humanity.

Notes:
1. Margaret Canovan, *The Political Thought of Hannah Arendt* (London: J.M. Dent, 1974), p. 16.
2. Hannah Arendt, *The Origins of Totalitarianism*, 1st ed. (New York: Harcourt, Brace, 1951).
3. See Franz Borkenau, *The Totalitarian Enemy* (London: Faber, 1940); Andre Gide, *Retour de l'U.R.S.S.* (Paris: Gallimard, 1936); Arthur Koestler, *Arrival and Departure* (New York: Macmillan, 1943); André Malraux, *The Fascist Threat to Culture* (Cambridge, Mass., 1937); Ignazio Silone, *The School for Dictators* (London: J. Cape, 1939); and George Orwell, *The Collected Essays, Journalism, and Letters*, 4 vols. (London: Secker & Warburg, 1968), 1: 532, 376, 459, and, in vol. 2, his review of Borkenau, *The Totalitarian Enemy*, pp. 24–6 – thus all references within the period 1936–40. William Steinhoff's recent *George Orwell and the Origins of 1984* (Ann Arbor: University of Michigan Press, 1975) makes clear that most of the fundamental ideas in Orwell's totalitarian thesis were formed in this earlier period, not in the cold war and above all not as a combination of cold war and death wish, as if he hadn't thought about it before he wrote in 1948.
4. See Carlton J.H. Hayes, ed., 'Symposium on the Totalitarian State, 1939,' *Proceedings of the American Philosophical Society,* vol. 82 (Philadelphia: American Philosophical Society, 1940).
5. George Orwell, 'Freedom of the Press,' *Times Literary Supplement,* Sept. 15, 1972, together with my note, 'How the Essay Came to be Written,' pp. 1037–40.
6. See Benjamin Barbour's contributions to Carl J. Friedrich and others, *Totalitarianism in Perspective: Three Views* (New York: Praeger, 1969).
7. Notably Carl J. Friedrich, ed., *Totalitarianism: Proceedings of a Conference Held at the American Academy of Arts and Sciences, March 1953* (Cambridge: Harvard University Press, 1954); and his and Zbigniew Brzezinski's *Totalitarian Dictatorship and Autocracy* (Cambridge: Harvard University Press, 1956), a book which, it is fair to Brzezinski to say, became more and more Friedrich's in the second American edition (indeed, Brzezinski vanished from the title page of the German edition), and became more and more conceptually rigid ('my model is . . .'), less and less historical.
8. See Arendt, *The Origins of Totalitarianism* (1951), p. 159, for her clearest definition.
9. Alexis de Tocqueville, *The Recollections of Alexis de Tocqueville* (London: Harvill Press, 1948), pp. 67-8.
10. See A.J.P. Taylor, *The Origins of the Second World War* (London: Allen & Unwin, 1962), for a picture of Hitler as a normal politician; and see Bertold Brecht's play *Arturo Ui* for a picture of Hitler as simply a political Al Capone seizing power by force and fraud alone.
11. Arendt, *The Origins of Totalitarianism,* p. 124.
12. *Ibid.,* pp. 431–32.
13. *Ibid.,* chap. 9, 'The Decline of the Nation State and the End of the Rights of Man,' pp. 266–98.

14. *Ibid.,* p. 159.
15. I discuss various possible senses of 'ideology' in 'Ideology Openness, and Freedom,' in Dante Germino and Klaus von Beyme, eds., *The Open Society in Theory and Practice* (The Hague: Martinus Nijhoff, 1974), pp. 217–37.
16. Arendt has somewhere remarked that there is, indeed a functional equivalent between religion and ideology, but the content, she mildly remarks, is somewhat different: It does make a difference whether one believes in Jesus Christ or in Adolph Hitler or in Joseph Stalin either as teachers or as models of behaviour.
17. See Hannah Arendt, *The Origins of Totalitarianism,* 2nd enlarged ed. (New York: Meridian Books, 1958), p. 468: 'Ideologies – isms which to the satisfaction of their adherents can explain everything and every occurrence by deducing it from a single premise – are a very recent phenomenon and, for many decades, played a negligible role in political life. Only with the wisdom of hindsight can we discover in them certain elements which have made them so useful for totalitarian rule. Not before Hitler and Stalin were the great political potentialities of the ideologies discovered.' I believe that she was correct and that her remark about 'only with hindsight' shows that she did not believe in a causal chain of explanation anyway, which she is alternately criticized for having and for not having. But there are other valid senses of 'ideology' – the term arose from a common set of needs, but has crystallized into several different, clear, and useful meanings. See my 'Ideology, Openness, and Freedom.'
18. Martin Seliger, *Ideology and Politics* (New York: Free Press, 1976). This is a very scholarly book in the sense of identifying and summarizing scores of different usages of ideology, but weird in its banal resolve to show that they all merely mean that even to think about politics is to have practical implications, which I don't think is true anyway – except in very trivial senses.
19. Under interrogation in captivity Goering said that the liquidation of the Jews was a vast political blunder; many would have made good nationalists and joined in the liquidation of the Communists. If only Hitler had not confused these two issues, he said! (G.M. Gilbert, *The Psychology of Dictatorship* [New York: Ronald Press, 1950], p. 246). But this only shows how important racialism was to Hitler, a matter of faith, whereas to an immoral adventurer like Goering it was simply a matter of expediency.
20. Taylor, *The Origins of the Second World War,* and Alan Bullock, *Hitler: A Study in Tyranny* (London: Penguin, 1952). A perspective that sees the importance of the ideology even while it studies the effect abroad of 'the tactic of legality' is Brigitte Granzow's brilliant and neglected *A Mirror of Nazism: British Opinion and the Emergence of Hitler, 1929–1933* (London: Gollancz, 1964).
21. Arendt, *The Origins of Totalitarianism,* 1st ed., p. 159.
22. William Hepworth Dixon, *New America* (London: Hurst & Blackett, 1867), pp. 171–72, 200. Superficially this is an ordinary travel book, but Dixon (a barrister who became a judge of the High Court) had as his travelling companion Charles Dilke,

Gladstone's political heir (if scandal had not ended his career), a keen political mind.

23. William Montgomery McGovern, *From Luther to Hitler: The History of Fascist-Nazi Political Philosophy* (Boston: Houghton Mifflin, 1941).

24. Canovan, *The Political Thought of Hannah Arendt*, is a judicious repository of these.

Five

The Sovereignty of Parliament and the Irish Question

*From Desmond Rea, ed., *Political Cooperation in Divided Societies* (Macmillan, Dublin: 1982).

Much depends on how one perceives the problem. Certainly to see it as the relation of Ulster to the rest of Ireland is too narrow and begs the question. When it was seen that way by Liberal governments, however belatedly, as in 1886 and 1911, the Protestants of Ulster began to arm, effectively and respectably. Rival politicians have forgotten their history if they can seriously hope or seriously fear that Great Britain could either give or sell Northern Ireland to the Republic. The Republic could not accept such a gift without guaranteed free service in perpetuity: the British army could alone enforce it, even assuming (as it was assumed until the Curragh incident of 1913) that it would; and the Irish taxpayer might jib at the 30 to 50 pence in the Irish pound increase in the standard rate of taxation that it has been variously estimated would be needed to keep the North at its present highly subsidised welfare levels. Never to forget that the great constitutional lawyer, A.V. Dicey, expounder of 'the rule of law' and 'the sovereignty of parliament' as the two foundation-stones of the constitution, signed Carson's Covenant and put himself openly on the side of the 'respectable rebels'.

The true political problem, put in its most obvious and banal form, is that a large number of people will stick at nothing (or at least will tolerate violent actions by a smaller number) to achieve the unity of Ireland, and that a large number of people will stick at nothing to maintain their homeland as part of the United Kingdom. Even that is too simple; Republicans do not seriously hope to achieve a lasting unity by force of arms, only to render Northern Ireland ungovernable by the British. And many, possibly most, Unionists would favour unilateral independence rather than loyally obey Acts of Parliament that appeared to move them constitutionally toward a united Ireland, even a federal or confederal Ireland.

Perhaps only the two extreme positions, the unity of Ireland or the unity of the present United Kingdom, are clear and logical. And these positions are surely contradictory. As a human being, I freely admit to

57

feeling the intense plausibility of both positions, indeed to sharing the pain of being torn between not injustice and justice, but two rival views of justice. This is not unique to Ireland. Albert Camus was torn between the justice of the case of the Arabs in Algeria and that of fellow *colons*, even though they were only third-generation settlers. Those who are committed utterly to 'One Ireland' or to 'No Surrender' can feel none of the moral agony of sharing two apparently incompatible perspectives. Sometimes such people, for all their long, miserable faces, seem in fact to enjoy the storm and the conflict: violent deeds and violent words become a way of life, ends in themselves. But the student of politics must start from these two incompatibilities: that Northern Ireland is part of the United Kingdom and that it is part of the island of Ireland. Even if we accept fully the 'two nations' thesis, the Protestant nation of Northern Ireland seems in English, Welsh or Scottish eyes to have essential links with, and characteristics of, Ireland as well as with Great Britain.

Talk of immediate solutions is fatuous. But possibilities of political containment of the worst symptoms exist. If there are no agreeable solutions, there might be acceptable frameworks established in which future changes, even if not fully predictable, could at least be accepted as fair; or at least accepted. Any such frameworks have to face the fact that Northern Ireland does face two ways. Straightaway this ensures that there can never be any simple 'unity of Ireland', a straightforward extension, as some have imagined, of the jurisdiction of the 1922 Dublin government, with a few vague mutterings about 'guarantees' for the 'minority' (i.e. Ulster's majority). But we must also remember that from 1920 to 1972, Northern Ireland was by no means an ordinary part of the administration of the United Kingdom. If legally she was, political and administrative reality was very different, was, in fact, what I can only can quasi or *de facto* federalism. And even direct rule has not meant an integrated administration – no more for Ulster than for Scotland after 1707. I will suggest that the apparent contradition of the two extreme viewpoints only involves a total incompatibility on a traditional but now very suspect and self-deluding view of the sovereign state. The theory that every state must be sovereign and possess absolute power is as suspect as the theory that every nation must be a state. People may want it passionately, that is a fact of political life; but it is not necessarily true. All sovereign power is understood by those who operate it at the time as being limited by well-known political and economic contingencies. This essay will suggest that British constitutional history needs re-interpreting to show that the doctrine of and belief in 'parliamentary sovereignty' has been a response to peculiar political conditions as hinted at in the very formula 'United Kingdom', not a necessity of law and order. If 'the sovereignty of parliament' can be seen as a useful myth, helpful at times but dangerous if accepted as a general truth about the minimal conditions of political order, both sides might begin to be impressed by the overlapping edges rather than the solitary extremities of their boxed-in positions.

Talk should begin about whether new forms of government or of inter-government relations could not emerge to reflect the fact, not change the fact, that Northern Ireland faces two ways. The role of the student of politics is to speculate, not to take sides, and to talk freely in long time-scales, not rivalling journalists in hard-headed realism about the next election, not simply talking about possible federal or confederal relations. And as if such talk is not reckless enough, the dominant constitutional ideologies of both the Irish and the British state also need questioning to see if they are, indeed, general truths or simply responses to past political conditions. Has the Irish constitution reached its final form? Has the United Kingdom ever been as centralised and as unitary a state as its statesmen have claimed and its textbooks have loyally or thoughtlessly and uncritically repeated? My remarks are mainly limited to the United Kingdom.

Historically the very formula 'United Kingdom' was developed to stress the primacy, first of the crown, then of parliament, in the practical business of holding together the different historical communities of England, Wales, Scotland and Ireland (two of which, indeed, had themselves never had common government, any sense of being states, until conquest). The formula developed into a conscious exaggeration, for clear political purposes, of the unity and homogeneity of the realm. 'United Kingdom' implies that Great Britain is not a conventional state. The English may dominate, but their domination must take unusual forms. Perhaps there is an English state, but not a corresponding English nation. Some have seen this oddity as simply a colonial mentality, or 'internal colonialism', an imperial English heartland imposing not merely its military and commercial power but also a hegemony of all cultural values upon a Celtic periphery.[1] This is too simple, or it smacks of a racial anti-racial interpretation, for so long as English political conventions were accepted, Scottish, Irish and Welsh notables were readily allowed to make their careers on the Westminster and Whitehall stages, and to live, in various ways, in two cultures. And the colonial thesis ignores both the success of the English parliamentary ideology and the willing price it had to pay. No specifically English nationalism was developed; there was patriotism to United Kingdom institutions in the eighteenth century certainly, and imperialism towards the 'lesser breeds within the law' in the nineteenth century, but an English nationalism as a public ideology had to be foresworn. Indeed national sentiments were tolerated in Scotland, Ireland and Wales, even at times officially encouraged and preserved, even to the level of distinct local administration, so long as national sentiment stopped short of nationalist claims to separate states.

The doctrine of the sovereignty of parliament arose not merely in opposition to the powers of the crown as seen in 1688, but because after the Act of Union (that is the managed voluntary suppression of the Scottish parliament) parliament was intolerant of any other legally constituted authority but its own. Indeed, the legal doctrine of sovereignty (that no court or other assembly can override legislation passed by parliament according to its own rules of procedure) was almost consciously confused with an empirical, pseudo-historical doctrine: that political stability, indeed law and order themselves, depended on parliamentary sovereignty. The Irish parliament began to appear as a threat in theory more than as a practical and reasonable effective way of governing the country, even before Grattan's Parliament and the rebellion of 1798. Just as divided powers seemed impossible to practical men in 1775, so the 1798 rebellion must have seemed in large part at least a consequence of divided powers, not a case for reforming and trusting a subsidiary legislature.

The great Blackstone in his *Commentaries on the Laws of England* said that parliament

> hath sovereign and uncontrollable authority in the making, confirming, enlarging, restraining, abrogating, repealing, reviving and expounding of laws, concerning all matters of all possible denominations, ecclesiastical or temporal, civic, military, maritime, or criminal: this being the place where that absolute power, which must in all governments reside somewhere, is entrusted by the constitution of these kingdoms. All mischiefs and grievances, operations and remedies, that transcend the ordinary course of the laws, are within reach of this extraordinary tribunal. It can regulate or new-model the succession to the Crown; as was done in the reigns of Henry VIII and William III. It can alter the established religion of the land; as was done in a variety of instances, in the reign of Henry VIII and his three children. It can change and create afresh even the constitution of the kingdom and Parliaments themselves: as was done by the Act of Union and by the several statutes for triennial and septennial elections. It can, in short, do everything that is not naturally impossible.[2]

But is there really such absolute power? There is, but only in a legal sense: that no other body can make enactments. But politically no government or parliament can 'do everything that is not naturally impossible'. In any other sense but a narrowly legal one concerned with jurisdictions, the phrase is mere rhetoric. But politically it is not *mere* rhetoric; it is meant to impress, just as Thomas Hobbes' *Leviathan* was meant to frighten people into obedience, but not to do much else except keep the peace. And must such power, rhetorical or not, 'in all governments reside somewhere' (Blackstone clearly means in one determinate and sovereign institution)? Young Jeremy Benthan in his *Fragment on Government* famously mocked Blackstone. Did he not think that the Switzers had government in their federal cantons?

Even after the founding of the United States of America, even after the war of 1812, English statesmen and lawyers continued to assert that 'divided power', 'divisions of power', and federalism especially, were somehow inherently unstable, tending to breakdown and anarchy, from which we British (or English?) were preserved by sovereignty of parliament and the rule of law. This was part of Whig ideology: the regime needed to argue thus precisely because in political and economic reality the United Kingdom of Great Britain, Scotland and Ireland was anything but united. This cloak of legitimation had so many obvious holes in it that the practical need was recognised for a constant skilled management of Scotland and Ireland, both by and in parliament. If religion was often felt to be a major binding factor of civil order, this only made the problem more acute. Many Scottish historians now take the view that opposition to the suppression of the Scottish parliament was relatively muted because the Assembly of the Kirk was felt to be the true popular, national institution. And it is clear that Catholic Emancipation in Ireland was passed, much like the Reform Act of 1832, not out of principle or dislike of anomalies, but largely as an attempt to keep the country governable at all. (In the same way objections to proportional representation as incompatible with the basic principles of the British constitution did not override the political need for institutionalised PR in the elections for the Northern Ireland Assembly of 1974, the Convention of 1975 and the European Parliament of 1979; this alone created any realistic hope of these unusual institutions ever working). Even the mild ecclesiastical proscriptions in nineteenth-century Wales stirred up civil disobedience over Church taxes, and led to disestablishment as a political response.

The memory of the 1745 rising made management of Scottish affairs from Whitehall and Westminster a conscious, constant and delicate matter. Even minor removals of Catholic disabilities to recruit Scottish highlanders for the American war could have unexpected and formidable side-effects, stirring up a Protestant mob in the Gordon Riots. The cabinet not merely ordered a reluctant George IV to Edinburgh for ceremonies of reconciliation stage-managed by Sir Walter Scott himself, but persuaded him to wear the kilt (once); and it was state policy that Queen Victoria should reside in Scotland for a noticeable part of each year, as well as changing her religion when she crossed the border. The establishment of the Scottish Office and substantial measures of administrative devolution to Scotland in the last quarter of the nineteenth century were conscious attempts to stop Home Rule agitation growing up there. The Scottish question was not felt to have ended with 1707 and then Culloden and the clearances: an historically-minded political elite was conscious of the need for conciliation and special treatment of Scotland for longer than most twentieth-century accounts of practical politics would allow to be possible. An articulate doctrine of English nationalism had to be consciously restrained, unlike in all the other nation-states of Europe, as part of the actual politics of governing the multinational United Kingdom.

By the 1960s both Westminster and Whitehall seemed to have lost this skill in practising either a *de jure* quasi-federalism, as in the former colonies, or a *de facto* quasi-federalism, as in Scotland and Wales and in Ireland before independence. Each decade saw the old experience of imperial administration grow less and less tangible. If Northern Ireland still remained, and with a constitutional and political status wholly anomalous to sovereignty of parliament doctrine, it was resolutely ignored by parliament until the troubles of 1968. And in most student textbooks and elementary works of constitutional law, it vanished almost entirely.

The contradiction between theory and practice in British political opinion is almost schizophrenic when one considers that the cabinet and the Colonial Office in the nineteenth century seemed to accept as part of nature that Canada, Australia and South Africa, even, could only be governed with federal structures of public law. Almost unthinkingly a federal form of three-tier government was offered to the colonies in New Zealand, and astonishment was great when they rejected it as grossly extravagant. Many of the post-1945 new constitutions followed suit, notably India and Nigeria. But in the homeland the belief was strong that any relaxation of the sovereignty of parliament could lead to disintegration. Joseph Chamberlain feared in 1886 that 'Home Rule for Ireland' could lead to demands for 'Home Rule All Round', as by 1910 it did; and it was touch and go whether Liberals would proceed with a general act or a specifically Irish act first. After the First World War, the Irish rebellion and civil war, this was forgotten; but for a brief moment of power the Liberal Party had broken from the old Whig parliamentary ideology, now taken over by both Tory and Labour. Since Labour only came into government after the Irish question was held to have been solved, and since Wales and Scotland were distressed areas, needing central help, and heavily working-class and heavily Labour, the Labour Party has never developed a distinctive constitutional theory. The promotion of the Scottish Devolution Bill was an extraordinary piece of opportunism on Harold Wilson's part, and its drafting showed that it had been put together without any clear lines of principle by men who mostly did not believe in it and who certainly lacked the experience of thinking federally, as had the generation of Churchill, Amery, Milner and F.E. Smith in relation both to the Irish question and to the broader imperial 'great game'.

The dog that does not bark behaves most peculiarly. Specialised and now popular studies of objectivity and merit have been written on the Irish question, but most British textbooks on politics and law have simply ignored Northern Ireland (until after 1968) and Scotland (until the Scottish National Party polled 30 per cent in the two general elections of 1974). Even the President of Harvard, A.L. Lowell, said of Scotland and Ireland in the preface to his book *The Government of England (1908)* that:

> The British Constitution is full of exceptions, of local customs and special acts with which town clerks must be familiar. They fill the path of these men with pitfalls, but they do not affect seriously the general principles of the government, and no attempt is made to describe them here. Even the institutions of Scotland and Ireland, interesting as they are in themselves, have been referred to only so far as they relate to the national government or throw light upon its working.[3]

And not much light did they throw apparently. Even our contemporary, Richard Rose, who has put us all so much in his debt with research work on Northern Ireland, called his first book *Politics in England*. Perhaps Rose could only make British politics appear as systematic as his social science models and frameworks demanded by ignoring initially the Celtic context of English politics. Members of his school tend, like Lowell, to see 'the periphery' as an exception to the normal practices of the English centralised, unitary state. Now local politics in Scotland, Wales and Northern Ireland are very different from local politics in England. But the separate identities of Scotland, Wales and Northern Ireland are not exceptional to the United Kingdom; they have posed major problems for the British state for hundreds of years and have radically affected the structure of the machine, as well as the states of mind of statesmen. Nationality problems are not exceptional to British politics: they are a characteristic part of it. Most of the great leaders of the past have been constantly aware of how integral was 'the Celtic fringe', and a large number either came from or made their reputations in the affairs of 'the periphery'. Only in the post-Suez generation of British politicians has this experience been lost. Among the old Tories this can still linger on, but among the new Conservatives the tradition is gone. And even in the Republic of Ireland, the British heritage (deliberately the wrong and the provocative word) still lingers on to an unexpected degree in many administrative and political practices.

All of this appears paradoxical only on two counts: firstly, if we try to write the history of the British state or even of the comparatively new Irish state as if they are wholly separate entities and experiences, as if the ideology and rhetoric were historical truth, and do not look at the political, social and economic relationships of – to use an historical and geographical expression – the British Isles as a whole; and secondly, if we adopt too rigid a language of 'parliamentary sovereignty' or 'the sovereign state' or (like some social scientists) develop abstract expectations that political systems, national and local, must be highly systematic and share a common 'political culture' or 'consensus' if they are to work at all. That states cannot work *at all* without a common political culture or consensus about basic values is observably false: think only of Belgium, Canada, Italy, Nigeria. What most people who say this must really mean is that they cannot work *well*, in evaluative terms, by modern Atlantic liberal, democratic standards. Even Northern Ireland can, after all, be governed, after a fashion, without consensus. And so can many other countries.

Self-deception goes deep. In a debate on the Government of Ireland Bill (1893) the Duke of Devonshire said:

> In the United Kingdom, Parliament is supreme not only in its legislative but in its Executive functions. Parliament makes and unmakes our Ministries; it revises their actions. Ministries may make peace and war, but they do so at pain of instant dismissal from office, and in affairs of internal administration the power of Parliament is equally direct. It can dismiss a Ministry if it is too extravagant, or too economical; it can dismiss a Ministry because its government is too stringent or too lax. It does actually and practically, in every way, directly govern England, Scotland and Ireland.[4]

My objection to this is not merely the familiar realist critique that parties try to do all this, if at all, not parliament. For the statement could simply be rephrased to speak of the need for working majorities of parties within parliament and governing through parliament, not literally government by parliament. I point to the flagrant falsity, long before that Duke of Devonshire's time and still not true today, of his last sentence: he was perfectly aware that Scotland had its own ecclesiastical, legal and educational systems, which parliament might amend but would never abolish. Government administration in Scotland and Ireland (as now in Northern Ireland) was highly devolved, peculiar and in indigenous hands. For obvious and well-known political reasons parliament was loath to interfere unless the local administration came near to breakdown. But for less obvious political reasons, the truth was always denied. Parliamentary sovereignty was the ideology of an imperially-minded governing class, not a universal truth about or necessity of British politics (or of any other, for that matter).

British constitutional lawyers, reacting against Dicey, have been teaching their students for at least twenty years how narrowly legal a doctrine is parliamentary sovereignty, cheerfully regarding the claim to political sovereignty as absurd, noting the large number of bodies 'out of doors' that parliament handles most gingerly if at all.[5] But this critique did not penetrate far enough. Many advanced English socialists (who might have other reasons for scepticism about sovereignty theory) began to invoke it again, as if plucked from the folk unconscious, in their campaign against British membership of the EEC. They may have had better reasons for opposing membership than a confusion of legal sovereignty (which parliament was in fact exercising) with political sovereignty which, in the sense of power, it notoriously lacked anyway, notably because of the declining economy, internal political factors and international realities and obligations. Indeed some of the Left wing still talk both of 'parliamentary sovereignty' and of the authenticity of 'extra-parliamentary democracy', as sublimely unaware of the inherent contradiction as when Dicey went on and on about 'the rule of law' *and* 'parliamentary sovereignty'. And like Dicey, they are not above justifying direct action when some actual results of two contradictory beliefs and modes of behaviour appear.

I should make clear that personally, if slightly irrelevantly, I favour both more power for parliament and more power for extra-parliamentary representative institutions. But I talk about *power*, not sovereignty, that is something to be balanced politically, uninhibited and unconfused by beliefs that there are any non-negotiable positions (such as, for instance, *the* constitution of the Republic of Ireland or *the* constitution or territorial integrity of the United Kingdom). Political power has to be seen not as a unique institutional locus or as symbolic events, to which legal theory and romantic nationalism respectively can become attached, but as a process constantly responding to changes in the actual situation. Political power comes neither from the barrel of a gun nor from a lawyer's mouth: it always comes from compromise between continuity and change. Guns can sometimes wreck political power, or provide the marginal increment of destruction if a government is losing its power, in the sense of losing that authority which people ordinarily (in most respects) obey and respect or at least accept. But guns cannot govern. Quite simply, as Hannah Arendt remarked in her short book, *On Violence*, 'power is acting in concert':[6] public opinion has to be carried for orderly government to take place. Violence occurs when governments lose their power, it is seldom the cause of the loss of power; and it is obvious that most governments resort to violence only when their habitual political power begins to break down. Equally no amount of constitutional ingenuity ('politic words', as the poet said) can patch up an impossible situation, or provide more than a temporary patch pending long-term structural repairs and alterations.

To see power as a process should make us look at the widest possible context of a problem, and neither to be in awe of the gun nor inhibited by the lawyers. Certainly at some stage we need to begin to consider not just the peculiarity of the United Kingdom and of the Republic of Ireland as separate sovereign states, as in legal senses they obviously are, and in nationalistic senses too; but also consider the anomalies in British-Irish relations as so conceived. There are an extraordinary number of things in common between Britain and Ireland (quite apart from Northern Ireland) when compared to almost any other pair of sovereign states conceivable.[7] It is not for me to comment on the interplay of English and Gaelic culture in the Republic, reaching even more widely than political and commercial institutions with common roots and practices. But consider only the most obvious anomalies on the British side, the openness of the ballot box as well as employment to Irish citizens. One would be hag-ridden by definitions if one used this as evidence that the United Kingdom is not fully a sovereign state, rather than simply noting that the actual state has responded shrewdly to unusual historical and political circumstances in specific ways. What are anomalies in the light of sovereignty theory are, on both sides of the water, readily understandable in terms of both history and politics. And politically the case for building on them, quite apart from the problems of Northern Ireland, seems far more convincing, more likely to occur in fact, than the case for seeing them as purely residual anomalies that should be tidied up and out. And similar considerations apply to existing levels of cross-border co-operation, both formal and informal.

I must labour this point of theory. So many limitations of leadership arise because politicians pride themselves on being purely practical and do not recognise how much they view the world through theoretical presuppositions. Lack of self-consciousness can often lead, as J.M. Keynes famously argued, these practical men to carry with them out-of-date theory, not no theory. If power is seen as a process, then we must gradually abandon the old thick true-Brit way of looking at institutions and ideas as if never the twain shall meet, as if institutions are simply the inert carriers of ideas, never suffering any change of state by contact with the ideas themselves. Such a view is that parliament is sovereign and can do anything. Neither is its power politically sovereign, it can be predominant but never omnipotent; and nor has it ever been able to suppress the non-English national cultures of the United Kingdom. Acting inflexibly, it lost most of Ireland, but its flexibility has so far kept the constitutional connection with Wales, Scotland and Northern Ireland.

The conventional theory has not gone unchallenged. Harold Laski went so far as to argue in his once famous *Grammar of Politics* that all power is inherently federal, using that term in a broad sense where many would use 'pluralistic'. He argued, following Figgis on the role of churches and Deguit on the role of trades unions, that the theory of the sovereign state only had relevance to periods of state formation and nation-building: that otherwise any institution that claimed a monopoly of decision-making was both oppressive and unstable; that a realistic approach to order always meant recognition of a plurality of quasi-autonomous corporations or societies within the state – churches, trades unions, pressure groups and sub-cultures of various kinds. The state itself was a unique institution, but only in that it had the initiative to set the terms of processes of conciliation between other groups, not that it was absolute, able to make or break other groups.

To some such a view of the state as mediator or as 'group of groups', is inadequate. The emergency powers of the state, that to Laski are residual or only usable for the defence of the state itself, not for resolving problems within an inherently pluralistic society, to others are central and perennial. Even the sociologist Max Weber defined the state as that social institution which held a monopoly of legitimate means of violence. He at least stressed legitimacy, whereas some super-realists, like Hobbes, Mosca and Pareto, thought that the coercive power of the state could actually create legitimacy (a view that is as empirically debatable as it is morally dubious). On such a definition of the state some might hold that the United Kingdom is hardly a state at all, unable to enforce its monopoly of legitimate violence in Northern Ireland. Since it cannot govern, these realists might say, it should get out. But even Thomas Hobbes, while he argued that obligation ceases when the sovereign can no longer keep the peace and protect the lives of his subjects, carefully added that obligation is then only transferred to another sovereign if he can clearly do better. All conditions in between must be a matter of political judgement. In fact, none of these definitions are definitive. Beyond the traditional minimal functions of a state, the defence of the realm and the enforcement of law and order, and modern maximalist views of industrialisation and the welfare of the inhabitants, lie a vast range of political alternatives, so little that is relevant can be inferred from such definitions. Even territorial integrity is negotiable and ideas of what it constitutes change through time. Unionists must be aware of that; indeed it is their deepest fear though their fear need not be so obsessive when everyone (well, nearly everyone) can see the impossibility of coercing them. And as territorial integrity immediately leads to definition and control of borders, it is worth saying that there are borders and borders. 'Necessity of state' can sometimes close or tightly control borders, but sometimes states have to relax their borders, even turn a blind eye on the movement of, for instance, nomads or, in more complex societies, people with a dual culture or allegiance, with two passports in their pockets (say British and Irish).

All states will defend themselves if threatened by armed force. Weber was right on that point. Americans fought to preserve 'the Union' when faced by military rebellion, but somehow 'the Union' (*ex pluribus unum*) was not, in a traditional European sense, 'the state'. My argument is that the 'United Kingdom', though it has pretended to be a sovereign, centralised state, has had in practice to allow a kind of informal federalism. It could be said that the Ulster workers' strike threatened the power of the state, but more precisely it threatened a policy of the government. I think that even the prevaricating and indecisive Harold Wilson would have let the police and army tear down the barricades had he felt the safety of the state to be threatened (he never seemed to care much for the integrity of the government so long as it survived). Many modern states have to show similar remarkable discretion where they attempt to enforce their 'sovereign power', in case it is challenged: many Emperors stay in bed for lack of clothes. Edmund Burke once asked the House of Commons over proposals to coerce the American colonists: 'I care not if you have a right to make them miserable, have you not an interest to make them happy?'

It would be easy if the concept of 'consensus' could replace sovereignty as the hypothetical, mystical cement that holds societies together. 'Consensus' and 'pluralism' are often linked, but if one is serious about pluralism, if one recognises that, for instance, Protestant and Catholic *do* hold different values, then what becomes of consensus as a necessary condition for government? Either one must say that good government is only possible where there is a consensus about basic values, which would lead to even more governments and even more instability and intolerance than nationalism has created as an ideology of government; or one must say that consensus is an ecumenical Hindu-Unitarian-Latitudinarian-Muslim – Catholic-Protestant-Jewish-Humanist mishmash. Personally I think that toleration and reconciliation involve mutual respect for, and recognition of, differences, not excessive ecumenical fervour. It is indeed possible to govern without consensus and amid a diversity of values. Lord Acton actually thought (in his famous debate with John Stuart Mill) that government over different nations and religions was of a higher ethical order than national states, though one is bound to say that most such governments are of a more rough-and-ready nature. 'Consensus' is best reserved to point to the need for agreement about means, not about ends, about procedures, not about their results. Good government is impossible when people either cannot accept that decisions are made fairly or will not accept some decisions, however fair the procedures. Nobody in Northern Ireland is against elections, for instance, so long as they yield the desired and predictable result. Some people even favour institutional innovation to settle 'the problem': a referendum, says one, of all the people of the United Kingdom; or a referendum, says another, of all the people of Ireland.

Most actual government is to be found in the ground between the two extremes: Hobbes saying anarchy if no final and absolute sovereignty, or Adam Smith and Talcott Parsons saying that there is only a minimal need for government *if* values are shared and systematically related. There might be some sense, then, in taking Laski's admittedly vaguer 'all power is federal' as a starting point, rather than half hoping that Britain could be truly a state after coming to fear that the actual political system may not be that systematic after all.

It is thus necessary to destroy the myths of both 'sovereignty' theory and 'political systems' theory and their alleged empirical entailments, if any progress is to be made. To put it simply, the beliefs are widespread that basic order is always threatened if, says one theory, there is not a common culture or, says the other, a truly sovereign state. So the temptation is either to try to enforce the conditions to fit the theory (sometimes politely called 'integrated education' or elsewhere 'moral leadership') or deliberately to restrict the boundaries of the 'sovereign state' to correspond with the area in which norms can be enforced with minimum effort.

I favour an English state in the heartland of old Mercia, south of the Trent and east of the Wye. Some Ulstermen favour a Protestant state within redrawn, diminished and tight boundaries (though with Conor Cruise O'Brien as king). Sinn Fein presumably want a state of their own on the West Bank of the Gaeltacht. However, in the real world there might be something to be said for examining how federal a state the United Kingdom already is and whether *de jure* institutionalisation of *de facto* practices might not be advantageous.

If Mr. Enoch Powell MP succeeds, for instance, in keeping the Official Unionists solidly behind an integrationist policy and they are not swallowed live by the DUP, the most likely result would be to increase radically British (that is English, Scottish and Welsh) opinion in favour of withdrawal. For the attempt to impose the British state on Northern Ireland, in Powell's sovereignty and unity sense, would simply over time prove too wearisome and bloody to be endured, even though nothing catastrophic might happen. And integration would reveal to Unionist supporters that once they forsake their peculiar institutions, they are but a small minority in the whole United Kingdom. But a federal recognition of likenesses/differences, common and rival interests, could work, might prove acceptable even if never fully agreeable. At least the White, Green, Buff papers of the last three years have moved from the Convention period language of 'agreement between the parties' to a more realistic 'solutions acceptable to the people of Northern Ireland'. The present British government could yet, if it acted with half of the zeal and firmness that some of us feel it is showing against trades unions and the working class,

impose an acceptable framework of parliamentary government –
certainly not on an unwilling majority in Northern Ireland, but probably only upon reluctant and hostile political leaders. What is
acceptable and what is agreeable can prove very different in actual
politics.

Both the *Working Paper* of November 1979 (Cmnd 7763) and
Proposals for Further Discussion (Cmnd 7950) show a sudden, almost a
frenetic, increase in what one can only call 'institutional inventiveness'. Some less inhibited minds, better educated about historical
constitutional proposals, showing something of the old skills, have
penetrated the Northern Ireland Office compared to the period of the
Convention when the machine sat back and hoped that something
would emerge from the *Sittlichkeit* and *Volksgeist* without external
stimulus. But the old sovereignty myth dies hard: the exclusion of an
'Irish dimension' is obvious (and more apparent than real), but a Bill of
Rights, entrenchment and judicial review are still obviously felt to be
'anomalous' if done for Ulster alone, likely to 'set a dangerous prece-
dent' for the rest of the United Kingdom. This last point was very
evident in 1974 and 1975 when any bilateral suggestions from the
Northern Ireland Office of federalism or quasi-federalism for Northern
Ireland were blocked by No. 10's fears that it would *encourager les
Ecosses*. Only a year later Wilson did his U-turn and went for Scottish
devolution in the teeth of a then largely reluctant Scottish Labour
Party.

Three years ago I tried to set this as a University of London 'A' level
question, but the teacher assessors rejected it as too difficult: 'The
concept of "devolution" was invented by Harold Wilson to obscure the
hitherto reasonably clear distinction between Federalism and Local
Government. *Explain and discuss.*' Top marks would have gone to the
candidate who saw clearly long-term dangers of uncertainty. After all,
if Stormont was *de facto* federalism for so long, an ordinary Act of
Parliament, passed at great speed, could abolish it. That 'special offer'
would not be bought again, either by majority or minority.

Even if inter-party talks were resumed in Northern Ireland, there
may be very little hope for a genuinely federal constitution emerging
there. What might have been *acceptable* to SDLP voters three or four
years ago, even if never *agreeable* to their leaders, a Bill of Rights, committee chairmanships, the need for two-thirds majorities, etc., etc., even
short of power-sharing, in other words a Pyrrhic victory for the
Unionists and a noble defeat for the SDLP, all this now seens part of
history, or a history that never was. The minority is more determined
than ever on 'an Irish dimension'; indeed it is doubtful if the leaders of
the SDLP could now carry their followers even into power-sharing in a
purely United Kingdom context. So I only make the speculative
comment that *if* Northern Ireland came into a clear federal relation-

ship with the United Kingdom, implications would follow for the rest of the United Kingdom constitution such as Wilson feared but some might hope for: a Bill of Rights, Scottish and possibly Welsh devolution, proportional representation even. But these would not flow from liberal pressure of principle, rather from the need to carry on the Queen's government, a political response to a crucial recognition that the unity of the United Kingdom could now depend more on federalising power than on repeating historical formulas, however useful they were in their day in strengthening central authority amid the quadruple diversity of nations. Do Scottish separatists really want to separate? Do Ulster integrationists really want to integrate and lose their own institutions? Do Westminster opponents of devolution really fear the break-up of the United Kingdom or simply the diminishment of English dominance?

Of course *if*, equally if, a British Conservative government tired of trying to reach agreements, whether in Belfast or Dublin, and simply gave the Unionists what most of them want, the old majority Stormont, then it would be overwhelmingly likely that if the majority in the North felt secure in the conduct of what they hold to be their own affairs, that say in two generations time such a new Stormont would have become, if economics, geography and propinquity have any meaning, deeply involved in close working relationships with Dublin. This would probably stop short of any overall institutional expression, simply close inter-state functional co-operation in a dozen or so joint agencies. But it might be enough to satisfy and pacify – if only time would stand still in the meantime. But the minority will not wait. They want to see something change in their lifetimes, not those of their children's children. Functional co-operation seems, indeed, to have been the real substance of the Anglo-Irish talks, and the meetings of the civil servants. And it is fair to remind people in Northern Ireland that the United Kingdom does have other problems and interests in common with the Republic. People in Northern Ireland are understandably somewhat obsessive about the Northern Ireland problem. There is much to be done by way of regularising a special relationship quite apart from Northern Ireland. Nonetheless it must be hoped in Dublin and feared in Belfast that institutions of such functional co-operation would become imperceptibly constitutional (somewhat like the first theories of a way to European integration through the Coal and Steel Community), however much a Conservative government in London is determined that that should not happen. If such institutions were to emerge, who knows what the outcome would be? This might be a fair and sensible procedure to adopt, irrespective of different views of what the outcome would be. It would also be a very long process, whatever the outcome; but it is the remotest chance of this happening that stirs extremism in Unionist ranks.

If I speculate about a possibility of federalism in a United Kingdom context (which is as important for Scotland as for Northern Ireland), one must note a remarkable outburst of such speculation in an island-of-Ireland context by Irish politicians and what I will boldly call the more literate and reflective activists. What it has in common is a recognition that any possible unity of Ireland could not be a unitary sovereign state, as in the old Fianna Fail doctrine. Garret FitzGerald's argument for confederalism (with a 'British dimension') is only the most sophisticated of a large literature. In newspapers and in pamphlets there has been a noticeable growth in the last few years of, as it were, 'middle-brow' political speculation, not entirely unlike what Perry Miller once called 'the citizen literature' of the last few years of the American colonies and the early years of the Republic. It is written for activists by activists. It is neither philosophical nor usually explicitly theoretical. As yet nothing comes anywhere near the standard of *The Federalist Papers* nor seems especially likely to convince those it most needs to convince; but it is not all purely polemical. The end may be 'Irish unity' or 'negotiated independence for Northern Ireland', but the means are often moot and speculative; and some brave souls try to square these two circles. Both the publications of Sinn Fein and the New Ulster Political Research Group (the spiritual arm of the UDA) are now showing a sense of time-scales, moving beyond next-electoral perspectives into much more realistic generational ones. Certainly most people now envisage 'a solution' less as an event in time (like a benign revolution) than as a long drawn-out process. Very few people in fact believe in the original content of the once most commonly argued 'solutions': that the six counties would become part of the Republic, or that they would simply be ordinary parts of the local government of the United Kingdom (what, after all, the Unionists originally fought for). The Provisional IRA proposed in its manifesto, *Eire Nua*, a federal Ireland of the four historic provinces with its capital in Athlone, not in hated Free State Dublin. The UDA has at least repudiated neither the official policy of its leaders, which is to seek negotiated independence, nor the remarkable content of their draft constitution: a kind of reinvention by themselves alone of the American constitution of 1787 replete with devices to ensure no effective government at all except with minority consent. The last bid of Her Majesty's Government in the late Atkins inter-party discussions, although it excluded talking to the UDA officially, at least moved on interestingly parallel lines: majority government with minority veto.

The SDLP also consider federalism: John Hume sees it as a way of reaching not the classic republican 'unity of Ireland' but an 'agreed Ireland', an 'Ireland of the future'; Seamus Mallon, their deputy leader, believes that, even so, some form of power-sharing would still be needed; and even Paddy Duffy has said that 'there would have to be some form of federal type of government, not a Republic-type of government as envisaged by former Republican leaders'. In June 1978, Mr. Denis Haughey, the chairman of the SDLP, proposed a deal with the Northern Unionists: a federal union of Ireland but with a strong parliament still in Belfast, devolution of all local matters, a Bill of Rights and continued British citizenship. (Needless to say, this fell on politically deaf ears.)

Senator Kenneth Whitaker, the former Secretary of the Department of Finance and Governor of the Central Bank (often called 'the father of the Irish economic miracle') wrote an interesting article in the *Irish Times* (20 June 1978) in which he argued the impossibility of fully integrating Northern Ireland into either the Republic or the United Kingdom in any foreseeable future: he too, therefore, argued for an intermediate solution in which two separate governments would establish a constitution creating a limited number of common institutions and the possibility of adding to them by mutual consent (shades of Calhoun). So from the *Irish Times* to discussion among and between the paramilitaries, the concepts of federalism and confederalism, even involving three 'states', has gained currency.

However vague much of this is, it is ahead of official thinking by the two governments most concerned and points to characteristics of some modern states, both in their internal and external relationships, that have been much obscured by the theory of sovereignty of the textbook writers.

The objections to a federal or confederal approach to Ireland are practical, not theoretical. With great respect to Professor Maurice Vile's paper,[8] while I see the great difficulties of a federalism with only two units, I also see the great peculiarity of the problem. Federalism is not a pre-existent formula, but a dynamic response to situations of divided power. If the majority in Northern Ireland wanted such a bilateral or trilateral relationship, it should not defeat human ingenuity if the will was there. But it is not, and even strong advocates of Irish unity recognise this. Consider for instance, Mr. Haughey's speech to the National Executive of Fianna Fail (as reported in the *Irish Times*, 27 March 1981):

> For my part, I have no hesitation in reaffirming openly and proudly that I am working actively for Irish unity. I have said before and I repeat now that progress towards the unity of all our people is my top political priority. I will not be deflected from pursuing that noble goal sensibly and patiently.
>
> In statements on February 10th and 25th last the Secretary of State for Northern Ireland spelt out what the British government mean by the constitutional status or position of Northern Ireland. He defined it as being that its position within the United Kingdom cannot be changed without the consent of a majority

of the people of Northern Ireland and of the Westminster Parliament.

Our position on this should be perfectly clear. As I have already brought out, the studies are part of a process initiated when I met Mrs Thatcher in London on May 21st last year.

Reference to the communique issued after that meeting will show that I agreed that change in the constitutional status, the present factual state of Northern Ireland, would only come about with the consent of a majority of the Northern people. In my Dail speech on May 29th last I pointed out that this simply recognised the practical realities of the situation.

Ulster can no more be coerced in 1984, even, than it could be in 1914. Certainly he 'will not be deflected from' that 'noble goal' but he will proceed 'sensibly and patiently': shrewd political words indeed.9 What could Dublin possibly do to gain the consent of a majority in the North to either a federal or a confederal solution? Can such a circle ever be squared? No Irish leader before Garret Fitzgerald has ever asked. It is hard to imagine why a Protestant majority should give up its British connection. And the matter would not be the least easier if Britain, which is most unlikely, were to give them up. As the SDLP realise, thinking of the 'troops out' movement, the matter might even be worse if the British army withdraws. Even the 'removal of the guarantee' would not alter the facts on which the guarantee is based. The IRA is a terrorist organisation that makes some aspects of government and ordinary life difficult; but the UDA, if unrestrained by the British army, would appear in the form of the old UVF militia that would actually take over first the streets and then the government.

Perhaps the circle can only be squared if a wider context is grasped and if we go back to our original point: that Northern Ireland *does* face both ways, and that many people in Northern Ireland do have dual allegiances: most Catholics have a clear dual allegiance and most loyalists would go for independence if Whitehall and Westminster ever tried to sell them out, even by nice stages and with baited hooks.

A *Guardian* editorial said in March 1980: 'It is more generally acknowledged in Dublin than is often realised that the two islands cannot be thought of as entirely separate units.' Who knows how true this is? But it could point to the wider context. What if political leaders could eventually grasp a sense of these islands as a whole as they have of Europe as a whole? Talk of the Republic rejoining the Common-wealth seems utterly unrealistic (when it will not even join NATO), even if the slow stages by which she left it are a salutary reminder that 'final' constitutional solutions are often remarkably fluid in long historical periods. Everything I have masochistically argued about the British need to think again about the 'sovereignty of parliament' could also be turned against some aspects of constitution-worship in the Republic. Even the territorial clauses of the constitution are, any scholar knows, far vaguer and less committal than both Nationalists and Loyalists make out; but the religious clauses are not.

The Guardian's remark points in a different direction: speculation about the possibility of a Nordic Council-like institution, or the slow growth of one: not a federal constitution for Northern Ireland with an Irish dimension, nor a confederal constitution of all Ireland with a British dimension, but a Council of Britain and Ireland whose component members would be at least the Republic of Ireland, Northern Ireland, England and Wales, and Scotland. Even this is near fantasy, for it begs the question as to whether even in the context of such a definite but minimal framework (the Nordic Council demands unanimity of its component nations before proposals can go to the national parliaments), an acceptable representative institution could arise in Northern Ireland; and it adds the additional dimension of Scotland if only as a make-weight to the size and dominance of England and Wales (and Wales?). What common institutions would arise would depend on the agreement of the nations, but it would not in any sense govern the separate nations, whether they were themselves separate states or federal entities.

All this is speculation. But speculation is needed. There are no short-term or final solutions. Once it is realised that the sovereign state is not sovereign, new and flexible forms of political relationship could emerge. A confederacy of these islands is almost utter fantasy, but a Council of the Islands seems at least a reasonable speculation.

If Northern Ireland cannot come to find some form of mutually acceptable representative institution, the only other hypothesis is that neither the Haugheys nor the Thatchers will get their way, but that the full complexity of accepting that Northern Ireland faces two ways would begin to be mirrored in dual citizenship (which many Catholics already exercise), inter-governmental administrative agencies, even alternative jurisdictions. It is just possible that the only practical response would be the two governments creating what to tidy-minded constitutional theorists would be sheer muddle, unworkable anywhere else (but where else is there quite such a problem?). I could imagine setting in 2000 (though more likely someone else in 2020) those same 'A' level candidates a rather different question: 'Is Northern Ireland constitutionally more a part of the United Kingdom or the Republic of Ireland?' I am not talking about 'condominium' which would need a far more comprehensive and deliberate agreement and exercise of power at one time by the two governments together than either seems capable of even alone. I am suggesting that a slow evolution of a thorough but tolerable muddle could occur. The line between the institutional and the constitutional could be thoroughly blurred and bi-lateral or tri-lateral functional agencies replace much national and territorial administration. Speculatively I slightly favour *The Guardian's* hypothesis, however.

All this essay has really tried to do is to remove some conceptual obstacles to facing a situation that cannot be conciliated in terms of either traditional state sovereignty theory or nationalist theory. And for the meantime more people must analyse and speculate, not take sides. I think of what Albert Camus wrote of the Algerian crisis:

> The truth, alas, is that a part of French opinion vaguely holds that the Arabs have in a way earned the right to slaughter and mutilate while another part is willing to justify in a way all excesses [against the Arabs]. To justify himself, each relies on the other's crime. But that is a casuistry of blood, and it strikes me that an intellectual cannot become involved in it, unless he takes up arms himself. When violence answers violence in a growing frenzy that makes the simple language of reason impossible, the role of intellectuals cannot be, as we read every day, to excuse from a distance one of the violences and condemn the other. This has the double result of enraging the violent group that is condemned and encouraging to greater violence the violent group that is exonerated. If they do not join the combatants themselves, their role (less spectacular, to be sure!) must be merely to strive for pacification so that reason will again have a chance.[10]

Notes:

1. See M. Hechter, *Internal Colonialism: the Celtic Fringe in British National Development*, (Routledge & Kegan Paul, London: 1975).
2. W. Blackstone, *Commentaries on the Laws of England*, (London 1776), Bk I, pp. 82
3. A.L. Lowell, *The Government of England*, (Macmillan, New York: 1908), pp. v-vi.
4. House of Lords, *Hansard*, 5 Sept. 1893, cols 33–4.
5. As most brilliantly argued by R.F.V. Heuston, *Essays in Constitutional Law*, 2nd ed., (Stevens & Sons, London: 1964), in the first chapter on 'Sovereignty'.
6. Hannah Arendt, *On Violence*, (Allen Lane, London: 1970).
7. See Patrick Keatinge, 'An Odd Couple? Obstacles and Opportunities in Inter-State Political Cooperation between the Republic of Ireland and the United Kingdom', in Desmond Rea, ed., *Political Cooperation in Divided Societies* (Gill & Macmillan, Dublin: 1982), pp. 305–53.
8. See Maurice J.C. Vile, 'Federation and Confederation: the experience of the United States and the British Commonwealth', in Desmond Rea, ed., *Political Cooperation, Ibid.*
9. The British Labour Party has now joined him, in their policy statement approved at the 1981 annual conference – but with similar reservations and realism.
10. Albert Camus, quoted by Norman Jacobson, *Pride and Solace: the Functions and Limits of Political Theory*, (University of California Press, London: 1978).

Six

Northern Ireland and the Theory of Consent

From Carol Harlow, ed., *Public Law and Politics* (Sweet and Maxwell, London: 1986), a *Festschrift* for John Griffith.

Texts for a Lay Sermon

The Guarantee itself

1. It is hereby declared that Northern Ireland remains part of Her Majesty's dominions and of the United Kingdom, and it is hereby affirmed that in no event will Northern Ireland or any part of it cease to be part of Her Majesty's dominions and of the United Kingdom without the consent of a majority of the people of Northern Ireland voting in a poll held for the purpose of this section and in accordance with Schedule 1 of this Act.

(Northern Ireland Constitution Act, 1973)

The Guarantee guaranteed by both Governments.

The two Governments (a) affirm that any change in the status of Northern Ireland would only come about with the consent of a majority of the people of Northern Ireland; (b) recognise that the present wish of a majority of the people in Northern Ireland is for no change in the status of Northern Ireland; (c) declare that, if in the future a majority of the people of Northern Ireland clearly wish for and formally consent to the establishment of a United Ireland, they will introduce and support in their respective Parliaments legislation to give effect to that wish.

(Agreement between The Government of Ireland and the Government of the United Kingdom, November 15, 1985)

Mr. Robert McCartney, Q.C., distinguishes consent from rape

In criminal law there is a crime called rape. Rape means having sexual intercourse with a woman without her consent. Consent in this circumstance, or the absence of it, is defined in three ways. It is not consent if you have her by force, and everybody agrees that in relation to Northern Ireland force is out. It is not consent if you have her by fear ... And it is not consent if you obtain her agreement by fraud ... because people will not accept Northern Ireland's refusal, Unionists are now worried that her consent will be obtained by fraud by a series of careful structurings ... After a

77

period of these closer working links she will be ... so committed, so bound and attached that she will not be able to say no. And this, I think, breeds a lot of distrust ... That's not the way to win her. If Northern Ireland is to be wooed, it has to be done honestly.

(Interviewed in 1981 by Padraig O'Malley in his *Uncivil Wars: Ireland Today* (Boston and Belfast, 1983), pp. 41–2)

A dangerously optimistic text for seducers

'And Crying, 'No, no, I'll ne'er consent,' consented.'

(Byron, *Don Juan*)

The Theory of Consent

When is consent actually needed for government, and what kind of consent in what kind of circumstances? The Northern Ireland question is at least intellectually interesting.

When the men of Massachusetts and of Virginia affirmed in 1775 that 'all government is based on the consent of the governed', they knew perfectly well that most government was not. Most human government was based, as both St. Augustine and David Hume had seen in different ways, on coercion, hopelessness, habit and interest. Most thoughts of rebellion are stifled, Machiavelli observed, not by lack of courage but by lack of hope. The Americans plainly meant that good government is based on consent (the consent of 'citizens,' at least); and they also had learned that consent, if construed as giving power to a majority, was not a sufficient condition for good government: the majority had to act prudently, as Burke lectured a restless Parliament, or better, they thought, should be bound by restraints in public law and widespread belief in individual rights. Power unchecked by constitutional law and by a belief in rights was held to be, whether in the hands of a few or of many, tyrannical and corrupting.

'The strongest', said Rousseau, 'is never strong enough unless he can turn power into right and obligation into self-interest.' He was certainly wrong on the first count, unless he meant it, as he probably did, as a moral precept rather than an empirical generalisation. Only in very special circumstances do self-interest and right coincide as constitutional democracy. By 1775 in Massachusetts, Virginia and their neighbours, white adult males with some freehold or substantial leasehold property (the laws of each colony varied) had not merely long enjoyed the franchise, but for very special and complex historical reasons had long constituted, to the frustration and annoyance of royal governors, an opinion and a power without whose compliance, co-operation and, indeed, active consent, orderly government could not be conducted. Not even taxes could be gathered if they collectively thought them to be unjust. But that was exceptional. Most people in the world, then and now, settle for peace, hope that bad government will at least be predictable and not arbitrary, and have little hope for justice based on an active consent.

Thomas Hobbes taught that for the hope of peace and to die in bed of natural causes, that is to minimise the incidence of violent death, we should surrender chimerical notions of rights in unconditional obedience to the state (which, to be fair to him, he thought had little reason to do anything else but enforce the peace, and would cease to be a state if it failed in that). To most people this is common sense; even to some permanent minorities in nominally democratic regimes. And if it is not acceptable as a sufficient condition for good government, it is a minimal condition for any kind of government.

The Lockean theory that government must rest on the consent of the governed is, fundamentally, not empirical but moral. It moralises political theory and obligation. We should act like human beings, at best as fellow citizens, or at least, if ourselves citizens, should treat mere subjects as equal human beings. A much used student textbook in political theory says, 'consent theory admits the legitimacy of authority ...only when it satisfies certain moral criteria'; but it then goes on to say, of course, 'people may differ on whether any particular government satisfies them', and, indeed, on what these criteria are.[1] One of the difficulties of the Northern Ireland question, for instance, is whether to treat 'nationalism' as among moral criteria like 'freedom', 'individualism', 'conscience', 'tolerance', 'justice' and 'rights'; and, if so, is it an overriding principle? A large dose of nationalism seems able in the modern world to make up for a large amount of what the best minds in the eighteenth and nineteenth centuries would have seen as intolerable injustice. And, of course, to say that a government is intolerable or illegitimate is not to say that it is about to wither away. Some flagrantly unjust regimes are remarkably stable. We may accept them for the sake of peace, or as a lesser evil than the consequences of trying to change them by external pressure; but acceptance is not agreement. Indeed to be an effective realist in politics one has to have some moral distance and to keep it.

The application of principle in the real world of policy, as well as for an individual's political actions, always involves some empirical calculation about consequences. Part of the concept of 'responsibility' is demanding that people try to think through the probable consequences of their actions. Even though we know that to be certain is impossible, we know that some degrees of risk and uncertainty are irresponsible. As Hobhouse once said, 'the ethically desirable must be the sociologically possible'. All political principles or values must claim to be workable. In fact we rarely argue directly about other people's principles, sensibly we argue about the acceptability of probable consequences. I fully accept everyone's nationalism, so long as I can question how it applies to those living in the same area who do not feel the same passionate sense of identity or read the same history books. Illegitimate governments may often be strong because people who do not identify with them nonetheless can see no practical alternative. Sometimes basically moral arguments take on a kind of 'empiricist rhetoric' in order to achieve this effect.

When Mr. Charles Haughey, for instance, says that 'Northern Ireland has failed as a political entity', he really means to make, in his light, a moral statement. His view of nationalism renders Northern Ireland illegitimate and, further, the values of most people in the North affront the specific values of his party's traditional nationalism. But he puts his argument in an empirical, or at least a pseudo-empirical, vein — 'has failed'. There have certainly been some instances in the modern world where organised government has broken down; but Northern Ireland for all its terrorism, bigotry, troubles and travails, is not one of them. There is a dangerous tendency, both in political and legal thinking, to move away from difficult but honest moral arguments into apocalyptic prophecies, masked as projections of social trends, of impending social breakdown if my case is not accepted entirely and at once. The debate about Northern Ireland is intense and deadly enough without such perpetual stage thunder.

What makes the question of consent in Northern Ireland so unusually complex is that, of course, there are two different concepts of 'the constituency' to which the consent pertains: all-Ireland or else Northern Ireland (the Unionists are very wary of relating consent to the United Kingdom as a whole). And the moralising of consent is certainly a factor of political power. Many people do not first think in Hobbist terms before they then seek Lockean solutions; many are willing to risk (so they say, and seem to behave as if they mean it) a breakdown of government in order to gain or defend the right constituency of consent. Yet it is mildly comforting to note that over the last fifteen years opinion polls solidly report that a majority of people in both communities have given as their second most acceptable constitutional or institutional option, the continuance of some form of direct rule; better at least than rule by the other side.[2]

Nevertheless, it is more helpful to use a moral vocabulary of consent, if we can do so with our eyes open; that is to be able to recognise and admit that some illegitimate governments are remarkably stable, rather than to say with Hobbist cynicism (or minimal humanism) that stability is all one can ever mean by legitimacy. By Lockean (and American) standards the religious clauses of the Irish Constitution make it a thoroughly illegitimate regime; but nonetheless it seems, in common sense, a reasonably civilised place, intolerable intolerance cannot be inferred from the letter of the law. No one's consent is total, however, nor can continuing consent be inferred by the stolid law-abidingness of the vast majority.

Locke famously attempted to deal with these questions and difficulties by distinguishing between 'explicit' and 'virtual' or 'tacit' consent. Explicit consent is to say freely (that is voluntarily and without coercion, as in a valid contract), 'I will'. When a state demands such explicit consent, it shows that there is a need for active support rather than mere passive obedience. Although republics are more difficult to manage, it was this, Machiavelli thought, that actually gave them more power in time of war than autocracies. When explicit consent is needed, whether for war or peace, it is a sign that a society has a large citizen body, and that a government to carry through anything extraordinary has to persuade many people politically rather than by command or coercion. 'Virtual' or 'tacit' consent is simply relative contentment, the absence of conscious and expressed disorder or dis-affection; even democratic governments rely on this for nine-tenths of their administration. But there are some things that demand more positive support. Some legislation is unenforceable without a high degree of positive agreement: road safety and statutory incomes policies are obvious examples, as was military and industrial conscrip-tion, or attempts to control deadly alcohol and nicotine addiction.

Constitutional change? But of what kind and where? Everyone seems to agree that fundamental constitutional change in Northern Ireland would need not merely the explicit consent of a majority but also the consent of the minority. Perhaps only tacit consent would be needed from the British and the Irish electorates. Her Majesty's Government says to 'institutional change' from Westminster, 'yes, certainly', so long as it commands 'widespread acceptance in both communities' (that is tacit consent); but no 'constitutional change' without the explicit consent of a majority. Does the 'Agreement' of November 15, 1985 between the two governments, establishing a consultative 'Intergovernmental Conference' to consider all aspects of Northern Ireland, itself constitute 'institutional' or 'constitutional' change? We must return to this question, but for the moment just note that the Irish government firmly avoids the issue, the British Govern-ment firmly says 'institutional,' and the Unionists cry 'constitutional.' The Unionist view is reasonable in light of the unprecedented extent of such an innovation, but more arguable when they say it is a 'surrender of British sovereignty' and 'the thin end of the wedge towards United Ireland'. Their feelings are so strong that they don't even trust Mrs. Thatcher on sovereignty. The great issue is distorted by the Irish habit, North and South, of talking of 'the constitutional issue' as if it was only the issue of the border and a united or a divided Ireland; and anyone knows that that cannot be changed except by consent (hence the Guarantee). But what of a constitutional change for Northern Ireland that does not raise the border issue? Or possible forms of half-life between two sovereign states, extensive 'co-operation' even short of 'joint authority'? It might seem that if the 'Inter-governmental Conference' proves acceptable, does not break down or cannot be destroyed, then what is 'constitutional', in the broad sense, to us on the mainland and 'constitutional' (and hateful) to them in the specific, Ulster and Irish sense, will be treated by most commentators and future writers of authority as 'institutional'. But proof of the pudding will lie less in definitions and recipes than in what happens in the eating, and the digestion.

Clearly consent of any kind has broken down when there is such a powerful negation of the concept as 'open rebellion' or, in the past, civil war. But where there is 'disaffection' (I find this old political and legal term less slippery than pseudo-psychological 'alienation'), it means that some have withdrawn their support from the state, and while not in open rebellion themselves, nonetheless tolerate and occasionally participate in obstruction, threatening demonstrations, small riots and political strikes. Some actually tolerate violence and terrorism. Different lines are drawn. As distinct from civil war or open rebellion, some lines are drawn. The toleration of violence is most often passive, expressing itself not in participation or active support but simply in non-co-operation with the police, in not informing on violent and murderous neighbours. These are measures of disaffection more deadly than the fanaticism of the relatively few active terrorists.

There is, of course, a lot of tacit consent for direct rule in Northern Ireland in terms of law-abiding people who are not so disaffected with the regime, but are disaffected with the choice of political parties offered them, or simply by the combative manner in which they are led. This is particularly the case in the Protestant community. Many people will only vote for a Unionist Party because they do not trust the others on 'the constitutional issue'; but they want no part in the membership of such a party. The phenomenon is not limited to Northern Ireland of party membership declining while voting levels remain high, so that people of extreme views find it easier to dominate the local parties and drive off the moderates. But at least they are limited in their abilities, whatever their threats, to turn their people out threateningly on the streets. (In fact, the politicians always claim that 'the people' are pushing them, but that is usually untrue; it is their party rivals who raise the stakes.) Politics does not always need agreement or high levels of participation, sometimes acceptance is enough; both for better and for worse.

Thus in Northern Ireland, to begin to come down to earth, explicit consent does not exist among a majority of the minority, and the level of tacit consent varies with political events. At times even that tacit consent, which is normally a sign that a government is (all things considered in context and by comparison with world standards) reasonably just, is wanting. Also the active consent of some of the majorit⌐

can be highly selective. 'Loyalism' is, in its origins and history, a very discriminating form of consent to Acts of the United Kingdom Parliament.

Ulster Realities

If Protestant Ulster had not threatened rebellion in 1912 and 1920, against the wishes – as nationalists always remind us – of the electorate in the last all-Ireland elections ever held, there would be no Northern Ireland today. Kevin Boyle and Tom Hadden have put this harsh truth clearly:

> The truth in crude terms is that both the Republic of Ireland and Northern Ireland were created by a combination of military force and popular will. The idea of partition was first seriously raised when it became clear that very large numbers . . . were prepared to fight in Carson's UVF against the imposition of Home Rule by Britain on an all-Ireland basis... The underlying reasons for partition were thus that the vast majority of the inhabitants in the North and in the South of Ireland had expressed incompatible loyalties and commitments and... had shown their willingness to fight.[3]

At least today it has not come to that. 'The Agreement' was not seen (if judged by how Unionist politicians behaved and not by what they said) as 'constitutional' (in the Irish sense), not really the ending of the Union, the great betrayal, but as a possible threat in that direction. Their 'withdrawal of consent' meant, of course, the active consent of participation in legally established institutional politics. In terms of our analysis, this is (or would be) to stop any process of change going beyond the consultative 'Agreement' towards 'joint authority' or even the weakest version of confederalism or federalism (and the very word 'process' can seem partisan). Such change would need active consent to make it workable. Coercion, on the scale needed, would not be workable and is outside the peacetime character of both the British and the Irish Governments. But active consent is not needed for the continuance of direct rule by Westminster even in the new consultative mode, only tacit or implied consent: the absence of mass civil disobedience or rebellion. People can accept as a realistic second best, out of fear of something worse, what they would never agree to formally. Such fear is not just of a new and hated regime, but the deepest and most conservative fear in us all: of a breakdown of any law and order. Revolutions more often take place because governments break down than for the reasons subsequently written into history by whatever group climbs fom chaos into the saddle.

Opinion polls tell us that a majority in the Republic favour a united Ireland. But they also tell us that a majority only wish this to be done 'by consent of the North', and that the issue is itself not very high in the order of issues in general elections.[4] Conor Cruise O'Brien poured out a cold-bucket of commonsense when he said in 1978:

> Just as in the Republic the aspiration to acquire Northern Ireland is a low-intensity aspiration, so in Great Britain the aspiration to get rid of Northern Ireland is a low-intensity aspiration. Both have therefore low priorities in terms of practical politics.[5]

This was written before the *Forum Report* and the Intergovernmental Agreement of November 1985. The Forum did create a speculative agenda, but not an immediate political agenda. The Agreement gave a large personal boost in opinion polls to Dr. Fitzgerald and a small one to his party. But O'Brien's general point remains true, despite his do-nothing pessimism. Most Irish opinion is wedded to the belief that unity can only come through consent – hopefully tacit consent but realistically, as most people realise in light of actual opinion in the North, it would need active consent, positive agreement. The American 'Friends of Ireland', former President Carter, Senator Kennedy, and Congressman O'Neill etcetera (now with mild Presidential support) openly favour 'the unity of Ireland with consent'. So did the *Forum Report* (the 'consent' should have been the surprising word not the 'unity'). The British Labour Party favours 'unity with consent'. But, once again, the difficulty is not just the self-deceiving unreality of such an aspiration (not deserving the name of policy) in light of present circumstances and past history, but the way the context or constituency of 'consent' keeps on shifting – within Northern Ireland, all-Ireland or even the whole United Kingdom. All very nice and democratic; but since active consent would be needed to make such fundamental constitutional change work, to stifle armed resistance, consent in Northern Ireland itself is the necessary, though not the only, condition for this.

The dogmatic nationalist is apt to ignore consent: 'no man has a right to fix the boundary of the march of a nation', said Parnell (and some English socialists still treat any one else's nationalism as holy). The teleology of that kind of remark is flagrant. Some people can hardly imagine how countries were ever governed before the rise of nationalism as a distinctive and modern ideology. Elie Kedourie in a classic work has characterised it as the belief that for every nation there must be a state, and dated it no older than the French Revolution.[6] National sentiment can be very strong, think of Quebec, Scotland, Wales and 'Ulster' itself; but a majority of the people in those countries wish strongly to preserve their national characteristics but not to form a separate state. They may not think it feasible or they may actually not desire it, pursuing their political aspirations through federal institutions or unusual types of regional government.

Nationalism and Sovereignty

Nationalism assumes, moreover, a sovereign state. It is the combination of these two concepts that can cause so much harm and blind allegedly practical and pragmatic politicians to any view of possible alternatives. Lord North is not thought of as a thinking man or one, like Lord Haldane, of a metaphysical bent. Yet he asserted, in response to the Franklin-Barclay unofficial peace proposal of 1776, that 'sovereignty cannot be divided'. Burke had, of course, argued in his great speeches on conciliation with America that the sovereignty of Parliament should be exercised with prudence; 'I care not if you have a right to make them miserable; have you not an interest to make them happy?' But not for a moment did he concede or believe that it could be limited in law. As is well known Blackstone regarded federalism as an impossiblity and if even Austin did not go quite so far, he did think that 'these United States' were inherently unstable. Both Mr. Haughey and Mrs. Thatcher seem to believe with Robespierre, for history makes strange bedfellows, that 'sovereignty is indivisible'.

The creation of a myth of parliamentary sovereignty was extremely useful to British Government after the Act of Union with Scotland in 1707 and again in Ireland at the end of the century. What it actually meant was something as Hobbesean as this: 'if you don't surrender all power to Parliament we can't stop you getting your throats cut by Catholic highlanders or bog-dwelling Irish peasants', But in fact Scotland was left to govern itself to an astonishing degree, and to have the Presbyterian Church established (an elective and popular body at every level) probably meant more to most lowlanders than the presumption to govern of a central but aristocratically dominated Parliament. The Kirk and the Law were the great national institutions. To this day textbooks both in constitutional law and in politics continue to present 'the United Kingdom' (the significance of that very formula is usually ignored) as a centralised, unitary state. This is simply old Whig English ideology. At the heart of actual political and constitutional practice in Britain there is an historically complex, but until the postwar generation, well understood, context of the management and consent of nations not simply of classes or individuals organised in electoral constituencies. Thus to this day the special status of language in Wales and of law, education and the machinery of government in Scotland, let alone the old quasi-federal devolution of Stormont, simply does not fit the usual English picture of central government in an homogeneous society.[7]

During the Irish Forum hearings Mr. Haughey blundered into interesting territory when he said that the North in a United Ireland could keep its peculiar institutions as did Scotland; but he was foolish to imply that this would not need any change in the Irish constitution. Scotland's institutions arose from the Treaty of Union of 1707 and a unique national history. To create anything in Ireland remotely analogous to existing Scottish administrative devolution would plainly need a new and federal constitution.

If we believe that the sovereign national state is the best form that national sentiment can take and the almost unavoidable form of human government in the modern world, there is probably no lasting acceptable framework of government for Northern Ireland. But there are a few areas of the modern world that cannot be governed peaceably or justly within such a conceptual framework: Cyprus, Israel-Palestine and South Africa are obvious examples where for a state to claim, in Weber's famous definition of the modern state, 'a monopoly of allegiance' is itself part of the problem, not the solution. The beginning of wisdom may be to see that Northern Ireland both historically and in the foreseeable future faces both ways. I mean not just the obvious political and confessional divisions, but the fact that there are few people active in politics whose behaviour is not a compound of both British and Irish influence.[8] If Ulster Protestants do not notice it, they need telling. In English eyes they are far more different than the Scottish or Welsh; and the average Englishman finds his immigrant neighbour from the Republic less strange than an Ulsterman. This may be irrational but it is so. (Indeed the Irish immigrant into Britain is an interesting person to consider, since he or she shows a wide spectrum of allegiance to 'Ireland' or to 'Britain', and sometimes not just differences between individuals but differences within individuals according to the situation or the company.)

To say that there are two traditions in the North, both of whom would have to consent to any constitutional change, is not to say quite the same thing as Conor Cruise O'Brien when he argues that there are two states in Ireland (and that's an end of it). Even if we accept his way of looking at things, which is a powerful and bold way, the difficulty is that one of these states is geographically contiguous but the other not. The Protestant-Orange state is uncomfortably mixed with Irish-Green enclaves – most imperfectly partitioned for 'a state' that could reasonably (unlike Israel in the captured territories) claim a monopoly of allegiance. O'Brien is bold but he simplifies. To discredit the Sinn Fein and the IRA for their violence and lack of negotiable political policies is not to discredit the non-violent nationalism of John Hume and the SDLP.

Boyle and Hadden are closer to the ground in Northern Ireland than O'Brien. In a number of thoughtful papers and a book they have argued that the fact of two very different communities in Northern Ireland has to be faced and that they should be faced (leaving all their careful detail aside) in two ways: by legislation in the United Kingdom Parliament which would virtually give equality of esteem and status to the two traditions (symbolically in flags and emblems, realistically in public employment and education); and by some joint administrative agencies between the two governments, a few bilateral projects of obvious mutual benefit that could attract a trilateral dimension.[9] They argue that this can only be done from the present starting point, within the framework of British administrative law and 'the Guarantee', They see this as a starting point which could, in the next generation, be a finishing point too: it could go no further or could develop into – quite what is hard to predict, except that it could not be a united Ireland in any traditional sense of a centralised, sovereign state.

The Irish and British governments did not follow the Boyle and Hadden line in their negotiations. The prospects of getting agreement to practical steps towards equality between the two traditions seem poor; so they have chosen for the moment to bypass any area which needs active majority consent. But Boyle's and Hadden's ideas are likely to be influential in the future. And once the extreme sensitivity of the Falklands debate is over, British governments may cease to think that joint administrative agencies necessarily impugn their sovereignty (having accepted the Treaty of Rome, this view grows less and less tenable – as worries and torments the logical Mr. Powell). Joint agencies may be acceptable even when they are not agreeable (indeed some exist already, the Irish Tourist Board and the Foyle Fisheries Board, for instance; and very close degrees of cooperation also, as in railways, long-distance bus transport and peat bog drainage).

Governments may have to proceed cautiously in such situations as Northern Ireland, but they are not mere passive reflectors of opinion or 'consent'. All governments try to build support for their policies. That most acute of American observers of British politics, Samuel E. Beer, once referred to one of the prime functions of Parliament as being 'a device to mobilise consent'. There is nothing wrong in this. Tails should not believe that they can wag dogs. It is perfectly fair of governments to try to influence people, so long as people are free and able to answer back, have reasonable access to publicity, and are not silenced either by deliberate acts or deliberate neglects of the state (unless the state itself is in danger, which it less rarely is than it claims). Consent needs to be mobilised if governments would attempt rapid social change. Britain could no more be made socialist by legislation in the first hundred days of a Labour Government with a majority (of whatever size) than Ireland could be united by simultaneous legisla-tion in the Dail and at Westminster. Consent to change involving allegiances, confessions and deep traditions, needs, as do changes involving fundamental working habits and income distribution, a great deal of preparation and persuasion. Some things can only be done by persuasion however long it may take; and if not, then aban-doned. Not only should governments not lead people into fundamen-tal changes against their will or in ignorance by any gradual step-by-step long march of deceit, but they should realise that if people already have a tradition of free politics, they will fail.

There is a counter-argument about consent made by some Sinn Fein intellectuals and fellow-travellers. They say that 'unity by consent' means consent only to the form of unity, not to the principle of unity. They then decently offer to specify minimum criteria for unity. A Unionist has reasonably called this view 'imprisonment by consent'. The very existence of such an odd argument shows the intensity of ultra-nationalist feeling. But the argument cannot explain why one should ever consent to the other fellow's nationalism in the first place (his special view of history or obsession that God created natural boundaries – 'One Island, One Ireland!', or 'Ireland shall be free from sea to sea!'). A nationalist who scorns political compromise has no rational argument to offer. Rival ultra-nationalists can only trade bad history and cultural insults with each other. There is no reason on earth why an Ulster Protestant, making what is to him a democratic argument, should allow the context to be pulled from under his feet into 'all Ireland.' He could only be coerced into 'all Ireland' – at a price that no one is willing to pay, or live with the consequences. But most ultra-nationalist arguments are, of course, about origins (who got there first), and so are inherently anti-democratic if population patterns subsequently change.

The Agreement and 'The Guarantee'

The Guarantee is thus something that cannot, in this empirical sense, be withdrawn. John Hume used to claim that its very existence had, from the very time of partition, 'undermined any hope of political negotiation in Northern Ireland' giving 'a permanent exclusive power to one side'.[10] Others think that if it were withdrawn organised Unionism would be driven to violence. The force of it does not depend, however, on statutory declarations, still less on internationally registered agreements, but upon political recognition of historical facts. So little thought has been given, even among constitutional nationalists, about how to persuade Protestant opinion, that serious observers can sometimes wonder if they are all equally serious. John Bowman in a well-documented book found many grounds for doubting even the great chieftain's seriousness. Like the British Labour Party, De Valera had aspirations to unity but no policy.[11] And yet the Guarantee itself recognises a contingent not a necessary and inalienable connection. HMG has made quite clear, both by declaration and statute, that it will legislate for unity if a majority in a referendum desired. Demography is to have the last word (not that the North would then be any more easy to govern, simply that mainland Britain would have had enough). This is perpetual gall to the Northern Unionist. We view him as a Briton and a British responsibility, but not inalienably and nationalistically, only conditionally: so long as he keeps his diminishing majority. This is not a very satisfying relationship.

The Agreement Between the Government of Ireland and the Government of the United Kingdom, Cmnd. 9657 of November 15, 1985 has been presented by Unionist politicians as a surrender of sovereignty and the primrose path towards everlasting unity. Mr. Peter Robinson, MP, burnt Mrs. Thatcher's effigy outside Belfast City Hall as 'a traitor' and Mr. Enoch Powell, MP in the House of Commons described the Agreement as 'treachery'. But it cannot reasonably carry that construction. Article 1 begins:

> The two Governments (a) affirm that any change on the status of Northern Ireland would only come about with the consent of a majority of the people of Northern Ireland; (b) recognise that the present wish of a majority of the people of Northern Ireland is for no change . . .; and (c) declare that, if in the future a majority . . . clearly wish for and formally consent to the establishment of a united Ireland, they will introduce and support in their respective Parliaments legislation . . .

The Guarantee could not be reiterated more clearly and the mode of formal consent is still as specified in the Northern Ireland Constitution Act of 1973 (quoted at the head of this essay). And now it is a declaration of the Irish Government too.

The main purpose of the new inter-governmental Conference is stated to be to 'concern itself with measures to recognise and accommodate the rights and identities of the two traditions in Northern Ireland, to protect human rights and prevent discrimination' (Article 5 (a). As other articles make clear, anything relating both to Northern Ireland and to British-Irish relations can be raised, but in consultative not decision-making or executive mode. Article 2 clearly states: 'there is no derogation from the sovereignty of either the Irish Government or the United Kingdom Government, and each retains responsibility for the decisions and administration of government within its own jurisdiction'. The word 'decisions' is vital.

In Article 4 both governments pledge themselves to try to achieve devolution 'in respect of certain matters within the powers of the Secretary of State for Northern Ireland . . . on a basis that would secure widespread acceptance throughout the community'. Again humble 'acceptance' is specified, not stern 'consent'. Article 2 (b) makes clear that the powers of the Irish Government to put forward 'views and proposals' are only 'in so far as these matters are not the responsibility of a devolved administration in Northern Ireland'. Even if the 'reserved powers' of the Secretary of State would always, in such a situation, be formidable (security, administration of justice, economic policy, administration of justice and electoral arrangements – at least), this is a substantial exception to the Irish Government's unique right of consultation and power of formal initiative. In effect it was said to the Irish Government and agreed by them, you may advise, warn and encourage but not in these areas, though you may discuss with us first what these areas are to be. Politically it is a carrot to the Unionist politicians to return to the now perennial project of trying to find terms on which they and the SDLP can agree to work the present or some other assembly. If they can do that (as they've failed to do in recent years), they get the Conference and Irish Government off their backs. However Article 5 (c) states:

> If it should prove impossible to achieve and sustain devolution..., the Conference shall be the framework in which the Irish Government may, where the interests of the minority community are significantly or especially affected, put forward views on proposals for major legislation and on major policy issues which are within the purview of the Northern Ireland Departments and which shall remain the responsibility of the Secretary of State for Northern Ireland.

The draftsmen walked like cats on ice. Although only a consultative body, the Irish Government can put forward, certainly not legislation, but 'views on proposals for major legislation'. Read calmly this preserves, in terms of Northern Ireland, the distinction between 'institutional' and 'constitutional' or between what merely needs 'acceptance' (as the absence of civil disobedience) and what needs, both legally and politically, formal 'agreement' as active consent). The Agreement is not even an Act of Parliament, although it has been ratified both by Parliament and the Dail; nor is it an international treaty either; copies of the Agreement have simply been lodged with the United Nations. But in mainland British discourse, all this is a remarkable constitutional innovation: an institution is created in which it is solemnly promised that a foreign government will be consulted before any major decisions are made about the government of a province, and has a right to raise virtually any matter or make any proposal it likes. One can see both why Ulster Unionists do not like it at all – which is one of the difficulties of being a minority in a democracy like the United Kingdom; but also why they all find in it (without being, in their indigenous theories of textual exegesis, especially radical deconstructionists), a subtext of burning letters promising unity by stages.

Nonetheless, while anyone who visits Northern Ireland at all frequently passes through a stage of being told, and passing on, 'you've got to see how it looks on the ground', yet some of us emerge to say to them 'but you've also got to see it through our eyes – the majority of the United Kingdom' (and it wouldn't harm to lift up your eyes, if not your hearts, to look not just at modern Ireland and modern Europe but also, to avoid naming 'America', at the Atlantic Alliance). And in these wider contexts the Agreement, while unusual, appears as a reasonable mirror of hard political reality. In the United Kingdom context it is, to be quite specific, an extraordinary misreading of the British conservative mind, and of Mrs. Thatcher's especially, to think that there is a sub-text of 'sell out'. It would be just as plausible and just as politically tactless to argue that the sub-text from the British point of view is simply that the Agreement is a 'talking-shop' to get both Mr. Fitzgerald and Mr. Hume off their respective barbed hooks.

A relevant argument in construing the text is to consider its purpose. The purpose was to arrest any further decay of the SDLP vote in favour of Sinn Fein and, more generally, to achieve some diminution of Catholic disaffection in Northern Ireland so that the climate of tolerance towards terrorist operations is diminished. The SDLP boycotted the 'Prior Assembly'. This may well have been unwise on their part. Constitutional politics needs a constitutional forum, however imperfect: if the name of the game was abstention, some of the Catholic voters might prefer to vote for those with an untarnished record in that respect. But the judgement had to be that of the leaders of the SDLP If they had taken their seats in the Assembly, they might have split and their support diminished disastrously. What is overwhelmingly clear, however, is that during the three years or more of the Assembly the Unionists were not willing, despite some slight movement,[12] to make compromises of a kind that could have brought the SDLP in and avoided bilateral action, which had been on the cards for a long time, by London and Dublin.[13] They had their chance for compromise of the devolutionary kind, so in 1985 a compromise form of direct rule was imposed on them: direct rule by the British Government consulting publicly with an Irish Government who now hold, if the analogy is apt, a watching brief on behalf of the Catholic community.

The Agreement neither creates 'joint authority' in the North nor 'power-sharing' in the North. 'Close co-operation' is the key word of the Agreement and the attached 'Joint Communiqué', and the reiterated objective is 'diminishing the divisions' and 'achieving lasting peace and stability'. These words if banal were well chosen. 'Co-operation' between states may be a deliberate limitation of political power, but it is no derogation of legal sovereignty. 'Diminishing divisions' is more realistic and tolerant than 'seeking for agreement' or that old weasel word 'consensus'. And 'peace and stability' will have to do until the rights of the Irish question are finally adjudicated at the 'Last Judgement', and even then there will still be some in Fermanagh and Tyrone who will not attend to the trumpet call unless they are sure what the judgement will be. We need both Hobbes and Locke. Hobbes is the precondition for any kind of political order, Locke for a just and consenting political order (when happily possible).

The Agreement is a 'step forward' when some do not want to move at all; but it is not a move towards some teleological goal of unity and enforced reconcilaition but towards a plateau of wider *acceptance* of institutions of government. This is the only possible basis for future *agreement* between any possible leaders of the two communities. The next generation may rest on this plateau or move in some obvious or novel direction. Better for us to bury our dead and to leave some decisions to the future. But it is fairly clear that if a future generation did move 'forward" in a nationalist sense, it could not possibly be towards any simple form of unitary state in Ireland. Mr. Haughey, Mrs. Thatcher and Mr. Kinnock all need to observe that many parliamentary democracies are of a federal nature; and that it is unlikely that mankind has exhausted inventiveness in political institutions. If Northern Ireland inherently faces both ways, forms of government will have to be devised to encompass that fact. Perhaps consultation and co-operation will be enough. Perhaps not. But it cannot be anything less. Those who say they want to stay put, in reality want to put the clock back, or –among the leaders – simply to enjoy the storm.

Notes

1. S.I. Benn and R.S. Peters, *Social Principles and the Democratic State* 1st ed., Allen & Unwin, London: (1959), p. 328.

2. The best analysis of this is still Richard Rose, Ian McAllister and Peter Mair, 'Is There a Concurring Majority About Northern Ireland?' *Strathclyde Studies in Public Policy,* vol. 22, (1978) pp. 49–51. Later polls sustain their conclusion.

3. Kevin Boyle and Tom Hadden, 'How to Read the New Ireland Forum Report' *The Political Quarterly* (1984) 55 (no. 4) pp. 403–4. This was a shortened version of a paper submitted to the New Ireland Forum and which also had a wide and influential private circulation.

4. The evidence of opinion polls is well summarised by W. Harvey Cox *Government and Opposition* (1985) 20 (no.1) pp. 29–47. He concludes that 'it would be a conservative estimate' to say that 'certainly no more than two Irishmen to one' favour unification 'and that one of the two in favour of it is a 'low intensity unificationist'.' (p. 39). See also his 'The Politics of Unification in the Irish Republic' *Parliamentary Affairs* 38 (no. 4) (1985) pp. 437–54.

5. Conor Cruise O'Brien, *Neighbours* Faber, London: (1980), p. 39.

6. Elie Kedourie, *Nationalism* 2nd ed., Hutchinson, London: (1961), p. 9.

7. See my, 'The Sovereignty of Parliament and the Irish Question' (1982), reprinted in this volume, above; and more recently I have applied this argument specifically to Scotland in "For My Fellow English", in Owen Dudley Edwards, ed., *A Claim of Right For Scotland* Polygon, Edinburgh: (1989) and as a pamphlet, *Labour and Scotland's Claim of Right* East Lothian Labour Party, Tranent: (1989).

8. This is the broad conclusion of all serious historians, see especially Oliver MacDonagh, *States of Mind* Allen & Unwin,

London: (1983) and F.S.L. Lyons, *Culture and Anarchy in Ireland, 1890–1939* Oxford University Press, Oxford: (1979).

9. Boyle and Hadden, *op. cit.* and their *Ireland: a Positive Proposal* Penguin, London: (1985), probably the best short analysis of the problem that has been written.

10. John Hume, 'The Irish Question,' *Foreign Affairs, Winter 1979–1980* (1979), p. 303.

11. John Bowman, *De Valera and the Ulster Question, 1917–1973* (1982). He summarises De Valera's assumptions: 'unity, along with being inevitable, was always postponable' (p. 305).

12. This was supposed to have been visible by a very close reading of the texts of *The Way Forward* (1984), a discussion paper issued by the Ulster Unionist Council, and Peter Smith's *Opportunity Lost: A Unionist View of the Report of the Forum for a New Ireland* (1984), issued by the same body.

13. It is often forgotten that Margaret Thatcher's impatience with the unwillingness of Unionist politicians to compromise began very early. On November 12, 1979 she gave an interview to R.W. Apple of the *The New York Times* (even before addressing the House of Commons on the 'Aitkens initiative') in which she was reported as saying 'that she would not permit the squabbling of political parties in Northern Ireland to block her initiative,' and was directly quoted as saying that 'if they said "We don't like it and you can't do anything unless we all agree", she would impose a decision. Otherwise, she said, "you'll never get anywhere and we must."' *International Herald Tribune,* November 13, 1979, p. 1.

Seven

An Englishman Considers his Passport

From *The Irish Review*, No. 5, Autumn 1988.

I am a citizen of a state with no agreed colloquial name. Our passports call us citizens of 'The United Kingdom of Great Britain and Ireland'. But what does one reply when faced by that common existential question of civilised life, which is neither precisely legal nor precisely philosophical, found in foreign hotel registers, 'Nationality?'

If that question is meant to establish legal citizenship, then 'British' is correct, although that is the least used name colloquially for people as distinct from goods, except in the expletive form of 'Brits', now used not merely by Aussies but by both Prods and Taigs in Ulster. But, rather than 'British', many write in the register 'Scottish' or 'Welsh'. The question does, after all, ask 'Nationality?' And when those with an address in Northern Ireland write 'British' one reasonably assumes that they are Protestant and Unionist. And a few with similar addresses boldly write 'Irish', and some of those even carry, quite legally, an Irish passport instead of or even as well as a United Kingdom passport. Once or twice I've seen entries which slide around the question and write 'Citizen of the United Kingdom', which means that they are either a Catholic who is an Alliance Party supporter or that even rarer stubborn breed, a Scottish Tory. One I read 'Cornish' but I suspected, correctly, that it was a wag and not a nut.

The majority write 'English'. The overwhelming majority of UK passport holders are, of course, 'English'; but I have a suspicion that many of them write 'English' not as an assertion of nationality, as do those who write Irish, Scottish or Welsh, but out of a common but mistaken belief that 'English' is the adjective corresponding to 'citizen of the United Kingdom of Great Britain and Northern Ireland'. This angers me personally: my children are half Welsh, I live in Edinburgh from choice and visit Ireland frequently, often for pleasure. And it angers me intellectually: I believe that the United Kingdom is a multi-national state or a union of different nations with different cultures and different histories. For I like it that way – even though I note that school books in History and Politics south of the border (sorry, I mean that border just north of the Roman wall) are almost entirely Anglocentric.

Leave aside, for the moment, the question as to whether this union was a free and voluntary contract that would have satisfied the philosophical criteria of John Locke (plainly not). When I retired from London University to live in Scotland my colleagues gave me a Gillray cartoon called 'The Union Club' which shows satirically the living and the dead notables of English and Irish politics drinking wildly together, Pitt and Grattan hand in hand, rival bishops sharing pipes, a busty Britannia and a buxom Hibernia amorously lip to lip, Lord Edward and Wolfe Tone jigging towards a sodden Prince and a collapsed Fox, as if the Union were a cause for mutual congratulation (as the Act or Treaty of Union with Scotland of 1707 had been – well, on the whole: most Scots at the time, real history now tells us, thought that they had driven a sensible bargain). And even leave aside, for a moment too, the special problem of Northern Ireland. If the Irish remember their history too obsessively, ordinary English people forget theirs too easily; but when English politicians forget (as they have done in the last decade) that they are dealing with a union of peoples and not (whatever the state myths) a homogeneous society with a centralised and common administration (Scotland, Wales and Northern Ireland – not to mention, as trivial but extraordinary, the Channel Islands and the Isle of Man!), trouble can follow. Thatcherism represents a conservatism that has forgotten true history and is living its myths. She believes that formal sovereignty is not merely inalienable (shades of 'The Treaty'!) but is the same as effective political power, and that the liberating of market forces has removed any vestigial need for the political articulation of different cultures.

Even in documents more elaborate than a passport we English are very confused when we try to name our state. The Central Office of Information publishes an annual handbook on the UK which has all kinds of useful information in it, and has wide a circulation abroad. The title of it is bizarrely (though no one notices or complains) the name of a former Roman province, which has no modern legal or precise geographical meaning: *Britain*. The current Preface of *Britain* states:

> Care should be taken when studying British statistics to note whether they refer to England, to England and Wales..., to Great Britain, which comprises England, Wales and Scotland, or to the United Kingdom (which is the same as Britain, that is Great Britain and Northern Ireland) as a whole.

Indeed. But is 'Britain' usually understood to be 'the same as' the United Kingdom as a whole? When I say 'Britain' I mean, contrary to the COI, the 'mainland' only, and say 'Great Britain' when I want to include Northern Ireland. Perhaps usage varies. In the *OED* early usages of 'Britain' all refer to the island or the mainland of the archipelago. And *OED*'s summary of early modern usage is confused: 'The proper name of the whole island, containing England, Wales and Scotland, with their dependencies; more fully called Great Britain; now used for the British state or Empire as a whole.' That 'more fully' is as a dictionary entry politically very question-begging and pre-emptive. 'Britain' and 'Great Britain' are as often used to refer to different entities. Ulster Loyalists are always careful to proclaim their (conditional) loyalty to 'Great Britain' or 'The United Kingdom'; they rightly suspect that loose talk of 'Britain' can often mean the mainland alone, and thus prove a device to distance them, ultimately to separate them.

The fundamental problem is not, of course, even as simple as that of maintaining or recovering a true view of Great Britain as a multi-national society and, in many respects, a quasi-federal polity. For it is also a problem of the interrelations of 'these islands' or, since usage creates names more than justice, the British Isles. For this brief argument it is necessary to say no more than that the cultural and social relations of the Republic of Ireland and Great Britain have been and are likely to remain (whatever ultimately happens to or in Northern Ireland) relations of an intimacy unusual, though not entirely unprecedented, between different legally sovereign states. If the *Gaeltacht* had ever become all Ireland as the heroes of 1916 (forgetting Connolly) hoped, the situation would be different; but it didn't. And it would be different again, more difficult even, if standard English language and literature had not been profoundly influenced by the vigour of Irish, Scottish and Welsh English. There is much talk always in British political circles of 'the special relationship' to the United States. But this concept is as true for Britain and Ireland together. And, moreover, the special Irish relationship with the United States and the special British relationship to the United States coexist and condition each other; to see them only as rivals is simplistic, culturally and politically mistaken. Most American opinion values both and resents the jealous quarrels of its two most honoured elderly and difficult relatives.

An often forgotten aspect of the problem of national interrelations in the British Isles is a lack of clarity on the part of the English as to what constitutes their own national identity. They could perhaps deal more easily and justly with the others if they were more clear about their own nature. And, by the way, relationships are reciprocal: a knowledge of England and the English is necessary to deal with the English, even where knowledge is wholly unclouded by affection. Was it Orwell who said to Koestler of Koestler to Orwell, 'know thy enemy as thyself'? I'm often surprised how little, for instance, my old friends in the SDLP actually know about Westminster politics. Their dislike of the place, which is understandable, often makes them inept in influence, and incautious in the acceptance of false or posturing friends. The English Press shows little understanding of, and gives little space to, Irish politics. But one can learn far more about British politics from the *Irish Times* or the *Irish Independent* than from the *Belfast Telegraph.* I'm not entirely preaching to the unconvinced. Most Irish understand the English better than most English do themselves. More have had to and have had a lot of experience.

In all this one must distinguish, however, between feelings of national identity and 'nationalism'. By 'nationalism' I mean, no more or no less, than the doctrine that for every nation there must be a state. For about three hundred years the mainland United Kingdom, at least, and including those in Northern Ireland who want to be included in it, has shown that while the nationalist theory of the state is a common aspiration, it is not a universal rule. And there are many other contrary examples: Belgium and Canada, for instance. (And there would seem no possible peaceful way forward for South Africa and for Israel/ Palestine except as multi-national states; both are areas, like Northern Ireland, where claims to sovereignty are part of the problem, not the solution.) That question in the foreign hotel register does make a nationalist assumption that nation and legal citizenship should normally go together and be exclusive: that is why the different entries are emblematic of the difficulties in these islands, so long, that is, as one is only allowed one answer.

Most English Left-wing authors used to regard any discussion of their own national identity as subversive of the purity of the Word and a distraction from the Good News of the class struggle. I am nearly sixty. All my adult life I have found that my fellow English Left-wing intellectuals are suckers for anybody else's nationalism and contemptuous of (and what is sometimes even more dangerous, ignorant of) their own. Only recently have a few emerged who are not positively embarrassed by patriotism. As a political philosopher I use the word 'sucker' quite technically; I meant that they ingest other people's nationalisms whole as a conditioned reflex. Instead of being critical friends of liberation movements, occasionally asking whether one-party states always make the best decisions, whether autocracy is always efficient, whether bombs are always the best persuaders and terror always the best answer to terror, they tend almost to revel in justifying other people's violence. David Caute once defined the Fellow Travellers of the 1930s as those who believed in Socialism in somebody else's country.

If the Left were always true heirs of the Enlightenment and of the Declaration of the Rights of Man, as at their best they are, they would say that any nationalism has to be pursued by means compatible with liberty, justice and respect for the rights of others – whether individuals or groups, especially groups who embarrassingly regard themselves as nations but happen to share the same sacred soil. And the English Left-wing enjoy being made to feel guilty for the sins of their colonialist fathers. It is almost too easy to make us feel guilty. Some Irish writers are expert in this – and some Scots and Welsh too, only fewer people listen. But guilt for sins one has not committed oneself is an insecure basis (I am not Christian enough to believe otherwise) for what has to be a close relationship. Indeed guilt even for one's own sins is rarely a healthy basis for a continuing relationship of any kind (I am Christian enough to believe that repentance, forgiveness and mercy are necessary virtues, even in political life).

The only English Left-wing writer to defend English patriotism and to try to characterise its legitimate content, sardonically, sensitively and, on the whole, sensibly, was George Orwell in *The Lion and the Unicorn*. A few English Right-wing authors have celebrated England specifically, notably Arthur Bryant and A.L. Rowse and praised 'the English national character' with the shameless reverence characteristic of nationalist literature. Their fitting reward was large sales of largely unread books purchased for, if not specifically produced for, private-school prize givings. Yet there are very few serious studies of English character, still less of English dilemmas about identity. Considering that the English are not lacking in self-esteem and, what A.L. Lowell once called, 'a certain effortless sense of superiority', this is strange – but true. If you doubt this, try to compile a bibliography or look at any subject-catalogue in a great library: subheadings will show shelf-loads of books on Irish, Scottish and Welsh nationalism or national identity, not to mention French, German and American etc. etc.; but very few, and then mostly rubbishy, on England and Englishness.

Why this massive silence? Why did the bulldog not bark even in the good old days when it could really bite? The explanation could lie in a very obvious factor. It is the simple presuppositions that we usually miss. Consider what historically, since at least the accession of James I and James VI to the two thrones, has been the main preoccupation of English politics: holding the United Kingdom together. Scotland and Ireland posed great problems for England even in the eighteenth and nineteenth centuries. And they both provoked alternating spasms of coercion and conciliation, occasionally both together. The former is better remembered than the latter, for obvious grim reasons. But if we compare British behaviour or policy with some other empires, then the degree of conciliation and the extent of devolved administration according to local customs, is equally remarkable. 'Indirect rule' can be derogated as 'divide and rule' and dismissed as a mere tactic of colonialism. Whether the relationship of the English to the others is what is usually called 'colonial', whether it was that form of oppression, is a more difficult question than many admit. But most would admit that at least there is colonialism and colonialism. For that 'divide and rule' usually meant the recognition of pre-existing divisions, not their actual creation, which reformers would have rather seen swept away. But even if policies were colonialist in spirit, the specific tactics pursued, the conciliation as well as the coercion, had lasting consequences; and to pursue them at all, whether in Ireland, Scotland or India imposed certain limitations.

For the English to have developed a strident literature of English nationalism, such as arose, often under official patronage, everywhere else in Europe, and in Ireland and Scotland, eventually in Wales, would have been divisive. From political necessity English politicians tried to develop a United Kingdom nationalism and, at least explicitly and officially, to identify themselves with it, wholeheartedly. But from the experience of dealing with Scotland in the seventeenth century and at least with the 'Old English' and the 'new English' in Ireland, the political tactic pursued was not that of colonial assimilation, but a kind of cultural politics. Scots, Welsh and some Irish (all Irish after Catholic emancipation) were encouraged to have a dual sense of national identity. Tocqueville in his great *Democracy in America* saw this clearly in the contrast between French and British eighteenth century administration in North America.

When King James VI of Scotland had been proclaimed King in England it was not, as often said, as 'James I of England' but as 'James I, King of Great Britain'. And that same formula was used throughout the Act or Treaty of Union in 1707, almost a pretence that 'England' as a separate entity had gone out of business, whereas in 1603 a separate kingdom of Scotland was plainly acknowledged and in 1707 a formidable list of Scottish rights set down, including the establishment of the Presbyterian Church (which many Scots at the time saw as the real national, popular and representative institution rather than the aristocratically dominated and corrupt Parliament). Throughout the eighteenth century English Governments and courts, especially after the great scare of 1745, made conscious and strenuous efforts to establish 'British' as the general description, and to replace 'Scottish' and 'English' with 'North British' and 'South British'. Some Ministerial hacks even tried 'West British' for Irish, or at least for loyal Irish. But this early attempt at Newspeak collapsed through its own unreality, a collapse hastened by waves of satire and ridicule. Only a hotel in Edinburgh survives to mark the usage, and the memory of John Wilkes's satiric and Scots-baiting *North Briton*. Policy soon swung the other way: to take pleasure in cultural diversity. This was the time of *Ossian* and the political patronage of romantic poets inventing past glories for the Celtic peoples.

Perhaps the high points of this cultural politics was when, after the repression of Highland society, a cabinet decision was made to attempt toleration and reconciliation throughout Scotland. Sir Walter Scott, a firm but not uncritical Unionist, was given a commission by the cabinet to arrange and manage an official revival (sometimes invention) of traditional Scottish institutions, all to be ready for the visit of the appalling 'Prinny', now George IV, to Edinburgh where he wore the kilt once – to the ribald delight of all cartoonists in the greatest age of English caricature. A pattern was set for the management of Irish and later Welsh affairs. This is well known. Enough to say that it went beyond folk songs in London drawing-rooms and the wearing of the green by wives and daughters of some Viceroys. National cultural institutions were encouraged, up to a point. If one looks for the missing dimension in all this, discussions of the English national character in the nineteenth century, then one must turn to the English novel. Novelists were much concerned with the character of the nations as well as of the classes, and the psychology of cross-pressured individuals. There was in England no state cult of nationalism with its sponsorship of official history and self-justificatory philosophy as found in France and Germany, and envied by subject peoples (only Coleridge did his private and eccentric best to fill the gap). To say, however, that this lack of theoretical concern and philosophical explicitness was a product of English Toryism may be to reverse cause and effect. For royalists and absolutists in the seventeenth century had spilt as much ink and invoked at astonishing length quite as much scriptural authority and bad theology as did Parliament and Covenant men. If the main task of English Toryism was to keep the two, indeed the three, kingdoms together, a certain *lack* of theory as well as of theology was necessary, especially if theory could increasingly take a cultural and national form.

Burke was to skate brilliantly to scratch over and cross-hatch some very opaque thin ice. He defended the rights of Irishmen, as he had the rights of the American colonists; but only within the framework of parliamentary sovereignty. English Tories, indeed the old Whigs too, basically held to two propositions: loyalty and sovereignty. Anything else was negotiable. Prudence and interest, said Burke, argued that sovereignty should not always be exercised; but its residual existence was essential and it could not be divided. He saw clearly that the whole doctrine of 'parliamentary sovereignty' had arisen as part of the 1688 Settlement of the 'glorious because bloodless revolution' (bloodless in England, that is). Power could not be delegated; federations were impossible in principle; but all power must be used with a restraint flowing from respect for and knowledge of traditional liberties, local customs and beliefs. 'Magnanimity in politics is not seldom the truest wisdom; and a great empire and little minds go ill together.' 'I care not if you have a right to make them miserable; have you not an interest to make them happy?'. 'The use of force alone is but *temporary*. It may subdue for a moment, but it does not remove the necessity of subduing again: and a nation is not governed, which is perpetually to be conquered.'

Thus fudge and toleration were part of English high politics. As the mediating institution the Tories looked somewhat more to the Crown (and themselves) and the Whigs somewhat more to Parliament (and themselves). But neither wished to thrust a comprehensive English ideology on the other nations, so long as sovereign power was not challenged. The Irish Catholics posed a special difficulty to the English ruling class not because of their religion (the English rulers were not, after all, Presbyterians) but because of their international connections. So long as the Papacy even attempted, however spasmodically and ineffectually, to be an internal political force, emancipation was not thought possible. Only after the Napoleonic Wars and the Congress of Vienna, when Great Britain emerged as an ally of 'Legitimacy' against revolutionary principles, could she cease to fear continental intervention in Ireland.

What lay behind the cult of sovereignty as it was developed after 1688 by jurists and statesmen was something very deep in the English conservative mind. It was not the fear of any alternative social order but the fear of anarchy, of the sheer breakdown of authority. And the form it then took was not revolution, of course, but a fear of the breakdown of the new United Kingdom: successful Scottish or Irish rebellion. Logically this is an odd argument. Why should the breakdown of the United Kingdom into separate states and distinct peoples and areas necessarily affect political stability in England, or the trade, commerce and intercourse of its peoples? But in the circumstances of the eighteenth century, international politics and war were inseparable from these questions. They are still sometimes confused, if with less plausibility. Paul Kennedy's recent *The Rise and Fall of the Great Powers* became a best-seller probably because he sent a shiver of fear down the spines of affluent Americans: since all previous empires became economically overstretched, and so declined, must not American hegemony go that way too? But Kennedy never says that the decline of an Empire necessarily leads to instability in the homeland and to barbarians coming over the wall. He is naughtily less than cautious, however, in not avoiding that sensational impression. But Great Britain is, after all, a clear enough example to the contrary.

If the English for good reasons never developed a literature of English nationalism, they did develop a formidable substitute: in the late nineteenth century a literature of imperialism emerged which enjoyed considerable state patronage. Each of the nations of these islands could share in the imperial myth and reality. Most of Kipling's imperial stories contained a type from each of the nations: an English officer, a little slow and rigid but decent; a Scottish engineer, dour but resourceful; a Welsh N.C.O., cunning but dependable; and an Irish squaddie, coarse, comic but courageous. The English imposed their centralised politics on the other nations and the culture of their elite was on offer through the new Public Schools to the leaders of the other nations.

The English cult of the gentleman made its converts to a more political purpose in Scotland and Ireland than in France and Germany. But the old aristocratic ruling class tolerated, indeed often actively patronised and encouraged, Scottish, Welsh and Irish culture – so long as it did not threaten the unity of the state. And this was not purely instrumental. Tory district magistrates, whether in India or in Ireland, commonly studied and defended indigenous customs against the rationalising tendencies of liberal, Benthamite administrators, or sometimes against the Protestant missionaries and schoolmasters. Perhaps the old Tories were so secure in themselves that they could often live, for a while (as in India before the Mutiny and the coming of the *Memsahibs*) in two worlds, much as until the middle of the nineteenth century the gentry were virtually bi-cultural and bi-lingual even in England: town and country were very different. Metropolitan, middle-class authors might mock but the gentry were 'rougher' or closer to 'their people' when at home, and polished and remote when in town. And when this internal duality declined the very image of 'gentleman' still carried with it some tolerance, some scepticism, some concern for 'one's people', as well as a secure sense of superiority based less on birth than on manners (philistinism, cruel sports and snobbery). The defence of 'good form' was indeed a defence of conventions, not of principles. It was an echo of the empirical and utilitarian approach to politics, including the national questions. And I suspect that the anti-intellectualism, sometimes the pose of anti-intellectualism, had its roots in vague historical memory and fears of what had happened when ideas and confessional beliefs were taken 'too seriously', or 'out of proportion' in the seventeenth-century civil wars in these islands.

English historians in the late nineteenth century could not conceal, of course, like American historians of the time, that the Anglo-Saxon peoples clearly had a unique capacity for good government; self-government and representative institutions, indeed, when they were on their own. In the USA Mr. Dooley remarked that in Presidential election years 'Celts became honorary Anglo-Saxons'. But even these historians, tinged with racial though not racialist doctrines, did not argue a general superiority for the English suddenly become hands-across-the-sea Anglo-Saxons. (How I welcome the Anglo-Irish Treaty; how I dislike the weird, ignorant and insulting, to Scots and Welsh and new immigrants, first name of it.) They agreed with Matthew Arnold in his celebrated *Lectures on Celtic Literature* that the Celts, if lacking in a political tradition, were pre-eminent in lyric poetry, ballads and song. Some of these beliefs still linger as English prejudices long after their real political context has been forgotten, indeed changed – if not quite 'changed utterly'.

So I argue that it is my fellow English who have to come to terms with themselves, and to ask questions that Welsh, Scottish and Irish writers have been asking for much longer. What are the national characteristics and distinct social-psychological needs? What is distinctive in the culture? And until the English attempt to answer these questions sensibly, the others will somehow, however sincere and interesting, have to hang in the air. 'The owl of Minerva flies at dusk'. Just as Thatcher offers a passionate caricature of traditional Englishry (even if her two patrons appear to be King Canute and Adam Smith), some real thought at last begins. In a book that deserved far greater notice, *Englishness: Politics and Culture 1880-1920* (Robert Collis and Philip Dodd eds., Croom Helm, 1986), one of the editors made the point that 'Matthew Arnold's . . . lectures of the 1860s are a reminder that the definition of the English is inseparable from that of the non-English; Englishness is not so much a category as a relationship'. But what is good for the English goose should be good for the Celtic ganders.

That is why I believe, thinking of Ireland, that while nationalisms are real and authentic in these islands, yet none are as self-sufficient as most of their adepts claim. In Northern Ireland most people are, in fact, torn in two directions: 'torn', that is, while their political leaders will not recognise that people can, with dignity, face in two directions culturally at once, and refuse to invent political institutions to match. In the world before nation-states such dualities and pluralities were common enough, as still in some other border areas today. 'No man is an island': nor are nations when as intermingled as ours. We have not been able to be one people, but nor can we ever be fully independent of each other, even politically. We are all inter-dependent. Irish, Scottish and Welsh intellectuals have long complained about anglicisation. But there is less study or appreciation of how much whichever culture one starts with is itself so much a product of the others, and probably the richer for it. Not only intellectuals can live in, or in and out of, two or more cultures. The migrant poor have done it for centuries. But English intellectuals, on the whole, are the last of the four nations to begin to face this squarely. But at least they are ahead of their leading politicians. And that passport, anyway, is to change. And perhaps after 1992 all hotel registers will only ask our nationality if we are not citizens of the Economic Community, which I'll still call 'European'.

Eight

On Devolution, Decentralism and The Constitution

*From Richard Holme and Michael Elliott, eds., *1688–1988: Time For a New Constitutional Settlement* (Macmillan, London: 1988) under the title of 'Sovereignty, Centralism and Devolution'.

In my *The Reform of Parliament* of 1964 I argued with some vigour the simple thesis that the power of the government machine had increased so much that the powers of Parliament needed a commensurate increase. This increase was not to threaten an elected government, but to hold it accountable, to force it to think again about its measures, sometimes to amend them, and to open up both the policy-making process and administration to greater publicity. Specialised committees seemed the key to the matter, a scarcely original view even then. What was original (or perverse) was the attempt to combine two theories often thought to contradict each other: an Hobbesian view of sovereignty and a Millite democratic theory of consent. 'Strong governments need strong opposition', I argued; and further argued that the strongest governments are those who can best mobilise consent. I assumed that the consent would always be that of a majority of the electorate – well, more or less. It was joy to be young and to have one's cake and eat it. I took a tough-minded view of the electoral system. 'Governments must govern' (did the Iron Duke say that or Dick Crossman?) etc. Indeed I coined a glib phrase that gained some currency, 'Parliament is a continuous election campaign': such was the fundamental mechanism that protected our basic liberties, etc., not any constitutional fine print.

In other words, there was no conflict between the theory of the sovereignty of Parliament and liberty so long as a few minor adjustments were made (with plenty of rhetoric to make reforms of parliamentary procedure sound ever so important) and the informal rules of the parliamentary game were still adhered to strictly. The constitution was, and should be, what those who wanted to practise parliamentary politics agreed among themselves were the rules needed to play the great game. Had not Jennings amended Dicey to the effect that the conventions of the constitution are simply the informal understandings needed to work the constitution, as it is?[1] It was an ingenious attempt to blend consensus theory with conflict theory – or ingenuous I now think.

The mature wisdom of age need not blush for the follies of youth, but it can acknowledge them. Perhaps the theory was always self-contradictory. The Hobbists knew that given even a narrow parliamentary majority and a strong nerve, there were no restraints except (Britain being Britain) the next General Election and the relative unlikelihood of a government abolishing elections, except in time of national emergency. The timing was always fair game, as was a mild Callaghanesque chicanery over Boundary Commissions which, like adjusting the bases of unemployment and health statistics, were thought unlikely to lead to riot or rebellion. And Whigs or old Liberals knew that self-restraint and custom in the majority party in the House prevented what Lord Hailsham, in Labour times, had called 'elective despotism' – words he never even ate but simply ignored when Tory times came back again and even he became a bellman for Mrs. Thatcher's elective despotism. And after the Falklands War we can never again all be sure to agree what is a 'state of national emergency' in which normal liberties can be suspended.

The Decline of Informal Restraints

Perhaps I have changed my mind simply because of events – as Beatrice Webb said of the rationalist Herbert Spencer, his only idea of tragedy was that of a theory killed by a fact. But changed it I have. The year of the abolition of the GLC, the prosecution of Clive Ponting, and of the Westland affair changed my mind very rapidly, and not just on the one point that Parliament itself now seems an ineffective restraint on what our ancestors called arbitrary government. All these things, indeed, the protection of fundamental rights, the power of Parliament against the Government, electoral reform, freedom of information, the restoration and enhancement of local government, hang together. Being an intellectual, I can change my mind more rapidly than politicians: the broad alternatives for Britain were always there as mental speculation, and as known fact about so many other democracies.

My party leaders still pin their hopes in a working majority and total victory next time after one more great push. They show little interest in consitutional reform. But the surviving 'free spirits' (a phrase of Mill's) in the Labour Party, that is, those who are thoughtful and are not creeping for jobs in a future government (or the old days back again of the 'Think Tank' and political adviserships – the academics on working holidays), most of them are now at least fellow-travellers of constitutional reform. In the austere pages of *Marxism Today* and in the *New Statesman* these issues are openly discussed, even if party funding was withdrawn from *New Socialist* and the editor was sacked when, during the last General Election, he put the case for tactical voting rather than for blind faith, heroism and total loyalty. Hardly anyone in the Labour Party who uses their intelligence freely does not now believe that constitutional reform is a major issue. For rather different reasons, reformers in Eastern Europe, even in Russia, as well as Eurocommunists, are now writing seriously about constitutional law, something once peripheral to the socialist enterprise, in so far as it wasn't simply denounced as a bourgeois restraint on a united working-class movement.

The old informal restraints are withering. One mourns as well as mocks. After all, the parliamentary effectiveness of the Opposition largely depended on them. The old Conservative culture of the gentleman in politics, how Baldwin socialised MacDonald and the very ambiance of the House, among so many other examples, has given way to that of the power-hungry careerist. The political manners of the Tebbits, the Heseltines and the Lawsons now set the example. And much the same has happened in the civil service: its old sense of itself as a state within a state or as a 'corporation' (*Gemeinschaft*) of servants of the crown, against which we all protested, has given way to collective greed (the incredible *job* of the non-contributory inflation-proofed pensions) and an individualistic clamour for advancement, which has made them a soft target for politicisation.

There is now no majority of backbenchers on the 1922 Committee who care to tell the Prime Minister or even the Leader of the House that this 'will not do' or 'is not done': there is only a majority waiting for the call to minor office. The new breed simply don't know the old customs and have, unlike the old Tories, very little interest in history. Not to put too fine a point on it, they are often historically ignorant. The Left of the Labour Party used to bewail how 'the House' socialised the socialism out of Labour MPs. I've always doubted that – Ralph Milliband's unhappily influential *Parliamentary Socialism* was built on the dubious assumptions that if you don't drink out of a saucer you can't be serious, and that most Labour MPs started as Belgian revolutionary socialists rather than as British trade unionists. But it certainly socialised them into a belief in proceeding in a parliamentary manner, if they didn't believe that already, which was all to the good; but also into a belief in the sovereignty of Parliament (if only it were, after that next big push, in the right hands). There was no difference between Herbert Morrison and Michael Foot on that score, nor is there between Tony Benn and Bryan Gould. This is the heart of the problem.

Put it another way. The idea that there is a consensus of values has gone. I have long argued (since the first edition of my *In Defence of Politics* in 1962) that representative democracy does not need a consensus on *substantive values* at all, indeed it is itself a device for governing in a civilised manner societies with differing values. In Britain we have never had a consensus of values if we take differences of religious and political doctrines as seriously as their rival claims truly deserve; but we do need consensus on *procedural values*. We do not need to agree on *what* decisions should be made but only on *how* decisions should be made. After the London Government Act and the abandonment of Royal Commissions and interparty conferences as the established way of proceeding on major institutional or constitutional issues like local government powers and Health Service finances, any procedural consensus has plainly gone. The Government now habitually changes national institutions as if it assumes, from the purely political contingency of a divided Opposition, that re-election is as certain as the resurrection of the body after death. In formal terms of political theory the Government has become the State. Small wonder that she speaks of 'my Ministers'.

I make my conversion from 'sovereignty of Parliament' to constitutionalism sound too rational. In fact, a wild memory keeps intruding into my mind. Two years ago Norman Tebbit, then a cabinet minister and chairman of the Conservative Party, was addressing a Sixth Form Conference in Central Hall, Westminster. His typed speech was statesmanlike and mild in tone and quite Burkean in content, almost boring; it was the week of the pre-election suspension of monetarism. But the first question roused the sleeping Adam. A girl asked him: 'What is the Government going to do about AIDS?' He leapt to the edge of the platform, pointed his forefinger high in the air, 'What is *the Government* going to do about it, *you* ask *me*?', he shouted, 'I ask *you* what are *you* going to do about it!' About half the hitherto quiet and well-behaved audience jumped up and cheered, the other half howled and hissed with anger. What shocked me was that he did it deliberately and so skilfully: seeking to raise emotion on such a complex and sensitive issue, seeking to divide, seeking to destroy consensus, seeking to heighten disagreements. He only wanted to excite supporters – the rest of our fellow-citizens could go hang. He had an unexpectedly persuasive effect on the chairman. He helped me think again about the second part of the great perennial equation: the need for positive government power for the public good and the need to restrain government power for the public good. I can remember, of course, some orators in my own party who would say things designed only to have a similar effect on Tories.

Sovereignty and Centralism

For the welfare of the country and the relief of unemployment and poverty, one should not want less power in the hands of public authorities, but it would be better were it more dispersed: and dispersed on a basis of an agreement that could outlast changes of government.

Parliament was once closer to tackling this problem than now. A resolution of the House of Commons of 4 June 1919 set up a Speaker's Conference on Devolution:

> That with a view to enabling the Imperial Parliament to devote more attention to the general interests of the United Kingdom ... this House is of the opinion that the time has come for the creation of subordinate legislatures within the United Kingdom, and that to this end the Government ... should forthwith appoint a Parliamentary body to consider and report –
>
> (1) upon a measure of Federal Devolution applicable to England, Scotland and Ireland, defined ... by existing differences in law and administration ....
>
> (2) upon the extent to which these differences are applicable to Welsh conditions and requirements ....

To the surprise of Lloyd George, who expected it to fail easily, the conference readily reached agreement on the powers, areas and finances of devolved or subsidiary legislatures; but the parties were unable to agree about composition, whether nominated or elected assemblies, and if so how. In those immediate post-war days there were an appreciable number of Tory advocates of 'Home Rule All Round' so long as it was all round and not just limited to Ireland.[2]

After the Government of Ireland Act 1920, discussions of federalism or devolution vanished from British politics, certainly in Conservative and Labour ranks. The Irish question had, of course, finally been put to rest. In days when for so long it dominated British Politics, public men had to do a great deal of constitutional thinking, and bargaining. A few of those skills were still there to be applied to decolonisation after 1945, although in the main the drafting of the new constitutions was a Colonial Office matter that followed closely precedents in the Old Dominions. (Note, in passing, that the Mother of Parliaments, allegedly wedded for life to Sovereignty, yet had cheerfully accepted, indeed often actively fermented, Federal promiscuity and pluralism among her older sons and daughters – young New Zealand actually had to threaten to rebel in order to resist federalism being thrust upon her.) But by 1974 when a Labour government found the need to conciliate Scottish nationalism, there was a lack of experience and an incapacity in constitutional thinking both in Westminster and Whitehall. This was grimly apparent in clumsy construction of the Scotland and Wales Bills of 1978 and in the lack of any clear line of logic or principle in the drafting instructions.

Vernon Bogdanor headed his study of those Acts with a quotation from Lord McDermott: 'As a nation the British have no great interest in either the institutions or the principles of law which determine the structure of their society and the means whereby it may change or develop.'[3] Only the Liberal Party had kept up the older tradition of constitutional thought.[4] Yet this could be changing. And if so 'the credit must go to Mrs. Thatcher', Antony Wright has written: 'the Thatcher Government has provided a lesson in the nature and extent of concentrated executive power available to a majority party in Britain. As such it has provided a constitutional education for the Left.'[5]

Yet this 'education' may have to carry us very far: to question the need for the doctrine of 'sovereignty of Parliament' at all, or certainly to prevent it being confused with the basic idea of an effective state. The state could actually be stronger, in its ability to get things done and respond to people's expressed needs, if it was decentralised. There are two modes of power, as Bertrand Russell once argued: power as unchallengeability (it must be done by me or through this office, or not at all) and power as the ability to carry out premeditated intentions. On this analysis, over-centralised power, sometimes, indeed, the powers of the Prime Minister, can often frustrate intentions to get things done. (That is the theoretical explanation of the weakness of government under Wilson's idea of strong government.) Yet the idea of sovereignty as both unchallengeable and effective power, cuts very deep into the consciousness of even those English politicians who believe themselves to be purely practical men and women, almost proud of not having an idea in their heads: at least not abstract ideas like sovereignty. And even thinking politicians, like Enoch Powell on the one hand, or Michael Foot and Peter Shore on the other, were convinced that we had lost our sovereignty on the day or night of our accession to the EEC in 1970, although somehow we muddle on.

Sovereignty as Whig ideology

The doctrine of the sovereignty of Parliament arose not just in opposition to the prerogative powers of the Crown in the post-1688 settlement, but because after the Act of Union of 1707 (still called Treaty of Union in Scotland) Parliament could deny that any legislation could have the force of law coming from any body other than itself: and also claim that there were no controls on its own legislation.[6] Blackstone asserted in his *Commentaries on the Laws of England* that:

> Parliament has sovereign and uncontrollable authority in the making, confirming, enlarging, restraining, abrogating, repealing, reviving and expounding of laws, concerning all matters ... : this being the place where that absolute power, which must in all governments reside somewhere, is entrusted by the constitution of these kingdoms .... It can, in short, do everything that is not naturally impossible.

But is there really such an absolute power? Only in a legal sense; that no other body can make enactments. But Blackstone tells us nothing about what parliaments or governments in general can do, still less specific ones. That is an empirical and political matter. Blackstone makes a sound point about jurisdictions but offers a very dubious pseudo-empirical generalisation that 'absolute power ... must in all government reside somewhere.' In the sense that there could be held to be an absolute quantum of power, it may very well be dispersed (and in some situations the more effective for that). The young Bentham in his *Fragment on Government* of 1776 mocked Blackstone. Did he think that 'the Switzers lack government?' (Some Tories long suspected, after 1787, that 'these United States' were really an anarchy, or about to collapse for a clear lack of central sovereignty.) And in the cases where power is in fact found in one place, this does not ensure that it is absolute.

There is more than a whiff of ideology as well as rhetoric in Blackstone's celebrated passage. It meant to impress and overawe, just as Hobbes's picture of the state as 'Leviathan' – 'that mortal God' – was meant to frighten rational men into obedience, stopping all that destructive quibbling about 'conscience' that had led to the Civil War –'the worm within the entrails of the body Commonwealth.' But no contemporary was so foolish as to think that it gave free rein to a useable absolute power. The political context of the popularisation of the lawyers' and philosophers' doctrine of sovereignty needs to be remembered. Parliamentary sovereignty was invoked for two great purposes: to limit the powers of the Crown, when some of that power was still desperately needed for the defence of the realm and the Protestant religion; and then to hold the new United Kingdom (as it was called after 1707) together. Roughly speaking 'sovereignty of Parliament' meant to lowland Scots a guarantee of law and order and the absence of anarchy, or in more hamely terms a reasonable hope to die in bed and not from broad-sword or musketball, fighting Catholic Highlanders or Irish mercenaries on moss, moor or mountainside.

The Scottish Parliament was not widely venerated as the *national* institution – that belief came from nineteenth-century historians. Its career had been spasmodic and its composition was anything but popular. Yet the bargain it struck for the merger or takeover was a sensible and a stern assertion of national interest: free trade within all British possessions, the retention of Scotch law and Scottish lawyers – and, above all, bitterly resisted in the English House of Lords, the establishment of the Kirk as the Church of Scotland. The Kirk was far more representative of the common people than either Parliament, and remained so until this century. And the famous Scottish education system grew up after the Act or Treaty of Union.

According to the pure theory of sovereignty the new United Kingdom Parliament could in 1708 or any time afterwards have legislated all these peculiar Scottish institutions into oblivion; but in practice this was impossible. The Highland clans were brutally repressed after the 1745 Jacobite rebellion, but there were more Scottish soldiers than English or Hanoverian in the Union army at Culloden. Scotland flourished and flowered in the eighteenth century (apart from the Gaelic areas) both economically and culturally. But for three generations it was not forgotten in Westminster that a barbarian army with foreign support had got as far south as Derby. In George IV's reign a deliberate government policy was launched to conciliate and reconcile for ever even the Highlands. An official cult of 'Bonnie Scotland' was launched, by an English cabinet employing Sir Walter Scott as impresario. So even in the 1830s conciliating Scotland was still seen as a political imperative.

In other words, when we became, or attempted to be, 'the United Kingdom', the major perennial problem of imperial politics from 1688 to 1920 became that of holding the United Kingdom together. The doctrine of parliamentary sovereignty was the English ideology of unity. There is a story of power, coercion and English arrogance, as in the Highland clearances, the abolition of the Irish Parliament in 1800 and the successive Coercion Acts, indeed acts of coercion. But there is an equally real story of politics, conciliation and English tolerance, as in the restraint of sovereignty, the removal of Catholic disabilities, administration in Ireland according to local customs and increasingly in local hands. Scottish, Welsh and Irish national sentiments were celebrated, in song and story, a romantic interest in the Celtic lands became a kind of cultural politics. Unlike everywhere else in Europe the English did not develop a literature of nationalism – which would have been politically divisive. They developed instead a literature of imperialism in which, as in the tales of Kipling, representatives of each of the nations of the British Isles played their part – much as Shakespeare had portrayed in his scene of the army on the eve of Agincourt, a common soldier from each nation of these islands.

Perhaps these strategies led the French to see in us English a paradoxical propensity for both tolerance and perfidy. These policies failed in Ireland but succeeded in Wales and Scotland. The old English governing class were historically-minded and had considerable knowledge, strengthened indeed by landowning interest, of Ireland and Scotland. Our present masters are largely ignorant and dismissive of the territorial politics of the United Kingdom, are Anglocentric in mentality and Home-Counties suburban or mid-Atlantic in culture.

The Scots have continued to manage their own affairs. So much so that most lawyers and civil servants, in effect the Scottish establishment after the decline of the Kirk's authority, have had little enthusiasm to have a democratic Assembly placed over them according to the 1978 Act, even if it gave them new powers. But the decline of the Kirk exposed the lack of a clear national institution that could speak for

Scotland – a quite unexpected consequence of the Act of Union; and rougher elements in that land, the majority, are no longer inclined to accept the implicit view of the Society of Advocates and the civil servants of St. Andrew's House that they are 'auld Scotland to the life'.

Wales, the most assimilated and least troublesome part of the United Kingdom to England, gained numerous concessions, touching religion, language, education and local government, not only in the national revival of the second half of the nineteenth century and when the Liberals stood for Home Rule all round, but even in the 1960s and 1970s when Plaid Cymru made quite modest electoral gains. Until this decade the instinctive response of English Conservative leaders even to minor troubles (by world standards) was disproportionate pre-emptory conciliation (Welsh television, the equality of the language in the courts, signs and placenames etc.) – despite the wishes of the non-Welsh-speaking majority. There was no hysterical incantation from English Conservatives then that 'the sovereignty of Parliament' and 'the unity of the United Kingdom' was threatened – the kind of reaction that (thinking of 1688) George Savile, the Marquis of Halifax, nick-named 'the Trimmer', once called 'true heart of oak ignorance' or 'stout resolute nonsense'.

The extent of variation in national institutions makes the textbook picture of the United Kingdom as an homogeneous society misleading. It is itself exposed as more part of the Whig eighteenth-century ideology than a true description of the politics and societies of the United Kingdom. But as the regulatory machinery of government grew in the late nineteenth century and accelerated as a consequence of the two World Wars and welfare legislation, no attempt was made to devolve power. The relative powers of the regions to the centre declined still more. The legal powers of parliamentary sovereignty could be used against the component parts of the Union, and were used drastically in the prorogation of the Stormont Parliament in 1972. But ordinarily they were not used. Most of the new centralism came about by default, but now it is being added to by intention.

Yet history cannot be wholly rewritten or ignored. The United Kingdom is of such a nature that heavy-handed rationalising programmes from the centre can threaten its unity. Historically the United Kingdom after 1707 might be better described as quasi-federal in relation to its actual administration and to what is always extremely important, the sense of identity of its peoples: always a dual identity, Scottish and British, Welsh and British, Ulster Protestant and (whether the rest of us like it or not) British, English and British. But it is the majority English who today seem to be losing this appreciative or tactful sense of dual identity, and are revealing, perhaps for the first time, a dangerous lack of a sense of history.

We live with a dangerous conceptual confusion, especially those who believe in holding firm principles but not in speculation and critical thought. We confuse legal theory with political theory. 'Parliamentary sovereignty' does indeed mean that only Parliament can make or authorise binding laws, but it does not mean that Parliament cannot delegate and disperse power as political prudence would suggest it should. The distinction between theory and practice was deliberately blurred, as the quotation from Blackstone showed, as part of the Whig ideology which tried to hold together the United Kingdom in the days of Irish and Scottish rebellions and unrest. But have we not by 1988 outgrown the urgent needs of 1688? 'If sovereignty is questioned, things fall apart', was the old message. But empirically the contrary can often be equally true: 'If sovereignty is exercised arbitrarily and unwisely, things fall apart.' We lost the first British Empire because Lord North, though no philosopher, believed that there was a metaphysical entity called 'sovereignty' which could never be divided – so peace proposals in 1775 and 1776 were rejected out of hand. The chance to conciliate Ireland was lost with Conservative opposition to Home Rule both in 1886 and in 1911–14. No secure peace can be made with Argentina, to the peril of their fragile democracy because 'sovereignty is not negotiable' (the thoughts of a non-thinker). No lasting solution of the Northern Ireland problem is possible, either, while two governments both take that same high muddled view of sovereignty. Our rulers have ended up by believing their own rhetoric – the confusion of the legal power to legislate with the political prudence to devolve, sometimes indeed to renounce that legal right. The concept has become not the key to British constitutional thought but the rust in the lock.

Decentralisation and Citizenship

In the 1970s one common argument for English regional devolution and for Scottish and Welsh Assemblies was to prevent overload in the centre: not merely Whitehall but London and the South-East had grown too great. This is a real and still growing problem. Dispersal of some government offices to the provinces is quite irrelevant. The problem lies in the over-concentration of decision-making, publishing and communications, in one very powerful but myopic part of the United Kingdom – London and the Home Counties. It is almost as if the capital, in the eyes of most opinion-makers, because they live there to make their careers, has become the whole country. And this over-concentration both of economic resources and of cultural dominance ('hegemony'?) will continue, until a genuine and self-sustaining dispersal of decision-making to elected bodies helps revivify or create both provincial and other national centres of power.

Consider even our recent past. Consider Birmingham and Manchester as great cities and as both schools and arenas of citizenship and recruitment grounds for national leadership.[7] Their civic leaders, as of Edinburgh, Glasgow, Liverpool, Sheffield, Leeds, Newcastle, Swansea, Cardiff, Bristol were frequently national figures, exercising real power, not merely in local administration but in the councils of their national parties. When they came to Parliament or sent colleagues to Parliament, these men knew their local world, a different England (even just to consider England alone for a moment) than London and the Home Counties. One of the continual themes of the English novel from the time of George Eliot and Arnold Bennett, through D.H. Lawrence even into C.P. Snow, has been 'roots': the pull between provincial culture and metropolitan; but it was always a balance of gain and loss, sometimes of disillusionment and homecoming. Most self-made politicians of the older generation lived in two worlds. They made their name on a local stage before a national. The number who found seats any old where after making a national name in London has always been much exaggerated. Indeed the older type of Conservative MP lived in two worlds too, town and country, more often in the other order of emphasis. And both the industrialists and trade unionists were physically and psychologically close to their workplaces. But the newly-dominant world of finance capital in the City of London creates no roots and few loyalties of any kind.

Plainly citizenship needs more to thrive on than spasmodic public elections. It needs an active concern with local as well as national issues; and levels of concern and participation are very much a function of whether there are important decisions to be made and of uncertainty about their outcome. The way to revive inner cities is not to take away the powers of city governments; it is to give them more. The very number and calibre of people wanting to enter into local politics diminishes with the declining discretion allowed to local government and its overburdening with routine tasks dictated by the centre, both so dramatically accelerated by the deliberate policy of Mrs. Thatcher's governments. To have to administer the gathering of the unwanted poll tax is the crowning insult to local democracy.

Only party activists and MPs themselves now approximate to the ideal of active citizens rather than passive and spasmodically grateful (or not) good subjects. And MPs themselves are now a fairly cowed if loyally noisy lot. The old informal restraints on governments unchecked by constitutional law, very much depended on the political and constitutional beliefs, the ethics and code, of their own backbenchers. But the old Tory tradition of 'independency' among private members has virtually gone, with a few bold exceptions. The interparty opposition are now nearly all discarded Ministers, generals with the odd loyal bodyservant but with no regular troops; so the old Grandees can be discounted politically. Backbenchers are office-hungry and the only offices that now satisfy them are in Whitehall; the Town Hall is no longer an alternative and knighthoods for long service are now a sad, almost shameful, consolation. Their eggs in one basket, they walk very carefully like fat cats on ice. And recruitment has changed. The time needed for local government service makes firms increasingly reluctant to see their bright juniors stand for office, and there seem few advantages any longer to be got if they do. The most able Conservatives now look to business as a career, not to the House. Prominence in local government now offers few rewards for the ambitious, even those of esteem in the national party. In the House itself it is get on or get lost.

It is no verbal punning to link citizenship with the civic. The connection lies at the very heart of our whole western tradition of politics. As Labour and Liberal go on about the need to increase the participation of ordinary people in decision-making, in workplace, neighbourhood and so on, and denounce the narrowness of the base of existing participation in decision-making, even this inadequate base is being swiftly eroded. Despite the rhetoric, most politicians feel their constituencies to be more and more an encumbrance to their main career in Parliament, and feel too helpless in the face of national trends even to have much political effect on their own manor. This could, of course, all change utterly if local authorities and regions were given greater powers, including revenue-raising powers.

Conservatives who care about local government (and they usually control a majority of local councils) have themselves to blame, not just their obsessive leader. Unlike Labour and Liberal radicals, they have always been a little ambivalent or nervous about encouraging real citizenship. They have habitually preferred the image of the law-abiding, not law-changing, *good subject*. Historically they had to adjust rapidly to the new world of a democratic franchise (the legacy of Disraeli with the shrewd advice of Walter Bagehot). They stirred themselves and strutted around the country more, but they played the card, as Bagehot foresaw, of *noblesse oblige* in the confident expectation of widespread deference. How unsuited they were in the old days to politics in the colonies – the Irish and the Scots throve better. There was an envy of 'the gentleman' but it all came to dislike and distrust. This great cultural image played a large role in British politics, and education. Its positive side was a code of decent conduct, a certain (if limited) tolerance and a paternalistic care for 'their people'. It also acted as a restraint on their leaders, a restraint both self-imposed (as in Baldwin) and imposed by the party (as finally against Chamberlain). But this code is plainly in decline, whether because there are fewer gentlemen now (rather than, say, careerists), or fewer people who pay any attention to them. But this is, nonetheless, another informal restraint gone. Perhaps the idea that constitutional conventions were a sufficient restraint without formal constitutional law was itself part of this gentleman culture, so knowledgeable about personal codes of conduct, so distrustful of formal laws and intellect, so masculine, indeed male-dominated, in its enjoyment of parliamentary politics as mock combat or a kind of bloodless blood sport. Yet the popularisation of this cultural image often blamed for the gentrification of the Victorian 'industrial spirit', is less often blamed for the frustration in Britain of the idea and practice of citizenship. Citizenship is far more evident in France, Holland, the United States, Sweden, Switzerland and the postwar Federal Republic of Germany (a proof that conscious change is possible).[9]

An interesting example of Conservative ambivalence about citizenship is their attitude to political education in local authority schools. Ten years ago many Conservative leaders were not against it, as such – even if they tended to think instinctively that the real object was somehow to instil 'respect for the rule of law' rather than balanced appraisal of real political issues. I remember accompanying Kenneth Baker Mark I to wait on the then Secretary of State for Education, Shirley Williams, to press the case for urging more political education in schools. He pushed, warmly, on what then seemed an open door.[8] But ten years later Kenneth Baker Mark II produces a national curriculum (a bad enough piece of authoritarian centralism in itself) with no place in it whatever for civic education. This is partly the new intolerance, partly a crudely utilitarian view of the training (hardly education) needed for other people's children, and partly because political education is the very kind of activity that makes the new breed distrust local government as such. Some LEAs do, indeed, think it their duty to try to produce citizens. Local government itself is a school of citizenship. But officially all that is now wanted are skilled workers, occasional voters and regular taxpayers. The great republican image of men and women as citizens has collapsed into a philistine and utilitarian slum. They talk of 'higher standards' but they offer 'prolefeed'.

Decentralisation as part of constitutional reform is all the more needed because of the great Thatcherite paradoxes. When the central state insists on dealing directly with individuals, local institutions have to be rendered either powerless or unattractive. When the state in the name of liberty seeks to control local initiatives of government, it has to strengthen its own powers to a quite illiberal extent. So many Conservative councillors must now feel that their own feet have been shot off to remove a rotten toe nail on someone else. It is, of course, not normal politics: it is obsession, and what our ancestors called arbitrary government. We need institutions and laws to contain the obsessive, including our own obsessions.

Conceptual Reform

There is another way of looking at the whole problem of power. De

Tocqueville once reproved John Stuart Mill for linking liberty solely to the rights of individuals; he offered the opinion that there must be a sociological as well as a legal and philosophical condition of liberty. There must be a plurality of intermediary groups between the individual and the state. De Tocqueville admitted that many such groups enshrined privileges and vested interests, and however much reformed by public law some inequities and anomalies would remain; but that would be better for liberty than attempts by the state to deal directly and only with individuals by means of general legislation. That was more likely to lead to what he called (with Napoleonic plebiscites in mind) 'elective despotism'. Mill, being a reasonable and open-minded fellow compared to Thatcher, Tebbit and Baker, was persuaded. His future writings stressed the need to nourish communities and to extend, while reforming, local government, not simply to sweep it away.

Among socialists there was a debate similar to that between the two greatest liberal thinkers, though more public and less amicable – that between Marx and Proudhon. Proudhon at that time had a larger following than Marx and was to have a lasting influence too, though one still underestimated. He was not an anarchist, as Marx accused him and as anarchists were to claim: he believed in a minimal state, rather like some modern neo-liberals, with largely administrative and coordinatory functions; but alongside the state there should be the most active network of self-governing co-operative communities. His vision was idealistic in sweep and fanciful in detail; but underlying it there was the good sense that power, if both sovereign and centralised, is inherently despotic, that democratic power can be active and powerful but should be dispersed in 'communities'. Ideally communities would be small enough for everyone to know everyone else, or in practice at least to know the community intimately – like a neighbourhood in its literal sense. And these communities would then group themselves into federations.[10]

Harold Laski went so far as to argue that all power is inherently federal, using that term in a broad sense where many would say 'pluralistic'.[11] He argued, following the Anglo-Catholic Figgis on modern church-state relations and the French socialist Deguit on trade unions, that the theory that the state is sovereign only has relevance to periods of state-formation, nation-building, and to times of real national emergency. Here he differed from the syndicalists to whom the state was simply a group among other groups and only productive groups were important. No power is in fact absolute, and attempts to enforce claims to a monopoly of decision-making are both oppressive and, in the long run, destabilising. He thought that both the Fabians and the Leninists had made the same mistake as Thomas Hobbes: confusing sovereignty as a minimal necessary condition for political order with a full and sufficient account of the normally highly political mode of operation of states dealing with, indeed partly composed of, a multitude of interest groups.

To Laski, local government was not simply an historical relic or a limited grant of powers by the central state subject to good behaviour; it was part of a seamless web of power, stretching up and down. It was the primary manifestation of popular power. Local communities seek to preserve themselves whether their formal powers are tightly proscribed or residual; and many 'sovereign states' are, in fact, either in pitiful vassalage to greater states, or preserve their internal autonomy only with constant difficulty, compromises and trade-offs. This he regarded as a realistic analysis of what actually happens in the governing of states, and he relegated the doctrine of sovereignty to the melodrama of preserving the state in crisis (and warned against the deliberate creation of crises to justify the production of melodramas). The ordinary life of states is the continual necessity of balancing or conciliating group interests, economic and geographical, religious and sometimes ethnic: the image of applying central sovereign power to obtain clear solutions is a misleading, even dangerous, picture of political life.

What Form of Institutional Reform?

I may have seemed to be taking a long time reaching a practical point. But reform can only follow from looking at the problem in its most basic and simplest perspective. The detail is fortuitous and variable: the starting point is crucial. Part of the problem is centralist attempts to legislate detailed good for others; and part is a mistaken formulation of the nature of the British constitution. The solution lies not simply in emancipating ourselves mentally from the old Whig ideology of sovereignty, of sovereignty invoked to help hold the new, precariously united kingdom together. We must also appreciate that we are a union and not a monolithic nation state; and understand the need to disperse power and to avoid uniform rules if liberty is to be secure and if a diversity of popular demands are to be met. Most popular demands are best realised locally and therefore the results can never be equal, even if arguably they are equitable if people want such differences. My comrades in the Labour Party cannot have it both ways.

If the above analysis is correct it follows that there can be no one model of devolution throughout the United Kingdom. Scotland, Wales and Northern Ireland each raise different possibilities for constitutional reform, and each of these is different from England.

The case for Scottish home rule is obvious and lies in Scottish history, tradition and in a clearly expressed Scottish opinion which overwhelmingly favours a subsidiary parliament within the United Kingdom, rather than separation. The case against is based on the peculiarly English fear that any such parliament would necessarily lead to separation. This fear has little reality in Scottish opinion or circumstances but is simply abstract inference from uncritically-held sovereignty theory: an inference that is absurd when applied to stable federal states throughout the world. Scotland is a nation but only extreme nationalists (and their extreme opponents) argue that for every nation there must be a separate sovereign state. But nations must have some national, representative and expressive institution.

Debate about powers and composition can be endless. But it is obvious that whatever is done must be sufficient to be acceptable and also capable of evolution. For all its faults, the 1978 Act is still the most likely starting-point for a new departure, if revenue-raising provisions are added to it, as the Scottish Labour Party now argues. The late John Mackintosh was vehement in his attacks on the imperfections of the 1978 Bill, but he argued that it was better to set something to work that could be changed after experience rather than wait for ideal agreement.[12]

Even better, however, to proceed through a Constitutional Convention in which an elected Assembly would produce a Bill to bring to Parliament – even if that Bill was simply a reform of the 1978 one. Parliament would be wise, in the election of that Convention, as in subsequent elections for a Scottish Parliament, to insist, as for the abortive Northern Ireland Convention of 1975–76, the Northern Ireland Assembly elections in the 1980s and the Northern Ireland seats in the European Parliament, on proportional representation. The Labour Party in Scotland should think again on this if they really wish to be seen as generous, patriotic and prudent leaders of a national movement, rather than as partisan inheritors and exploiters of it. Consensus is not needed for policy decisions but it is needed for setting up procedural rules, especially a set so elaborate as for a subsidiary parliament; and also because in Scotland local government reform, both in the sense of areas and powers, is quite inseparable from constitutional reform. With a Scottish parliament, it would become unnecessary to have a region the size of Strathclyde; indeed, in the short run Strathclyde, by virtue of its size has and acts as an interest against reform.

In Wales the case for proceeding by a constitutional convention rather than directly by a Bill in Parliament is even stronger. The old Act was so overwhelmingly rejected in the referendum because there was no clear majority agreement as to what form any devolution should take to be acceptable and workable.[13] The language question is still an obstacle for most, even if an end in itself for some. Separation is no longer an issue. The Welsh Language Society are now well aware that if the language were not protected by Westminster it could be diminished by any Assembly. And it is hard to think of further concessions to the Welsh-speaking minority that would bring Plaid Cymru into any

Assembly that did not give equal status to the two languages in the Assembly. But this would be a stumbling-block to the Labour Party in Wales, and probably to the Liberals too. Simultaneous translation could, of course, be available on the floor as in the European Parliament and the Dail Eireann (where, in fact, Irish is rarely spoken). Polyglot documentation is only a technical problem. But this would mean that all the staff would have to be fully bilingual, which would mean, in fact, overwhelmingly sympathetic with either Plaid or the Welsh Language Society. And that would be politically unacceptable to the majority of non-Welsh-speaking Welsh members. Or could Plaid cease to be a political party running candidates and simply become a national movement? Since I have not argued, like some old Liberals, for an imposed uniform solution of devolution for the whole of Great Britain, it is enough to say that Parliament should be very tolerant of any agreement that looked half-way workable that would come from a Constitutional Convention for Wales – whether for a legislative assembly for the Principality, a consultative council or simply more powers for local government.

In Northern Ireland the immediate lines of constitutional policy are already clear and agreed between the British and Irish governments: the recreation of some kind of power-sharing or inter-community assembly in Northern Ireland, and the continuance of the Inter-Governmental Council. That Council, itself an interesting innovation (we can innovate when we have to), retains all law enforcement and formal sovereignty in British hands; but it gives the Irish Government the right to be consulted over any aspect of the government of Northern Ireland. And it reaffirms what is already in two statutes: that Northern Ireland is a part of the United Kingdom, until such time as a majority in a legally constituted poll vote otherwise. The British Government actually pledged itself as part of the 1986 Agreement to bring in legislation for separation should that day come. Northern Ireland is not then, as Unionists would wish, an integral and unconditional part of the United Kingdom like Yorkshire: it is a conditional part. 'The Guarantee' is a two-edged blade. Legal sovereignty can, after all, be a marvellously flexible thing when it is viewed politically and not ideologically.[14]

Our critique of the theory of sovereignty suggests, however, that any acceptable solution is unlikely while the question is put in the form of whether Northern Ireland be part of the Republic of Ireland, with guarantees to the new minority (and some form of weak external link to the United Kingdom), or remain part of the United Kingdom, with even stronger guarantees to the present minority (with some form of weak external link to the Republic)? And still less likely when put in the form, 'whose cause is just?' or those bloodstained ecumenical slogans, 'God Defend the Right!' and 'Not an Inch'. The facts of the case suggest that Northern Ireland could no more be governed peaceably from Dublin than it can be directly from London. In fact, of course, what is called 'direct rule' is not integration but overall British control of the policies of a Northern Ireland administration, itself as different from Whitehall in personnel and practices and as geographically removed as the Scottish Office.

The logic of the situation is that Northern Ireland inherently faces both ways. And the cussed two-headedness is not just that some of its inhabitants want to be Irish and some British, but that each individual also contains a different mixture of both, culturally and politically. The truth of this, so unwelcome to the zealots in both communities, is seen in the suspicion of Northerners in the South and in the maddening lack of reciprocity in England to the loyalism of the Loyalists. The logic of the situation, as already imminent in the Inter-Governmental Council, points towards some kind of joint responsibility for the level of decisions that would normally be taken by a central government in a formal federation, while an assembly in Northern Ireland handles at least the kind of powers of a normal federal province. The concept that is now common is 'joint authority', of course, tactfully not 'joint sovereignty'. Already, in fact, with referenda, constitutional conventions and electoral reform, the British Constitution has proved, in response to unusual problems, more flexible and inventive than as yet Conservative and Labour leaders will allow is possible on the mainland.

The main alternatives for a structure of regional government in England were set out briefly but clearly in the White Paper of July 1974, *Devolution Within the United Kingdom: Some Alternatives for Discussion* and *Devolution: the English Dimension: a consultative document* of December 1976. Because of the defeat of devolution in the referenda and the subsequent fall of the Labour Government, politicians have for the moment forgotten them. But they are likely to be the starting point of new initiatives. Neither put forward a precise scheme; the political will was not there. But the 1976 document ended with what could be the broad outline of the future:

88. To sum up, the case for change is seen to lie in:
    (a) lightening the burden on central govenment, enabling it to concentrate on matters of genuinely national importance;
    (b) bringing government closer to the people;
    (c) rendering the work of major nominated bodies subject to local democratic control; and
    (d) providing a layer of government to deal with such matters as may be better dealt with at a level intermediate between central and local government as they now exist.

The whole document hardly, in the words of the Greek anthology 'warms the blood like wine': and I would move the deletion of the last

four words. But even then the case was clear for a powerful intermediary level of regional or provincial government, just as now it is
clear that local government needs restoring and strengthening. A lot of
economic and geographical thinking went into establishing the boundaries of the seven Planning Regions of 1965. What was lacking was
any elective basis for the boards and a broad political perspective,
rather than already-outmoded ideas of economic planning and
development.[15]

New regions would need to be seen as having capital cities, existing
centres whose decline as informal provincial capitals, like Bristol,
Birmingham, Leeds, Manchester and Nottingham, can be reversed. If
we are to disperse power, both to the provincial or regional and to the
local levels, we must build on the culture and civic ambience of cities.
This would argue for the old eight 'New Standard Regions' of 1961,
especially as their more traditional criteria would separate East Anglia
from London and the South East (included for economic reasons in
1965), bringing Norwich into play as a provincial capital. In 1964 it
seemed rational to *accept* the growing dominance of East Anglia by the
London region; but part of the object of a new constitutional settlement should be to contain the power and excessive prestige of the one
city-region which is also the national capital. 'The city-region' is the
only viable political and economic concept. The power of London and
the attraction of it to people of ability cumulates not just because of a
centralised administration but because of the facilities of the city and
its region. The rebuilding of city centres elsewhere already gives something to build on. Capitals must look like capitals if power is to be
federalised.

I argue that power should be federalised, not that we necessarily
need a formal federal system. We need a Bill of Rights. We need electoral reform. We need a new structure of government for Scotland,
Wales and Northern Ireland, and we need directly elected English
provinces with revenue-raising options as well as guaranteed central
funding by agreed formulas. But the attitude of mind comes first. It is
more important to change some of our presuppositions about 'parliamentary sovereignty' and the nature of power than to state an intri-
cate case for a speculatively possible written constitution of the United
Kingdom with entrenched constitutional law and an American-style
Supreme Court. We would need a legal profession on the American
model before we would be likely to trust lawyers with such power, and
perhaps not even then. Both the democratic and the oligarchic spirit
work against it. We will probably proceed on the Stormont model.

That name is not enticing nor is the memory of the folly of its unchecked majorities, but the thought is serious. The difficulties of
Parliament legislating to bind its successors irrevocably in law are
immense. Sovereignty theory in the tradition of this country does, I

have noted, have a strong point on jurisdictions. Like the Act of Union, fundamental reforms could be gone back upon in theory; but because of the political difficulties and the popular support surrounding them, they would only be reversed in extreme circumstances: like the abolition of Stormont. Parliament will retain its legal sovereignty. It would create provincial assemblies by ordinary statute as it might create, for tightly-defined purposes, a constitutional jurisdiction. Such acts when passed would be politically difficult to amend, not legally so. The whole difficulty will be in ever getting them passed. Parliament would be overwhelmingly wise to devolve much power: for the sake of liberty, to avoid overload, to reanimate civic spirit and to maintain the fundamental nature of the United Kingdom as a quasi-federation. And it should legislate more and more in the form of enabling acts and delegated legislation, not for Ministers to complete, but to allow wide discretion to all subsidiary assemblies and councils. The remit to the 1919 Speaker's Conference used a phrase quite shocking and contradictory both to strict sovereignty theorists and to strict legal federalists: 'federal devolution'. But it was a politically sensible phrase. I like to think of myself now as a political federalist.

Constitutional reform and the devolution of powers will not, of course, come by reason, any more than the Reform Bills came by reason. It is only likely to come either when a government is frightened of the political consequence of not reforming or when a government cannot be sure of a regular majority in the Commons, and in any case not until the fall of Thatcher. But if that day comes, then I think it will all come quickly and come together, not piece by piece. We should, in memory of 1688, if we have any care for national constitutional celebration and continued reputation, prepare our thoughts so that we can get it right when the opportunity comes; as men in exile did before that fortunate year.[16]

Notes
1. Sir Ivor Jennings, *The Law and the Constitution,* Allen & Unwin, London, 1948, and see also Geoffrey Marshall and Graeme Moodie, *Some Problems of the Constitution*, Hutchinson, London, 1964.
2. Cited in J.C. Banks, *Federal Britain,* Harrap, London, 1971, pp. 81–5, an unusually thoughtful and surprisingly neglected book.
3. Quoted in Vernon Bogdanor, *Devolution*, Oxford University Press, Oxford, 1979, p. 163. The merits of his analysis of the problems of Northern Ireland, Scotland and Wales should *not* have been affected by the fact the book was published before the referenda on the assumption that devolution would pass.
4. See for example, *Power to the Provinces*, Liberal Party, London, 1968, and J.C. Banks, *Federal Britain,* op. cit., pp. 79–95, which reports a continuous drip and trickle of Liberal Private Members' motions and 'ten-minute' Bills from the 1930s through to the 1970s.

5. Antony Wright, 'The Politics of Constitutional Reform', *Political Quarterly*, October 1986, pp. 414–25. The article concentrates on the Bill of Rights. Wright sees its connection with electoral reform, but is silent (like many other Fabian writers still) on devolution. Richard Rose's remarkable *Understanding the United Kingdom: the territorial dimension in govenment,* Longman, London, 1982, is the pioneering modern textbook of the totality, not Anglocentric in the least; but conceptually it is weak on 'state', 'sovereignty' and 'power' and ends unexpectedly as an Ulster and a Scottish Unionist tract.

6. These next paragraphs draw on my 'The Sovereignty of Parliament and the Irish Question' in Desmond Rea (ed.), *Political Cooperation in Divided Societies.* Gill & Macmillan, Dublin, 1982, pp. 229–54. On the general question of 'sovereignty' and United Kingdom politics, the first chapter of H.V. Heuston, *Essays in Constitutional Law,* Second edition, Stevens, London, 1964, is profound and stimulating.

7. M.J. Wiener, *English Culture and the Decline of the Industrial Spirit,* Cambridge University Press, Cambridge, 1981, is magisterial, though he underestimates the purely political culture; see Antony Wright, 'British Decline: Economic or Political?', *Parliamentary Affairs,* January 1987, pp. 41–56 for a good survey of this whole controversy.

8. Following the Report of a working party of the Hansard Society, published as Bernard Crick and Alex Porter (eds), *Political Education and Political Literacy*, Longman, London, 1978.

9. Mrs. Thatcher has recently talked a lot about citizenship but she seems to mean not political involvement, especially in localities, but rather voluntary charitable work instead of public-funded professional social services – as if private initiatives can rationally calculate and effectively satisfy public needs.

10. See my *Socialism,* Open University Press, Milton Keynes, 1987, pp. 39–42. The whole book tries to restore the historical balance between pluralist and *etatist* socialist thought, as does David Blunkett and Bernard Crick, *The Labour Party's Aims and Values: an unofficial statement,* Spokesman Books, Nottingham, 1988.

11. In his early scholarly books on the theory of sovereignty and in his once-famous *A Grammar of Politics,* Allen & Unwin, London, 1928, not in his later Marxist writings.

12. See throughout in the posthumous volume, Henry Drucker (ed.), *John P. Mackintosh on Scotland*, Longman, London, 1982.

13. See David Foulkes, J. Barry Jones, R.A. Wilford (eds.), *The Welsh Veto: the Wales Act 1978 and the Referendum,* University of Wales Press, Cardiff, 1983.

14. As more fully argued in my 'Northern Ireland and the Concept of Consent' in Carol Harlow (ed.), *Public Law and Politics,* Sweet & Maxwell, London, 1986. See also W. Harvey Cox, 'Managing Northern Ireland Intergovernmentally: an appraisal of the Anglo-Irish Agreement', *Parliamentary Affairs*, January 1987, pp. 80–97; he concludes that while the Agreement was 'a fine and imaginative political enterprise', yet the two governments 'were themselves too much in the thrall of their own inheritance of

simplistic concepts of sovereignty and territoriality, which ill
fitted the peculiarity of Northern Ireland' (p. 97).
15. An excellent summary of the whole local government reform
controversy is found in W.A. Hampton, *Local Government and
Politics*, Longman, London, 1986, pp. 164–82.
16. Since writing this, two important documents have appeared, both
very congenial to my argument: *Scotland's Claim of Right*,
Campaign for a Scottish Assembly, Edinburgh: 1988, and *Charter
88*, New Statesman, London 1988. And in a volume of essays on
the *Claim of Right* (Owen Dudley Edwards, ed., *A Claim of Right
for Scotland*, Edinburgh University Press: 1989) and in a
pamphlet *(Labour and Scotland's Rights*, Labour Club, East
Tranent: 1989) I moved from a quasi-federalist to a full-blown
federalist advocacy, much influenced by Jim Ross (see his
"A Fond Farewell to Devolution", *Radical Scotland,* No. 36,
December 1988).

Nine

Can we Legislate Against Discrimination?

* From Richard Hoggart, ed., *Liberty and Legislation* (Frank Cass, London: 1989).

The general grounds on which legislation and the law can extend our liberties as well as protect established ones need to be considered more carefully than has sometimes been the case — especially among fellow socialists. The old cautionary chestnut is apt. Harry Pollitt is at Hyde Park orating about the shape of things to come. The rich ride by on their horses. 'None of that after the Revolution, eh Harry?' 'You've got it wrong, comrade. After the Revolution you'll all ride horses!' 'But I don't like bloody horses.' 'After the revolution you'll ride bloody horses whether you bloody well like it or not!'

Bagehot said that 'one cannot make men good by Act of Parliament'. But then he would, wouldn't he? We all know what sort of liberal he was. He was only in favour of the Reform Bill of 1867 because he thought that it would prevent mass democracy and that moderate democracy could be managed by those of us who know best what is good for others. But Harold Laski, who was *almost* a revolutionary, was forever saying that 'the state cannot make me happy, but it can prevent me from being happy'. We are on sounder ground when we legislate to remove obvious obstacles to human happiness than when legislating to make people happy or good. We legislate draconically to improve road safety marginally, and it took Enoch Powell to put the case power-fully against seat-belts in the name of liberty (without any illusion that the statistical case in favour was other than strong: he argued that accidental death was terrible, but that loss of liberty was worse). But is legislation meant to benefit minorities directly and specially, to discriminate in their favour (oddly called anti-discrimination legisla-tion), analogous? Any answer depends on defining both the problem and the key concepts carefully.

There used to be an American comic strip called 'There Ought to be a Law' in which a small town busybody demands a law whenever any-thing shocks, worries or irritates him. He probably invented 'Curb Thy Dog', 'Don't Litter' and 'Report Obscene Matters to Your Postmaster'. He was invented to parody the spirit behind the old 'blue-laws' of which the Prohibition Amendment was only the most famous. Now, of course he was a right-winger in any context. He first voted for Hoover. His politics would be Reaganite or Thatcherite today, anti-state, all for private action, but he is also famously quick — without showing the least awareness of the contradiction — to demand legislation against anything detestable. Left-wingers want laws of a different kind, but often with equal unhesitating frequency; and no censorship whatever, of course.

Law is, it is worth recalling, not the only form of social control. Banalities are sometimes hard to take seriously, but we should try. The rule of law is preferable to individual or group violence, but there is also tradition, education, example, public opinion, social pressure, enlightened self-interest, and even satire and ridicule. Satire can be extremely important, even in the minimal sense of mouth-to-mouth jokes in regimes where the law sets out to deny any freedom of speech, publication and assembly to criticise the government — sometimes even prohibiting anything that is not officially blessed. That Orwell in *Animal Farm* and in *Nineteen Eighty-Four* chose the form of satire to argue that liberty and equality can and must be reconciled was not merely a literary strategy; it came from a profound belief that the laughter of free men deflates the pompous and the proud, shows Emperors that they have no clothes other than those we make for them.

Laws need the support of public opinion; but public opinion can, of course, be intolerant, even oppressive, psychologically and physically; good laws and honest judges are needed to protect individual rights against some forms of public opinion and behaviour almost as much as against the state. But such laws are essentially a protection of liberties, constitutional law or protection of the procedures of public debate, not a prescription of substantive outcomes. Laws too far in advance of public opinion can stir resentment and prove self-defeating. Under what conditions can law go further than protection and be a positive enhancement of liberty as an instrument of public policy? Benevolent autocrats or old-fashioned Communist rulers of one-party states have no doubt. Law is to moralise and improve the population: freedom is being freed from servitude and superstition. So laws are then to be interpreted by underlying intentions, not by what is actually written. But a democratic socialist argument needs to be more subtle because more genuinely libertarian. To the democratic socialist liberty and equality are not to be confused and are both equally valued. An enforced equality would be unjust because unfree in principle, and anyway unworkable in practice and invariably an oppressive and often a bloody debacle when attempted. But liberty for the poor is, indeed, hideously restricted, not merely by their life-chances but in clearly measurable and dramatically different life-expectancies.

Therefore the quality and quantity of liberty will be enhanced the more egalitarian a country can become, if it becomes so in a voluntary and widely acceptable manner. But if either 'liberty' or 'equality' is made the sole criterion of public policy, the result is injustice.

So when should we legislate against discrimination and intolerance? It depends, of course, what one means by these two terms, and what one thinks can be and ought to be the role of the state.

Dr. Peter Morris in a thoughtful article, 'Being Discriminatory About Discrimination' (in *Politics*, No 1, 1986), has recently drawn attention to the existence of a pressure group called VOAD. Their name denotes the widest possible generality of protest — Voluntary Organisation Against Discrimination. And in September 1987 Mr. Ken Livingstone MP was reported as having a one-line Private Member's Bill up his sleeve: to declare *all* discrimination illegal. Such aspirations come close to what Albert Camus once called 'metaphysical revolt'. But VOAD, in fact, is a worthy voluntary organisation founded to obtain for the physically disabled legislation against discrimination analogous to that of the Race Relations Act of 1965. The name sounds, however, both to Dr. Morris's discriminatory ear and mine, meaninglessly general. Surely discrimination needs both a subject and an object, something specified done against a group described? But we readily understand what is meant by discrimination against the disabled and against the physically and mentally handicapped. We think, if we have ordinary human decency, that firms *should* employ people who *can do* a specified job irrespective of other physical handicaps or perhaps just appearance. We notice that some firms do it as a matter of deliberate policy — like the BBC — and others, like the High Street Banks, not at all or not up front. Certainly we think it unjust if the disabled or the disfigured are passed over for someone less, or even equally, qualified. But I suspect that VOAD would go further, quite understandably, and argue for either or both of these propositions: that if there are extra costs involved in enabling a disabled person access, say, to the desk or bench, these should be met either by the employer or the state; or that even if some physically or mentally handicapped persons are not quite as efficient as some others, yet firms over a certain size should be required by law to employ such and such a percentage. Unlike with race and sex discrimination, there is a problem when it is admitted and obvious that the job cannot be done quite as well, or without additional costs. Very deep water occurs almost as soon as one leaves the obvious shallows. For one could put the question: is the discrimination relevant to the task? And if so, should the state make some other compensation to the disadvantaged person rather than force, for however plausible a public good, an economic liability upon an employer whose efficiency is also commonly supposed to be a public good?

For 'discrimination' has come to have two quite opposed meanings. Obviously its basic meaning is simply to distinguish between things, but to many the term has now become entirely perjorative. One does not blink much, if at all, when someone boasts that they are 'against all forms of discrimination'. One thinks one knows what they mean, probably something like this: 'I am against all forms of discrimination which are not relevant to the task at hand or are motivated by irrelevant prejudices against certain categories of people'. If one says, 'I don't like the look of that chap', this cannot be thought relevant to judgement of the worth of his or her concert performance. (This is to leave aside whether it is prudent for a pianist at the Wigmore Hall to upset the conventions of the occasion and the expectations of that kind of audience by adopting the dress and manners of a Punk Rock personality.) And surely one does and must discriminate between one performance and another — however this is done, however difficult it is to talk sensibly about reasoning in aesthetic judgements, just as difficult but as necessary as in moral or political judgements?

For an older meaning of 'discrimination' is precisely the making of such judgements. Discrimination was seen as a virtue. To call someone a person of 'great discrimination' meant that they were sensitive to difficult distinctions. 'Discrimination' was a mixture of empathy and good judgement — an actual judgement has to be made, it is not simply understanding or contemplation; so one discriminates in favour of Bach and against Bartok. To discriminate even about moral matters is not always to moralise. The legendary actress said: 'I am no prude but I am not promiscuous. I discriminate'. And George Santayana said that he did not favour more chastity but simply more delicacy. To discriminate is not necessarily to condemn: 'For myself, I simply prefer post-modernism', or watching West Ham. Not everyone would agree, however. Some would say that all such discriminations are arbitrary even if they are not hurtful ('I know, you just think I've got no taste'). So it comes to be believed that people should not be hurt or disadvantaged by arbitrary judgements of any kind. 'Prizes for everyone', or no prizes at all and no competitive sport. ('Honorary degree, indeed; now can you see what they've done to you!') Such opinions are by no means a preserve of the ultra-Left. The folk philosopher Schulz sees it as endemic in bourgeois American society. 'Charlie Brown, Charlie Brown! Gee, you were dim in school today.' 'Whadda ya mean, "dim".' 'I mean you got the answers wrong.' 'I thought you only had to be sincere.' Lionel Trilling in a famous review of the Kinsey Report on human sexuality (reprinted in his *The Liberal Imagination*) saw it as exemplifying a democratic belief that all facts are equal, that all patterns of statistically significant behaviour are therefore valid. Such a belief was perhaps liberating in some respects, he said, but destructive of sensibility and discrimination in others.

Aristotle had said that the fallacy of pure democracy was the belief that because men are equal in some things therefore they are equal in all.

Discrimination is not merely a virtue in aesthetic judgements, it is very close to the idea of 'discretionary judgement' which Richard Titmuss once argued in a famous article in *The Political Quarterly* (Vol. 42, No. 2) was essential for the just application of the complicated rules of the Supplementary Benefit Commission by counter staff (and that therefore these staff were scandalously under-trained and under-educated compared to the framers of the discretionary rules themselves). If 'profiles' of pupils, for instance, are to supplement written and external examinations, discrimination will grow more important, not less. Without discrimination there is only inflexible bureaucracy, no individual case can truly be 'considered on its merits'. Discretion is also close to the idea of 'good political judgement', which plainly people possess to rather different degrees — even politicians. Ronald Beiner has cogently argued in a recent book, *Political Judgement*, that it is a virtue more often found among observers than among fervid activists. It is a rare player who can assess the strategies and tactics of a game as well as a knowledgeable, experienced and reasonably dis-passionate spectator — even if the spectator is powerless to intervene. Lionel Trilling saw discrimination as the supreme liberal virtue both in aesthetic and in moral judgements.

So it is foolish to think that all discrimination is unjust. It depends what one is talking about. All types of discrimination are prescriptive, positively or negatively; something is judged good or bad and an action is taken as a consequence (even if the action is only to express the judgement publicly, the attempt to influence). To say that all dis-crimination is bad, undemocratic, hurtful and/or elitist, is the same kind of fallacy as to say that any exercise of authority is authoritarian. Just as we should discriminate, relevantly, tolerantly, cautiously, wisely and well, so we should respect authority — when the person claiming or recognised as having authority is fulfilling a function that is widely accepted as needed and exercises it openly with some special skill or knowledge widely agreed to be in the public interest. But some-one is authoritarian, indeed, when he or she tries to generalise the authority they have for specific and acceptable purposes into other and irrelevant spheres. Our noble ancestors were more sensible than modern trendies to protest against the abuse and *extension* of authority, to demand *limitation*, specification and accountability, not to denounce any exercise of authority as authoritarian, or any act of discrimination as bad.

When is discrimination unjust? Eileen Fry has recently defined (in *Politics*, No. 1, 1985) two common but unsatisfactory accounts of unjust discrimination, which she calls 'the intentional view' and the 'proportional view', and usefully suggests a better one, which she calls the 'counterfactual criterion.'

The intentional view 'holds that a necessary condition of an action being described as discriminatory is that the agent's intention in acting is to discriminate.' If someone is not hired or is sacked because they are black the employer's action is plainly discriminatory. But if a university department offers places strictly according to merit as determined by GCE results which results in no black applicants being successful, this could not be called discriminatory by the intentionality criterion. So to make the absence of an intent to discriminate a condition of a policy being condemned as discriminatory is, she rightly argues, too restrictive as a guide to social policy. And, I would add, intentions can be frustrated and the unintended consequences of policies can be more significant than the premeditated intentions. Also someone may be racially prejudiced, but partly because he or she knows that we suspect and are watching, nothing much happens. And if we are wise we may think that it is easier to make prejudiced people behave politely than it is to 'eradicate prejudice' (as is sometimes proclaimed to be the object of teaching on race relations in secondary schools — for one, two or at the most three hours a week).

The proportional view holds that the intention of the agent is irrelevant and that only the result should be considered. 'An action is discriminatory if it results in a larger proportion of people of one type than another being treated in a certain way.' The university department, however fair, objective and dreadfully time-consuming are its selection procedures, is discriminatory if the result is 'a larger proportion of whites than blacks' relative to qualified applicants, or the society is discriminatory if the proportion of whites to blacks admitted is simply very different from that of the age group in society as a whole. This is, indeed, what people often mean by discrimination. I think Eileen Fry's example would have been even stronger, if put in terms of the employment of unskilled school-leavers in a supermarket or a High Street chain-store. Some would think that it is not the relative proportions that can constitute discrimination but the proportions of those with equal qualifications. Admittedly others say that one has to look at 'the system' as a whole, the huge discrimination against blacks as a whole; so it is no accident that they are poor and as under-qualified as most of the poor, and it is no better to discriminate against people because they are poor than just because they are black. Indeed, as a matter of fact, it is at the bottom of the labour market that racial discrimination in employment is most flagrant and obvious. Yet the difficulty with the 'proportional view' is, indeed, that it makes the class of discriminatory actions potentially an impossibly large one. You are being discriminated against both because you are black and because you are poor (and poverty is even more difficult to forbid by legislation). Yes, society as a whole is discriminatory. We could just as well throw in the sponge and sit down and wait for the revolution. And, even on an individual level of false consciousness, what if most of the friends I ask to my home are black, Jewish, homosexual or otherwise foreign — am I discriminating against the plods and the normals? Or what if I only ask a black to my house because he or she is black? This action is surely discriminatory, even if unimportant and silly.

So Fry invokes '*a counterfactual criterion*': 'an action is discriminatory if it results in people being treated differently than they would have been had they been different in some respect' — as in the common cry, 'If I was a man you bloody well wouldn't treat me like that!' or 'If I was white you'd be all over me'. I am discriminating against someone if I treat them differently than I would have done if they had been of a different ethnic group. If I refuse a job to a black fellow it is discriminatory if I could have offered it to him and would have offered it to him had he been a proper white man. My motive may not, of course, arise from overt racial prejudice, but from the tradition of employment or the known views of other workers (which is why intentionality is often difficult to pin down); or the unfortunate man may have been 'one black too many' in a strictly controlled, well-meant and enforced quota system (which then might not be discrimination on the proportionality view).

Yet if discrimination can be good or bad, is it ever right to discriminate racially? Some say it is, when we discriminate against a majority in favour of a disadvantaged minority: that reverse discrimination or *positive discrimination* should be enshrined in public law, whether for compensation, to overcome prejudice or to set a trend going. Under such a policy, to follow the useful counterfactual criterion, in certain situations blacks would be better off than they would have been if they were white and whites worse off than they would have been if they were black. Turning everything on its head may be what we often want to do, as in the anarchist imagination of Dario Fo, but it may not be either justice or what is popularly acceptable as justice; no guide indeed, as Bentham would have put it, to rational grounds for legislation.

Suppose we wished to legislate to end discrimination against blacks and women in employment. The grounds for doing this are obvious. Prejudice must play some part in explaining the dramatic disproportion of young blacks unemployed and women underemployed. Two strategies could be pursued. All firms over a certain size would have, subject to legal sanctions, to bring their whole work force over a period of time up to the proportionality of women and blacks actively seeking work. And where special qualifications of skills are needed, entrance standards could be lowered somewhat in the hope that over the years the same proportionality could be obtained.

With unskilled jobs there are not insurmountable problems, except political will. And I assume that a serious policy of positive discrimination would not leave it to individuals to have to prove discrimination, or — as at present — to an understaffed statutory body to take cases through the courts after exhausting conciliatory procedures. Employment statistics would speak for themselves. It is hard to see why there need be any real impairment of efficiency: certainly it would be an interference with the freedom of employers, but not in any manner necessarily harmful to their material interests in employing people at all. With semi-skilled occupations the effect could be appreciable: to shift some training from the schools and FE colleges to in-service or day-release training. But training for industry and training by industry is a shifty borderland at best, full of mutual delusion, deceit and humbug among employers, educationalists and politicians alike. And where objective entrance standards have to be lowered they might only be lowered marginally; and most of us are well aware that such differences can soon be made up. GCE results, for example, are not a good predictor of final degree results. And a National Curriculum will almost certainly do no better: many people do grow and mature over two, three or four years. Motivation and good teaching can make up for a lot of differences at the point of entry — as shown by the experience of mature students without normal qualifications at the Open University, Birkbeck College, Goldsmiths' College and elsewhere. Detail is infinitely arguable but if there was a will there would be a way and the practical consequences, whether for industrial and commercial efficiency or for educational standards, are unlikely to be great. It probably wouldn't make an appreciable difference at all. (At least no one is silly enough to claim that efficiency and standards would necessarily *improve* if such discriminations were ended — as the original suffragettes argued would happen to the whole tone of society, just as their opponents believed that Naval Estimates would never again pass the House of Commons). It is the *injustice* that is the primary issue even where systematic discrimination, as in South Africa, is also inefficient.

Objections of principle would arise, however, when better qualified whites or males were excluded from jobs or places by either a quota system or discriminatory lowering of standards in favour of the groups discriminated against. The United States Federal Courts, for instance, seem to be drawing a line (in an admittedly somewhat confused situation) between, on the one hand, legislation for equal opportunity and fair employment practices and, on the other, positive discrimination rules for college entry when unsuccessful but better qualified white candidates brought suit. It seems to offend against natural justice to make some individuals, as it were, innocent and accidental victims of measures designed to correct an historical collective wrong, a collective wrong involving deep-rooted social and economic inequalities. Certainly it offends against what ordinary people think is justice. It is quite another matter to use public law far more strongly than we have yet done in mainland Britain against employment practices and admissions procedures that deliberately and needlessly exclude some groups of people, even if they are not designed to be deliberately racially or sexually discriminatory.

The case of religious discrimination in employment in Northern Ireland is interesting. Since 1976 there has been the Fair Employment (Northern Ireland) Act which makes discriminatory hiring illegal and which encourages employers to subscribe to a declaration of intent to implement 'the principle of equality of opportunity'. More recently failure to subscribe to such a declaration entails a firm losing public grants and contracts. It has some effect, even if currently unemployment among Catholics runs at about twenty-five per cent and among Protestants at thirteen per cent (and that in a situation where one can assume a rough equality of schooling). Of course it will take another two decades before the results of the old blatant discrimination decline so far as to give, positively, anything like proportionality of employment in large firms and, negatively, an equitable proportionality of unemployment. Some would argue of such laws that the dogged officials of the Fair Employment Agency and of the Equal Opportunities Commission should have been given more teeth and have used them to bite hard more often. But all sides recognise that with majority opinion and behaviour still hostile even to the principle of equal opportunities, the limits of manoeuvre are narrow, and to apply positive discrimination on any large scale would result in bitter strikes at the best and violent riots at the worst.

Recently a series of American states have enacted the 'MacBride Principles'. These require American companies trading in these states not to do business with or invest in any firm in Northern Ireland which cannot prove that it has abolished religious discrimination in hiring; and, beyond that, prove also that it practices positive discrimination in favour of, some drafts say, 'the minority', other say 'minorities'. And the MacBride principles demand special training programmes 'to assist minority employees to advance to higher paying jobs requiring greater skills'. (This fits Eileen Fry's 'counterfactual' definition of discrimination perfectly. 'Sorry George, you're not eligible for the scheme. For one thing, you're over-qualified, and for another you'd have to be a Papist.') Now it is far from clear whether the United States Supreme Court will sustain these ventures of New York, Massachusetts and Connecticut etc. into foreign policy, nor whether the Bills are meant to destabilise Northern Ireland by wrecking investment rather than to steer it to the havens of the righteous. One standard clause demands that employees must 'guarantee the safety of minority employees travelling to and from work!' Americans opposed to such legislation, just as British Government spokesmen and even John Hume, all point out that the principle of positive discrimination would contradict the established principle of 'equal opportunity' in the 1976 Act. There seems no way around this dilemma. The basic problem is, of course, that the social conditions for genuine 'equality of opportunity' need to predate by far the morning of that individual job interview.

In general, quite apart from Northern Ireland, the argument is strong that positive discrimination is inequitable to other individuals accidentally disadvantaged. And the social costs of trying to enforce such a policy throughout British industry might well be too high: disruptive, stirring prejudice swiftly rather than allaying it gradually and lastingly. When the United States Supreme Court finally moved against statutory segregation in schools, in *Brown et al. versus the United States* (1954), it enjoined School Boards to desegregate with 'deliberate speed'. It did not allow deliberate prevarication and infinite delay, as a small multitude of subsequent actions and cases showed, but it recognised that, in matters of such deep prejudice and tradition, time is needed. Legislation can be effective, but only if conceived as one part of broad strategy through time — not as the single easy answer.

Short of legislation, there is obvious sense in the state itself setting an example (if the Government chooses). With regard to the employment of women in the civil service, to a large degree over the years it has; but as regards their prospects of promotion and share of higher level jobs, the occupational profile still demonstrates shameful injustice to women. The same is true of the judiciary and, most unhappily, the police service. But at least some black faces are through the station door and behind the counter. The police claim that recruitment endeavours are now strenuous but that sufficient recruits at the standard are not forthcoming — perhaps, indeed quite likely, as with recruitment of Catholics for the Royal Ulster Constabulary. So here, indeed, would be a case for some positive discrimination. Of course black applicants would have to be shown to have scored far higher on the personality factors in the entrance tests to compensate for a greater flexibility about the CSEs and 'O' levels, but as an experienced examiner, both in higher and secondary education, I'm reasonably sure the entry boards could fit that one up, quietly and without fuss, if the will was stronger and the views of the Police Federation were slightly more public-spirited in all respects.

Do we count the BBC and the Independent Broadcasting Authority as part of the state? In some senses, yes. They are statutory bodies, public quasi-monopolies. And with the exception of no other institution except Parliament they are treated as an embodiment of the national image and consciousness. They are often in a better position than the government machine itself to set a public example of positive discrimination; certainly they can act with greater speed and visible presence. Think of the emergence of black presenters and personalities, particularly on television. And we see remarkably more women in publicly prominent positions than a decade ago. Is this really a case of positive discrimination? Or is it actually tougher for them to get there, needing, like black footballers, more consistent merit? One simply will never know. But some of them must be the result of a quiet policy of positive discrimination rather than a timely consequence of demographic and educational change. There is no apparent diminution of standards. Perhaps the mark sheets of interviewing panels might show a difference, and positive policy directives could have favoured some blacks and some women over some white males. But such positions are not strictly competitive on purely objective scales of assessment, as are most public examinations and university and polytechnic entrance. It partly depends on what qualities you are looking for. Black skins and female characteristics should be highly relevant. In such employment procedures there must be safeguards against nepotism, favouritism, partisanship and corruption; but considerations stemming from broadly agreed public policy can be relevant, need not be excluded. One presumes it was not always a matter of marks that rather suddenly produced so many soft Irish accents on the airwaves and Ulster brogues giving us the bad weather. For a long time the BBC has tried, with obvious success, to de-emphasise 'RP' (received pronunciation), which must have involved some discrimination against well-qualified candidates with marbles in their mouths from the English public schools. Imagine, however, the difficulties of trying to achieve this through legislation. Government, through example and public policy, could do much more to combat unjustifiable discrimination even without bringing in new legislation and raising basic issues of liberty. It could put its own house in order first (as some local authorities have begun to do), in the civil service and perhaps one day even in the party itself, or at least the party machine over which it has more control. Example is extremely important as a trigger for social change. The role of television is essentially exemplary (and very important for that) rather than a serious contribution to reducing black unemployment.

Of course there is some mockery and cynicism about the search for a token woman and a token black for every damned committee. Professional black women are headhunted with indecent fervour. But if 'tokenism' is partly a fraud and often a deliberate delaying tactic or buying off, it is also a foot-in-the-door. It may not be enough. The motives of the white male majority may be suspect and self-protective, but their reaction shows that some general pressures of opinion can reach them. Politics works like that. The pressure just has to be kept up and increased. Once there is a foot in the door, it is far more difficult to close. A great deal more positive discrimination can be done informally by institutions that might offend principles of natural justice if attempted by legislation. In a modest way, for instance, I've quite often practised a form of positive discrimination in appointing or commissioning women. I mean that if two candidates are roughly or arguably equal in their claims, then gender becomes a relevant factor, especially if one glances at the male majority around one and thinks what a disappointment most of them have been compared to that early promise shown at interview. If the will is there. Or not. Once upon a time I was an external assessor for the appointment of a Statutory Lecturer at the University College of Galway. The language of the University of Ireland Act was clear. If two candidates were of equal merit in the subject, preference must be given to the one who spoke Irish, or spoke it better in a specially convened second interview. We were advised from on high that there could never be such a thing in nature as two candidates of exactly equal merit. But if the field had been tight at the final fence, I'd have discriminated in favour of a woman or a black — had there been one.

Legislation is more likely to be successful in removing or prohibiting obvious discriminatory practices than in attempting to obtain proportionality, still less a positive discrimination. On matters that depend on people's behaviour changing, it is difficult for legislation to work if it runs too far in front of public opinion. Consider the utter failure of statutory attempts to control prices and incomes. but also consider that when the proposals for the breath-analyser or nosebag and tougher speed limits came forward, the RAC and the AA's representatives advised Barbara Castle, then Minister of Transport, that the measures would be unworkable, would lead to a lack of respect for the law akin to the attitude of the respectable drinking public under American prohibition, would bring the police and the middle classes into similar and continual conflict. Her judgement that this was rubbish, that they either did not know or were misrepresenting the views of their members, was quickly confirmed by an opinion survey commissioned by her department; and eventually by the result of the legislation. The survey showed that few motorists liked the idea but they nearly all accepted the need for the new law dourly. It was still only the workers who felt that the police were getting at them the whole time.

This may be a good parable for racial and sexual discrimination. The rational target is not agreement to positive discrimination nor a fermented outbreak of spontaneous love between ethnic groups, but is simply acceptance of each other and of procedures for equality of opportunity. Any legislation intending a mass effect on behaviour can only work when public opinion will at least accept it. There is a lack of serious studies of kinds of legislation that actually need public support to work, or at least which are unworkable with widespread non-compliance. (We are much better at studying campaigns than at monitoring results.) In political life not everything is agreement or rejection: for many purposes it is enough that people will accept something. No Government, for instance, can hope for positive agreement to any constitutional settlement in Northern Ireland — a high level of mere acceptance would be grand.

Sometimes we set our sights, meaning well, too high. Let me illustrate by raising the related question of tolerance and intolerance. How far should we tolerate intolerance? Can we legislate against intolerance?

The trouble with Americans was, Martin Chuzzlewit's manservant remarked, that 'they have so much liberty they can't help taking a few liberties with it'. We only obey the maxim that what is good for the goose is good for the gander (or vice versa) grudgingly. We do not always approve of the use to which others put their liberty. Liberty, said Orwell, 'is telling people what they do not want to hear' - absurd as a general definition of liberty but a vivid characteristic of it.

People can use their liberties in ways of which we deeply disapprove, often with good reason. But when are the reasons strong enough truly to say, 'There ought to be a law'? The debate is endless but generally a minimal view (and views should be minimal) picks out actions which threaten the ability of others to exercise their proper liberties, clear and present danger to the safety of the state, assault and theft and - in the great language of the Common Law - 'incitement to a breach of the peace'. But short of actual violence it can sometimes be thought that to defame or abuse someone grossly and solely on the grounds of their race, religion or sexual identification, should be illegal. That people who do this should be reviled, morally condemned, even ostracised, I have no doubt; but should they be punished by law? The debate is familiar and it partly turns on our fears that to proscribe any opinion, even dishonestly held, can be the thin end of the wedge given the propensity to oppression inherent in all government; but to allow some things to be said publicly at all - for example racial abuse - puts an intolerable constraint on the objects of the abuse, always fellow human beings, often fellow citizens, to restrain themselves from striking back. And others single out obscenity and pornography as intolerably offensive to women.

It is worth reminding ourselves, therefore, that all tolerance, however benign, contains an element of disapproval. Tolerance historically is not the same as indifference (see *Political Theory and Practice*,

Crick 1973). People did care passionately about religious commitments, but sometimes were willing, partly for philosophical and partly for prudential reasons, to limit their reactions. And it was for God to punish heretics, not men. Think of the first statute of the reign of William and Mary, 'The Act of Toleration to Dissenting Protestants...' The power is there and the object of toleration is named. The country still felt threatened by religious diversity, official policy still frowned on dissent, but it was not to be persecuted or proscribed generally (except for membership of universities, commissions in the army, membership of Parliament and of most of the professions). It was not tolerant enough, by our standards, indeed to some of the best minds of the time, but it was tolerant in the sense that it gave an area of freedom to a group of which the state generally disapproved, and the state had the undoubted power to give or withhold. I cannot attach any meaning to my being tolerant about things over which I have no power or influence.

A tolerant society and a permissive society are very different ideas: the one limits disapprovals and the other manifests total indifference, or a belief that 'anything goes'. Actually a society using 'anything goes' as a rule simply couldn't work. There must be some conventional moral rules. We may not take all of them that seriously but we must observe most of them or else it would be collisions all the time — as if there was no arbitrary rule of the road. Now it is a fallacy to think that the opposite of tolerance, or the negation of tolerance, is intolerance: it is indifference. For I negate indifference not by intolerance but by caring for the issues, and consciously tolerating, to some degree, different behaviour. The opposite of intolerance is not indifference, but some firm rival view: the negation of intolerance is love or conversion, being taken over by the other side.

This logical point fits in with the observed psychological phenomenon that extremists often don't lapse into or achieve sweet tolerance and moderation, but can abruptly change sides, adopting some rival harsh fanaticism. The intolerant mind with the fanatic heart lives in an either/or world. (Alas, it is so hard to find truculent moderates; the old republican spirit needs reviving.) The tolerant person is a pluralist, he or she observes different moral codes or ways of life within a nation or wider community and has some familiarity, sympathy even, with several. She or he can manage this pluralistic moral economy by experience and by continual, usually conscious, compromises. If we did not have a consciousness of living among different and authentic moral codes, calling for disapprovals as well as limited acceptances, we would be accepting everything, therefore indifferent, permissive, dwelling in a kind of could-not-care-lessitude — wholly cynical and undiscriminating. The conservative accepts everything as he finds it, the anarchist accepts everything as it can be imagined as an arena for personality. For any such society of total scepticism to work, it has to have, of course, clear and rigid conventions (as Hume was well aware), like a Tory club or an anarchist commune.

I stress this element of *disapproval* in tolerance, rather than the equally real dimension of *acceptance*, because I hold to the view (to begin to summarise all this very simply) that if we modern liberals and democratic socialists were not so inhibited in expressing *moral* disapprovals publicly, there would not be felt so much need for public law in these difficult areas. I want to see far greater ethnic and sexual equality — they are parts of and test cases for the idea of an egalitarian society: but I am convinced that we have to do it for the most part by ourselves collectively, by persuasion, writing, education, above all by example. The courts can only deal with extreme cases and the public law can only provide a broad framework for social action, not itself a constant series of socially transforming legal interventions. For such interventions to work they would need, in any case, considerable and constant public support. State intervention is not always appropriate to social change. Some broad framework of legislation is needed to set standards, and some positive discrimination is desirable in symbolically important areas that can have an exemplary effect elsewhere. Why is it left to campaigning organisations to point to the fact that so few young blacks are to be seen in banks? Surely all shareholders and customers are not racist — more likely they are indifferent, when they should not be. They should be intolerant of their bank's indifference. I like Gellner's maxim: social tolerance and intellectual intolerance.

We need to condemn what we think is wrong and label what we think is nonsense, nonsense. Demands to censor obscenity and pornography (dangerous areas for law, indeed) would be less strong if those who oppose *all* censorship (or so they say) so strongly gave a little time to denouncing rubbish and condemning, indeed, much that is called pornography (see *Crime, Rape and Gin,* Crick, 1974). I sympathise with those feminists who sometimes use aggressive and direct tactics against people who make their living by pornographic images of the female body, indeed see most of this as not just offensive to women but as anti-sexual, the negation of eroticism. But if I call a play both pornographic and bad, this no more constitutes a cry to have it banned than if I call another trivial and silly (only a cry for sensible people not to waste their time and money). The trouble is that as soon as some idiot demands that a play or film is banned (not being able conceptually to distinguish between law and morality), another load of idiots (with a similar conceptual hang-up) spring up (usually in the ICA, *City Limits* or *Time Out*) to say that it is a work of art or 'authentic anti-art', therefore untouchable, or that something else like it one day could be a work of art, or have faint elements of authenticity about it. When elites turn permissive rather than tolerant, ordinary people give ready support to politicians and popular journalists who bellow, 'There ought to be a law'. They may just want it condemned, or to hear the healthy cry of the home supporters, 'What a load of rubbish!' I believe in public opinion. I far prefer it to constricting laws. But the literary and artistic elite have to try to reach it and influence it, not to demand both to be left alone and to be given a privileged position.

To think that tolerance is the antithesis of intolerance can actually lead to false optimism. Consider the most elaborate and large-scale study of race relations in modern Britain, E.J.B. Rose and associates, *Colour and Citizenship: A Report on Modern British Race Relations* (OUP, 1969). A survey was commissioned that ranked respondents on a conventional scale. At one end were the 'Prejudiced' (a mere ten per cent), at the other, thirty-five per cent 'Tolerant' (hurrah!); and in between came a shifty seventeen per cent 'Prejudice-inclined' and a wobbly thirty-eight per cent 'Tolerant-inclined'.

Theodor Adorno in his *Authoritarian Personality* first used such a scale, with authoritarian traits at one end and democratic at the other. But such conceptualisings can be very misleading. Adorno argued that a state was likely to be authoritarian when its leadership elite had those kinds of character traits, and democratic if democratic. But Edward Shils argued, in a famous review in *Social Research*, that no democratic polity was likely to hold together for five minutes that could not make use of both these allegedly antithetical personality types, socialise a fair number of the authoritarian types and make the democrats reasonably tough-minded in their own defense. In *Colour and Citizenship's* survey is someone in the ranks of the 'Prejudiced' ten per cent necessarily intolerant? He may be well aware of his prejudices, and lean over backwards to be nice to blacks, Jews or women or whatever. His expressed beliefs or even intentions could be awful but his actual behaviour could be impeccable, perhaps just the way he was brought up. I've known such people. Or is a man certified 'Tolerant' necessarily devoid of prejudice? Consider the editor of a liberal-minded quality newspaper who works among beautiful (white) people who detest what is happening in South Africa and North Balham, but he lives nowhere near Balham and happens not to employ any blacks on the editorial and senior management floor (quite a lot down below, however) and never entertains British blacks, only visiting heads of state or American actors. Can his behaviour be called 'tolerant' or 'unprejudiced' when the issue simply doesn't arise, or he doesn't let it? He is neither overtly prejudiced nor capable of running up any kind of score for intolerance on even the most subtle attitude survey; but does he deserve the accolade of 'tolerant' (if that is something positive, capable of disapprovals, and restraints) rather than 'indifferent'? I think employers have to be put to the behavioural, not just the attitudinal test. My imaginary editor would be in an excellent position to practise prominent positive discrimination.

Perhaps the darker point is that racial and sexual prejudices are very hard to eradicate, but easier to contain. I've used this example before, and it caused terrible misunderstanding; but let me try again. I could admit to some prejudice against homosexuals, and, indeed, rationalise it. Unfair to women. 'How will the world be populated!?' Sometimes a nepotic freemasonry. Absurd claims to pre-eminence in the arts. A code of behaviour impossible to generalise as a moral rule to satisfy Kant. Some worries about seduction of the young. And not merely no homoerotic feelings myself, but a tingle of revulsion. Finally, a great rage at their rape of a good and common English word to now render many great lines ludicrous. Never can the great joke come cleanly again, that the *Beggar's Opera* made Gay rich and Rich (the theatre owner) gay. But I was strongly for the abolition of section 40 of the Criminal Code, and am strongly against discrimination (except in a few cases where I think it relevant – teaching in single sex boys' schools, for obvious example). I cannot see any conceivable case for positive discrimination, however. Yet I know several gays as friends. Out of civility I reluctantly use the term they now choose. I had a very dear friend once who was a homosexual. My tolerance had a strong cognitive element, as they say, not simply moral: I needed to know his tastes and habits in order to know on what occasions to meet, when to stay and when to leave. I say 'my' tolerance, for the point is unavoidable that it is the majority who have to and should tolerate minorities, or in that case and in those days the one whose promiscuity was legal had to tolerate the one whose faithfulness was illegal. Of course some, for this reason, say that all tolerance is condescension: they don't want tolerance but full acceptance, even love. Sorry, that is too much. We live by our exclusions as well as our inclusions. Groups like individuals often get along best by knowing each other well enough to know when to keep a distance as well as when to mingle. In a pluralist society public law may need to be invoked both to help preserve communities, and also to ensure that the young of either sex can leave them.

Bagehot was right. One cannot make men good by Act of Parliament. We can and must use the state to create a *more* economically equal society so that people can exercise their liberties more fully, but it is better that it is done by enabling people to help themselves. Mrs. Thatcher is half right, in rhetoric at least; but to help everyone to help themselves as others can, means massive income support and redistribution of incomes through the tax system. Positive discrimination in taxation according to income is a sound principle of social justice. We need to combat mass unemployment and wages so low that many people in employment are also in poverty; but by devices like negative income tax, redistribution through the tax system for a guaranteed minimum wage, not by the state assuming or resuming direct control of industry or attempting to control prices and incomes.

There is a general revulsion from too much state control, state enterprise, standardised welfare and centralisation. Mrs. Thatcher has part caught the mood of revulsion from 'the gentlemen in Whitehall know best' and part fermented it, but like the 'there ought to be a law' individualist she has also added to centralisation by irrational dislike of liberties actually being exercised in local government and in public sector education. Her rate-capping, then her destruction of the rating system and her educational policies are creating a centralisation of power possibly greater than the decentralisation effected by her war on Quangos and her campaign for privatisation.

Yet things will never go back to what they were before. The post-war welfare state was too rule-bound and too apt to do good for people through professional social workers, etc., rather than finding ways of enabling people, in groups and individually, in a variety of forms, cooperative, municipal and commercial, to do good for themselves. The welfare state, the new Leviathan, was benign and well-meaning but it was inhabited only by civil servants, social workers and clients. There were also politicians, but they were only supposed to mediate, not to change anything; and there were taxpayers who were to pay for it all. Actually, despite Tory legend, the revolt did not come from the taxpayers. Several surveys have recently shown that while everyone says they would like lower taxes, most people also say they would rather pay more if it could restore the over-stretched Health Service and the run-down schools. I think the revolt came because people began to see the professionals not merely as too interventionist, but as a self-preservation society. Even occasional readers of the popular press will be aware that the NUPE campaign against Health Service cuts, like the NUT's to save the schools, was pictured as flagrant self-interest: jobs for the boys. Unfair, grossly exaggerated; but they could not see that they were not the people to make the case. The professionals by becoming too organised have then treated the public either as clients or as ungrateful and stupid dupes of a new rabble-rousing Conservatism and a popular Press, rather than as active agents. It may be less efficient to help people to help themselves than to help directly, but it is more democratic and likely to last.

There is a lot of talk now in the Labour Party about 'an enabling state', neither a command state nor a welfare-providing state. There is a reappraisal of the whole idea that the central state is necessarily able to achieve, or should even attempt to achieve, uniform social justice, including racial and sexual equality, etc. The dispersal of power, not its concentration, may actually get more done, though not always in the same way or even the same direction, let alone at the same speed. There will be much greater variation in outcomes than reformers previously

envisaged, whatever the actual reality – which they always attributed to
the failure of particular plans, not to central-planning in general.
Individualism and liberty are now taken back into the democratic
socialist Pantheon. Labour's version of an individual at his or her best
is still a more sociable and a less competitive animal than Thatcher's
Man (also more North British than pseudo-American), but the
difference is no longer absolute. Egalitarianism in many parts of the
country and in some sections of society is now the style, in dress,
manner's and friendships; but it is less tied to ideas of formal economic
equality. And respect for traditional communities is now a hidden
common bond between much Labour sentiment and the values of the
Old Tories among the 'Wets' – as can come into the open in bizarre
alliances for protests by local conservationists and radical environ-
mentalists.

Amid all these changes it seems to me reasonably clear that reformers will never go back to a simple faith that with the right legislation
from Whitehall and Westminster racial equality, sexual equality, positive discrimination for the handicapped can be achieved, the Health
Service restored and rendered uniformly swift and good, all schools
brought to a uniform level. We have now learned, the hard way, that in
a   civilised   society   we   do   not   just   want   unjustified
discriminations in public provision abolished, we also want to
discriminate more carefully about different kinds of provisions, and
therefore sources of provisions, for ethnic groups, women with
different views and with different circumstances, local preferences for
health and educational priorities, etc. Moreover, we do not all want the
same things.

More taxable income should stay in the regions to be taxed or be put
at the disposal of regional and local authorities. We shouldn't insist
that everyone bakes the same cake and cuts it into the same portions.
The state can enable more choices to be made and define an acceptable minimum (acceptable, by the way, to people in that position as
well as to those who imagine they are paying for it personally); but if the
state attempts a direct and universal equitable provision, it will fail. We
do live in a pluralistic society, not an homogeneous one. We do have
different cultures, values and interests quite apart from social class.
Therefore there are limits to what the general rules of law can achieve
by way of justice in such a situation. In such a situation one just has to
trust to political mechanisms of bargaining, conciliation and compromise, and to a culture that still has some general common sense of
equity or fairness and of altruism as well as individual self-assertion.
We don't want less local politics, we want more; only less national
politics. Politics doesn't always work well. But one can try again
without having to bring in a major piece of legislation in every instance
and hope that the courts will do what Parliament intended. Legislate

for reform, by all means, but to create devolved, enabling structures, functional as well as territorial, such that ordinary people can influence if not always operate directly. What's so bad in parent power in school government? Because it is her idea? But will it yield the result she expects? We must see.

Reformers must not automatically defend the professionals against the people. We must challenge the Prime Minister's assumptions about what people really believe, and can be persuaded to believe. Laws codify and express the necessary relationships of a society. Laws do not create these relationships.

Ten

On Liberty : For Fellow Socialists

* From Larry Gostin, ed., *Civil Liberties in Conflict* (Routledge, London: 1988).

We socialists, I am sorry to remind you in mixed company, can have a bad name with some libertarians. And, to the surprise of anarchists, 'libertarian' has become a bad name to many of us. Libertarian philosophy is often associated with those of the radical Right who believe in an uncontrolled market economy but who also, with greater logical consistency than traditional conservatives, dislike censorship and almost any controls on personal life and private morals. But it is equally sensible to talk of 'libertarian socialists' and of 'libertarian conservatives'. I simply want to restate the case why liberty is never a sufficient condition for social justice (unless you are an anarchist, whether of the left- or right-wing variety) yet is always and everywhere a necessary condition for social justice.

I am equally angry with neo-liberals who say that democratic socialists are either hypocritical or muddled to think that equality and liberty can go together, and with Marxists who say that individual liberty is possible only in a classless society (or that 'bourgeois liberty' is not really liberty). There are still fellow socialists who, despite all the awful object lessons of oppression using or misusing the name of socialism, take terrible liberties with liberty: no liberty, they say, for fascists, racists, perhaps even 'scabs' (the comprehensive term used to be 'no liberty for the enemies of the people').

Far from seeing equality as a pre-condition for a future liberty, the early socialists, the pre-Marxian socialists, saw the aggressive assertion of actual, existing popular liberties as being thwarted by gross inequalities. Greater equality of condition had to be achieved in order to maximize liberty. There was no glimmer of an opinion that popular liberties had to be restrained for the sake of equality. Poverty and oppression prevented people acting freely, or certainly limited drastically the effective limits of free action. But liberty, none the less, was seen as the greatest goal. A poor man, it was said, could scarcely call his soul his own. So an egalitarian society would allow much greater freedom of action for more people, not just freedom for the fortunate

146

few. Early socialists, like Proudhon in France and Robert Owen in Britain, believed not merely that the main object of the struggle against oppression and the class system was to maximise human freedom, but that the struggle must take the form of asserting popular liberties. And they believed that socialist communities would, in a decentralised society in which the role of the state was minimal, order their affairs very differently.

There were, unhappily, two other traditions of early socialism: that of the followers of Saint-Simon and that of Blanqui. Saint-Simon was the great rationalist: a just society would be created by the knowledge and administrative skills of a specially educated elite controlling the state in the true interests of society (not what selfish people clamoured for or the ignorant thought they wanted). Blanqui was the eternal revolutionist and militant (he spent over half his life in prison): a small band of dedicated working-class revolutionaries could choose the right tactical moment to seize the state power and use it to smash the old social order for ever. For once the artificial order was violently demolished, a natural order of spontaneous harmony would follow. (Some modern terrorists exhibit just this potent mixture of delinquency and innocence.)

Yet even Saint-Simon and Blanqui professed that part of their aim was liberty (though there were good grounds for not trusting either). They offered no unusual definition of it. Liberty for all was not to be attained in either a traditional or a capitalist system, but qualitatively the liberty there was and the liberty to come were much the same thing. It was only Marxists who began to argue (not even consistently Marx himself) that bourgeois liberty was not really liberty at all and that true liberty could be found only in a classless society after the revolution. Bourgeois liberty was used only against the working class and was only ever of tactical, temporary, opportunistic use to them. Parliaments were only devices by which the bourgeoisie made use of their leisure, gained from exploitation and surplus value, to deceive and control the working class. I am not concerned here with how this argument entered into socialist tradition. I want only to identify it and to point to some consequences. The international socialist movement became split between libertarian and democratic socialists, and authoritarian socialists who believed that the party embodied the will of the working class and that there must be no liberty to oppose or delay their emancipation.

Forcing to be Free

The Marxist view of liberty was, however, only a specific formulation in class terms of an older and more general argument. Saint-Just in the days of the Jacobin ascendancy had cried that there was no liberty to stand aside. 'Those who are not for us are against us', he declaimed to the Assembly, 'what are they but enemies of the people?' The fearsome concept was born that allows no appeal and leaves an individual no space in which to move. The idea of privacy as anti-social was invented almost at the same time that privacy itself became a concept to be valued. And you also had to be clerical or anti-clerical; middle positions of indifference or suspended judgement were dogmatically and violently denounced. Robespierre explained that:

> The terror is nothing but justice, prompt, severe and inflexible, it is thus an emanation of virtue; it is less a special principle than a consequence of the general principle of democracy applied to the most pressing needs of our country.[1]

But it was Rousseau who had given this idea its more acceptable classic formulation, actually intending to strengthen democracy. For his idea of the 'General Will' was that social justice was not to be found in reason by educated philosophers. Rather it was to be found in the hearts and sentiments of ordinary people, the common people, when they stripped their minds of all pre-conceived knowledge, of book learning, and of all vested interests. Thus what was good for all, not for one's selfish self or corporate interest, would prevail. The common man would be more able to achieve this empathy or uncorrupted innocence than the educated or the aristocrat. But what if some poor wretch was to be so insensitive as not to experience, or so perverse as consciously to disobey, this beneficent General Will?

> Whosoever shall refuse to obey the general will must be constrained by the whole body of his fellow citizens to do so: which is no more than to say that it may be necessary to force a man to be free – freedom being that condition which, by giving each citizen to his country, guarantees him from all personal dependence and is the foundation upon which the whole political machine rests and supplies the power which works it.[2]

Now, there are many occasions on which it is right and just to use force against a fellow citizen: to resist a violent attack or to arrest or detain a thief, and so on. But something is wrong when we say that the person who is forced is therefore made free. We may be more free when a killer is locked up, but it is dangerous to believe that constraints on others make them free. Many things limit freedom, but the idea of it as lack of constraint is essential. Rousseau does not solve the problems of 'dependence' and 'oppression'; he substitutes one kind of oppression for another.

Consider the consequences. Oppressive commands must be not merely suffered and obeyed but applauded and internalized. Everything is class ideology, and 'the ideologically correct' is determined not by Rousseau's imagined beneficent Legislator but by an actual political party. On this logic not merely is there no liberty to criticize the party of the people, but liberty itself becomes everything the party decides to do, and nothing else. Consider a poignant and astonishing example.

In 1936 a Russian music critic called Olesha was commanded to recant publicly his admiration for the music of Shostakovitch:

> The article in *Pravda* deals with a question of principle. It is the opinion of the Communist Party; either I am wrong or the Party is wrong. The line of least resistance would have been to say to oneself, 'I am not wrong', and mentally reject *Pravda's* opinion. In other words by keeping to the conviction that in the case in question the Party had not spoken correctly, I would have granted the possibility that the Party was wrong.
>
> What would have been the result? There would have been serious psychological consequences. The whole framework of our social life is very closely knit together, comrades. In the life and activity of our state nothing moves or develops independently ...
>
> If I do not agree with the Party in a single point, the whole picture of life must be dimmed for me, because all parts, all details of the picture are bound together and arise out of each other, therefore there must not be a single false line anywhere.
>
> That is why I agree and say in this matter, in the matter of art, the Party is always right. And it is from this point of view that I begin to think of Shostakovitch's music. I continue to enjoy it. But I begin to recollect that in certain places it always seemed to me somewhat, it is difficult to get the right word, contemptuous.'[3]

He must have been very frightened but he must also have been a very clever time-server. He was clever not to claim an implausibly sudden conversion to Stalin's dislike of modern music; and equally clever to grasp so well and state so slavishly the full logic of Communist theory of ideology. He exhibits the bottom of the slippery slope on which any one of us can find ourself once we get into the habit of telling lies for the good of the cause, or more generally accepting that free actions and judgements must always be an 'ideologically' correct calculation of class (more often party) interest.

Modern Marxists might dismiss this as the personal philistinism of Stalin. But the more profound problem arises if one believes that freedom is a mere product of material circumstances, not a means of shaping them. For then free actions can be only those that further the true cause, not those of critics or opponents. Their actions become not free but somehow unnatural, perverse, anti-social. Those who adhere to this ideological theory of truth can offer no guarantees against the abuse of power by whatever person or group is trusted to speak for the cause authoritatively, precisely what John Stuart Mill called 'the fallacy of infallability'.[4] It is dangerous as well as morally wrong to demand freedom for oneself but not for opponents. Single parties so often turn inwards to fight against themselves for power: 'the revolution devours its own children'.

I am, of course, discussing freedom of speech, assembly, and movement: the rights of citizenship, rights which if not exercised will wither away. I am not discussing rights of rebellion. Some states are so oppressive that it is the positive duty of their subjects to try to overthrow them, to act like citizens, if all other remedies have failed. But socialists have no special privilege, nor has anyone else, to break down laws or even to overwork non-violent civil disobedience (which if over-used as more than a symbolic gesture can hardly fail to involve or to provoke violence). Those who wish to transform society have a special duty to be tolerant and thick-skinned against criticism. It is not merely a question of tolerantly suffering 'reasonable criticism' or graciously welcoming 'helpful criticism'; one needs the civic toughness to accept slander. Our mothers well taught us that:

Sticks and stones may hurt my bones,

But names they never will do.

Again, Orwell said that 'Liberty is telling people what they do not want hear' – ridiculously insufficient but certainly a necessary part of any definition of liberty.

So liberty is liberty. There is no exclusive socialist, liberal, nor yet conservative liberty. One modern Marxist, Ralph Miliband, has seized this point well – in contrast to so many prudes among us who feel tainted by any talk of 'things in common' and will not, unlike Marx himself, praise the bourgeoisie for their great achievements in their time:

Regimes which depend on the suppression of all opposition and the stifling of all civic freedoms must be taken to represent a disastrous regression in political terms from bourgeois democracy.... But the civic freedoms which, however inadequately and precariously, form part of bourgeois democracy are the product of centuries of unremitting popular struggles. The task of Marxist politics is to defend these freedoms: and to make possible their extension by the removal of class barriers.[5]

If this is true, then it has implications for those of us who wish to defend and extend liberty as well as to promote particular causes.

Common ground can and should be found between socialists and non-socialists in taking up all cases where the civil liberties of anyone are threatened, whatever their politics. Even tactically it is usually best to make working alliances if the object is, indeed, to win a point of law of general application, to see that justice is done and not (as has sometimes happened in some famous campaigns) to make a martyr to publicize the cause. Socialists discredit themselves and devalue liberty when they make socialism a condition for supporting bodies like the

National Council for Civil Liberties. The insistence that the NCCL, for instance, moves beyond 'negative objectives' and 'campaigns positively' (for socialist objectives and trade union discipline) is damaging both to civil liberties and to democratic socialism. Bodies like Amnesty International sometimes face the same problems – that is, some members who are more keen to attack oppression in general with their mouths than to do what is more quietly and thoughtfully needed to help actual individuals in prison. Take-overs of voluntary bodies by socialists can be very damaging, obviously to the bodies in question, which need to be able to convince non-socialists, but also to socialists themselves. The public can come to view them as irresponsible wreckers and trouble-makers, as people who fail to demonstrate that 'socialist institutions' work but can demonstrate that socialists can stop coalitions for specific causes working. (I am sometimes tempted to think of much of this as play-acting at revolution in a safe playground in leisure time, in which no one will get hurt.)

Of course the defence and assertion of civil liberties are not enough. Everyone has other values and needs. Socialists have a quite specific combination of values. We think that society needs reforming towards both egalitarian and libertarian objectives, building through and towards a great sociability and sense of community. Society needs reforming. But everything can't be done at once, still less in the same forum. We need to differentiate and discriminate tasks and roles, if we are serious and not just play-acting. We need to keep the basic constitutional and procedural concerns of civil liberties apart from agitation for substantive socialist reforms. Otherwise the tragedy of Soviet communism, not just of Stanlinism, will be repeated for ever.

Social theories are invented to explain why the Soviet Communist Party proved, contrary to socialist expectations, grimly repressive. Most of them seem far-fetched, and many have always been special pleading. One reason at least why one-party states become one-party states is that the leaders of a determined party want it to be that way: a matter of human will. More subtly, they developed an ideology that at a particular point of time crudely conceptualized all civil liberties and constitutional restraints as part of the exploitative mechanisms of the superstructure of capitalist states. But we now live in a world in which there are many capitalist autocracies and many socialist autocracies, most of them not even pretending to be parliamentary, democratic, or liberal. Neither the mode of production nor the class structure determines everything (nor are they ever as simple as once thought).

Truth to tell, even the British Labour movement, while intensely libertarian, has always had a rather simple theory of the constitution: that if a party gets a working majority in the House of Commons it can legislate as it pleases. Popular sovereignty legitimizes parliamentary sovereignty. There has been little concern with limiting parliamentary sovereignty itself – despite its use to privatize vast amounts of public property and to destroy local democracy in the capital city itself. I fancy that this may be changing. A reaction against centralized planning and excessive state control in favour of more local autonomy is taking place. It begins to dawn on even the most traditionalist socialists that to protect local and community rights some structure of public law, entrenched in the courts, might be preferable to the alternating risk of everything being undone again next time. It is doubtful if there could be a thoroughgoing decentralization of the polity and the economy without something like a Bill of Rights. But that is, of course, some Marxists would object, a liberal concept; so it is. So what? We should not deny historical fact. But we should try to make something better of it for all.

A Real Difference in Emphasis

None the less, there is a real difference in emphasis between liberal and democratic socialist accounts of liberty. Sir Isaiah Berlin in his famous essay, *Two Types of Liberty* (1958), argued powerfully against what he called 'the positive theory of liberty' – theories that, in various ways, identify liberty with the positive achievement of some chosen state of affairs or, at least, with a comprehensive avoidance of error. 'In thy service, Lord, is the only perfect freedom' and 'The truth shall set you free' are both, whether in religious or secular mode, paradigmatic of positive liberty. A sociological version of the argument was Harold Laski's 'liberty is the existence of those conditions in society which enable me to become myself at my best'.[6] The fallacy of this is quite simply that not being unhealthy, not being unemployed, or not being in poverty cannot, however lengthy the benign list, constitute or guarantee freedom. (But in other writings Laski offered, as if he saw no difference, a negative formulation: that liberty is the absence of those conditions which can prevent me becoming myself at my best.)[7] Liberty, indeed, means being left alone and not interfered with, even if sometimes other values lead us to curtail but never to deny liberty. Said Berlin:

> The 'negative liberty' they strive to realise seems to me a truer and more humane ideal than the goals of those who seek in the great, disciplined authoritarian structures the idea of 'positive' self-mastery, by classes, by peoples or the whole of mankind.[8]

Yet something is missing from Berlin's account, not about the nature of liberty but about the conditions for liberty. Either we must say that Berlin puts too much stress on the protection of individual liberty, the liberal ideal of being protected by law from the state, and not enough on *the exercise of liberty* – the price of liberty is more than eternal vigilance, it is eternal activity. Otherwise, we must argue for an unobjectionable sense of 'positive liberty' which is not authoritarian at all but is republican. Authoritarianism identifies liberty with some chosen and obligatory version of truth or righteousness; but the republican tradition identifies liberty with the positive exercise of citizenship, popular participation, the perpetual challenging of authority, the election of leaders but always criticizing them and holding them to account. The republican tradition aggressively seeks to politicise issues and to democratize institutions; the liberal tradition gently seeks to take issues out of politics and to put a wall of law between a legislature and, say, education, religious observance, or property rights. To the republican while a good life cannot be wholly political, yet nothing can be taken out of politics *a priori*; and everything must be settled politically – that is, by public debate, argument, persuasion, bargaining, and compromise.

Free actions are the actions of individuals, not of organic groups of homogeneous classes. Socialists must never forget that. They are themselves individuals, usually rather innovative and unusual individuals. But individuals interact with other individuals. This the liberal sometimes forgets. My identity consists not in asserting the uniqueness of my wretched personality to the height, nor in repressing it sternly into some single and conventional social role, but in how I am recognized by others. When we act we interact. You are what you are because I, and many others, see you in that way. I am what I am because of the reactions and recognitions of others. Free political actions are not merely free actions, they are interactions between people acting in a political manner: citizenship. Acting in a political manner is not simply acting effectively towards realizing some policy or ideal, but it is acting through public debate, using persuasion, recognizing other people's differing values, reaching sensible compromises, being resolute about ends but open-minded about means, and seeking to avoid all violence except the counter-violence of self-defence.

In the republican tradition the sword of liberty, it was always said, will rust in its sheath if not used – the true socialist might add, not just for other people but *by* those other people. 'We are all here on earth to help each other', the poet Auden once gibed, 'but what the others are here for, God only knows'. The liberal is stronger on 'the shield of the laws', but the republican (and democratic socialists who inherit this Roman, Dutch, French, and early American tradition) is stronger on William Blake's 'sword of burning fire': assertion, challenge, positive action. Each is needed. In the republican tradition politics is not a minor disagreeable necessity, as it is to liberals; it is one of the marks of the good life and an educative activity in itself.[9] A person becomes more fully human by public debate and interaction with his or her fellows. Citizenship, free citizenship, acting for the common good, is the most noble image of humanity. Socialists in free societies commonly exhibit in their own behaviour this rugged and active republican individualism; but then they sometimes fatuously claim not to be acting freely but as the impersonal agent of some great abstraction like *the* people or *the* working class.

Politics, like freedom, in some thin sense can exist anywhere – in the Kremlin or in the court of the Great Dictator. But in a fuller, richer sense its existence as a public method of government, as a *system* is limited. Most governments in the modern world seek to repress political activity, some endure it, and a very few encourage it. Politics comprises the public actions of free people, and freedom can be maximised only in political democracies.[10] That is minimal political justice.

Social justice consists in the procedures of reconciling in a political manner the plurality of different values and interests found in any complex society. Socialism is one such substantive view, or rather, to be fully honest and let a cat go running from the theoretical bag, is many such views. Democratic socialists believe not merely that socialist societies can be achieved by democratic means, but that they can only be achieved thus. It may seem foolish not to call the Soviet Union a socialist society. This is not a very serious theoretical issue. For if we do call it socialist, then it is a bad socialist society in the primary sense that it is not a free society. Conservatives often argue like old Stalinists, that any socialism must impose changes so drastic that freedom suffers. But in the history of socialist thought, and in the possibilities raised by democratic socialist governments, this view is easily refutable — whether one is a socialist or not. It is as silly as to claim that all Conservative or capitalist governments are really, in some deep sense, authoritarian ('almost' fascist) or tend that way (according to a polemical pamphlet that Lenin wrote in a hurry in a peculiar circumstance).

Thus liberty deserves almost fanatic support from democratic socialists, not just if it appears to help a favoured cause of the moment. A truly socialist movement is so committed to liberty and open government that at times it can seem almost incoherent amid the multitude of voices who speak for it and the variety of different policies advocated. It can at times seem almost paranoid in its belief that anything less than totally open government conceals behind closed doors weapons of oppression and conspiracies against the people. And liberty is an unpredictable and exuberant thing. Give people liberty and you never know what they will do with it. The actions of free men and women are always unpredictable – which is why some teachers prefer teaching 'the rule of law' rather than the disruptive skills necessary for effective participation. Now, I am all for the rule of law. We should always give the benefit of doubt to laws that have been properly passed. But it is also in our tradition, in the republican tradition long before socialism even, to ask whether the laws are just and to challenge unjust laws. That is the difference between the good citizen and the good subject.

Berlin's concept of negative liberty does well to stress that many doors must always be left open. The socialist should know that many roads lead to Rome, not just one. Some may take longer, for instance, but prove less bloody. But it is not enough to purr with pleasure that there are so many doors; doors are to be passed through, though we should never slam them behind us. People who use their liberty in order to avoid political life are more often done down than left in peace. The price of liberty is active citizenship both in the formal polity and in all other associations.[11] The sword can never rest at our side until everyone can and will act as equal citizens: women in general, the Black population in particular, the Catholic minority in Northern Ireland, the Arab minority in Israel (or majorities in a different context).

Conclusion

The poor, the disadvantaged, and the dispossessed do not merely need injustices removed, they need positive discrimination to help them off the ground to act freely and politically for themselves. Freedom needs its antique, republican, pre-liberal cutting edge resharpened for modern conditions. Welfare is not secure if it is a gift and not a collective achievement. Freedom is positive action in a specific manner: that of a citizen acting as if among equals, and not merely to preserve the rights of existing citizens (say we socialists) but to extend them to the wretched of the earth. Far from there being an inherent contradiction between the ideals of liberty and equality, without social equality active liberty (which I call freedom) can never be achieved. But we need to watch it. It is so easy to take liberties with other people's liberties, especially if one means well by them. Without active liberty for all, the activists will always constitute a 'new class' or an elite of the elect – benign, arrogant, and reckless.

Lastly, without liberty truth can suffer. Socialists should not repeat the mistake of pre-industrial autocrats in seeking, grandly, to freeze knowledge and to hold it constant and, pettily, to excuse themselves from simple moral rules like telling the truth. What is 'ideologically correct', comrade, not merely has to be enforced but can then destroy the sense of reality of the leadership itself. That was Orwell's profound argument in his satires *Animal Farm* and *Nineteen Eighty-Four*. A somewhat similar egalitarian and libertarian to Orwell, Ignazio Silone attended the Comintern in the 1920s as a delegate of the Italian Communist Party. He provided a concrete example of all I have been warning against, quite as extraordinary as poor Comrade Olesha adjusting his views on Shostakovitch to those of Stalin.

They were discussing one day, in a special commission of the Executive, the ultimatum issued by the [British TUC] ordering its local branches not to support the Communist-led minority movement on pain of expulsion. After the representative of the British Communist Party had explained the serious disadvantage of both solutions, because one meant the liquidation of the minority movement and the other the exit of the minority from the trade union, the Russian delegate Piatnisky put forward a suggestion which seemed to him as obvious as Columbus' egg: 'The branches', he said, 'should declare that they submit to the discipline demanded, and then, in practice, should do exactly the contrary.' The English Communist interrupted: 'But that would be a lie.' Loud laughter greeted this ingenuous objection, frank, cordial, interminable laughter, the like of which the gloomy offices of the Communist International had perhaps never heard before. The joke quickly spread all over Moscow, for the Englishman's entertaining and incredible reply was telephoned at once to Stalin and to the most important offices of State, provoking new waves of mirth everywhere. The general hilarity gave the English Communist's timid, ingenuous objection its true meaning. And that is why, in my memory, the storm of laughter aroused by that short, almost childishly simple little expression – 'But that would be a lie' – outweighs all the long, heavy, oppressive speeches I heard during the sittings of the Communist International, and became a kind of symbol for me.[12]

I have never forgotten hearing that fine, scholarly socialist Harold Laski reading that passage from the newly published book in one of the last lectures he ever gave. It worries me because laughter is usually on the side of liberty, it is a form of liberty, so often satirizing autocrats. But the Kremlin's laughter was not the satirical laughter of free men, which makes a moral point, but the laughter of cynics, which sees nothing in the world but naked power. 'They that live by the sword shall die by the sword.' Any socialism that neglects the liberties of others destroys itself.

Notes:

1. Quoted in Talmon, J.L. (1952) *The Rise of Totalitarian Democracy,* London: Secker & Warburg, pp. 114–15.
2. Rousseau, J.J. (1947; first published) in Barker, E. (ed.) *The Social Contract*, Oxford World Classics, pp. 261–2.
3. Olesha, P. (1936) 'On Shostakovitch', *International Literature* 6 (June), pp. 85–7.
4. Mill, J.S. (1947; first published 1859) *On Liberty and Considerations on Representative Government,* Oxford: Blackwell.
5. Miliband, R. (1977) *Marxism and Politics*, Oxford: Oxford University Press, p. 212.
6. Laski H. (1948) *A Grammar of Politics,* London: Allen & Unwin, 5th edn., p. 142.

7. Laski, H. (1937) *Liberty in the Modern State,* London: Penguin Books.
8. Berlin, I. (1958) *Two Concepts of Liberty,* Oxford: Clarendon Press, p. 56.
9. Crick, B. (1982) *In Defence of Politics*, London: Penguin Books, 2nd edn.
10. Crick, B. (1973) *Political Theory and Practice*, London: Allen Lane.
11. Crick, B. (1984) *Socialist Values and Time,* London: Fabian Society, pp 13–16.
12. Crossman, R.H.S. (ed.) (1950) *The God That Failed*, London: Hamish Hamilton.

Eleven

The Character of a Moderate Socialist

* From *The Political Quarterly*, January 1976. This was a revised and expanded version of five short articles which appeared in the *New Statesman* while someone was on holiday in August and September 1975.

GILNOCKIE   Aha, ha. But you *are* ane whoor?
LADY   I'm no *your* whoor.
             — From John Arden, *Armstrong's Last Night.*

'Moderates stand up!', indeed – as Mr. Roy Hattersley has just cried. I Am a moderate, indeed a rather truculent and aggressive moderate, someone who has always thought that the average citizen should have his sleeves rolled up and his fists lightly clenched, not sit wincing behind this or that newspaper. But I want to say something before I stand up: that I am a moderate *Socialist,* or rather a Socialist who is moderate. I hope I am still with Mr. Hattersley, or probably a bit beyond him, keeping my distance but not too far ahead.[1] I am not moderate, however, in the sense that the editor of *The Times*, Mr. David Wood, Mr. Ronald Butt, Miss Nora Beloff, Mr. Robert McKenzie, even, and all in the Liberal Party over the age of forty are moderate. And Roy Hattersley should beware of the motives of these Greeks when they come bearing gifts, praising him as moderate. They said all this to Reg Prentice and unhinged him politically. And when in September, *The Times* called Mario Soares a moderate (catching correctly that he believes in parliaments and persuasion, but missing utterly that he wishes to achieve a planned and egalitarian society) they drove the editor of *Tribune* into acute dialectical contortions: for Dick Clements seemed to accept that anyone whom *The Times* called moderate is not fit to be thought of as a Socialist.

This silliest usage of 'moderate,' however, is simply to mean 'what I approve of' - or as the *Daily Telegraph* editorial writers use it, to refer to any *others* whom they can on occasion mildly tolerate. The commonest use is to define an alleged centre of the political spectrum. (I always remember that Arthur Schlesinger, Jr., once wrote a book called *The Vital Centre*, which seemed to me to be simply dead centre.) This dead-centre-of-the-political-spectrum view soon gets muddied up with talk of coalition (immediately jerking several points to the Right all those radicals who are flattered into that premature senility of being 'responsible fellows,' *i.e.* unresponsive to popular pressures). What would they do with a coalition if they had one? Or 'moderate' can be given the more theoretical-seeming and less practical-politics import of 'consensus' – a belief that we must have 'fundamental values' in common in order to survive. This view is usually advocated by people without any clear beliefs in basic values themselves: so probably the moderate-as-consensus-politician needs to reformulate his case to say that other people, that is the People, should hold values in common (like a bit in the mouth of a horse), but that they are not necessary for us, pragmatists all. Values should restrain (difficult) people, not animate them into positive citizenship. The confusions arise because 'moderate' can be applied either to means or to ends, to goals or to values. And when it refers to substantive goals, it can refer to the centre of the national political spectrum or to the centre of the Labour Party – a rather different calculation. And when it refers to means or to procedural values (like parliamentarianism, toleration, respect for simple truth, liberty and democracy, not the contortions of ideology), it can treat them simply as means towards many different ends or it can treat them as ends in themselves – which is the most sophisticated argument, the argument that any pursuit of rational and clearly defined goals is ultimately going to prove coercive, so we should best carry on simply managing, administering, politicising, with decency and humanity, not hope for too much, and never treating people as if they could be better, either more altruistic or more rational, than they are.

Now there is much to be said for this view, if we believe in the Myth of the Fall, are naturally pessimistic or rationally believe, through reading what Sir Keith Joseph calls 'the noble philosophy of Hayek', that there is little chance of us all bettering our lot in this world of scarce, indeed, diminishing resources, particularly in our British economy of today. I simply want to say that as a moderate and a socialist this is not my view for one. I believe that our society needs to be changed, should be changed and can be changed. But that it can only be changed in desirable directions through time and by what are essentially moderate means. When this has happened, there may be a point at which we can look back and say that there has been a revolution (as for world health or scientific technology, for example), that is both a change in the conditions that shape social and economic arrangements and in human consciousness. But revolution is rarely the most probable means to ensure a good end. Violent revolutions are a response either to the breakdown of government or to intolerable oppression: at best they create the opportunity, which then has to be taken deliberately and carefully, for comprehensive social change. More often revolution can only sensibly be understood as a process and not an event. In other words, moderate but naked and quite unashamed, I am an evolutionary (i.e. revolution-through-time) Socialist. Please do not call me moderate at all, though call me tolerant and libertarian (if I deserve it) any day, if this then leads you to believe that I want to maintain the same kind of present society (cleaned up a little) as the centre of the political spectrum both desire and enjoy. Which of us would then have been deceiving the other? And please will the Left stop deceiving themselves that socialist legislation without mass support can transform society (at least without an intolerably – and usually self-defeating – degree of coercion); and will they stop calling any who doubt this either backsliders or Fascist beasts? Ordinary people still need convincing, and convincing freely, that socialist ideals are worth trying, perhaps not necessarily only in alternating electoral spasms, but always in such a way that while advance continues the possibility of peaceful retreat is never closed. Yet if once ordinary people were convinced, then a democratic socialist regime would have far more power behind it to transform society genuinely than have the imposed socialist regimes of East Europe.

So let me try to restate in its broadest and most commonsensical terms the case for democratic Socialism (to use George Orwell's careful lower and upper case). But is this necessary – when we have had a Labour Government for about a decade, with one short interruption?

Lack of Thought

They (I mean the leaders of the Labour Party) find it hard to think at all (apart from being too busy, except perhaps in August) because of (a) a constitutional debility; and (b) a mistake in logic. The constitutional debility is the castrating or muzzling (as the case may be) of leadership by the doctrine of collective responsibility. No Minister may safely state any principles that the Prime Minister might dislike or might feel put himself in the shade, nor apparently produce any evidence which might ruffle the belief of the Sir John Hunts of that world that the least said the better. Harold Wilson himself may break the doctrine (a) by writing his memoirs (which contain no thought in the whole of the book, only a day-to-day celebration of his own cleverness); and (b) by the agreement to differ in the Common Market referendum campaign. But the others may not break it. And civil servants watch that they do not.

The others, it is said, collectively constitute (with a bit of ballast) the most intelligent, certainly the most highly educated, Cabinet in British political history; and yet they cannot talk freely and speculate publicly abut the aims of political activity. They may only, by permission, defend set positions. Only the briefest and most enigmatic signals are allowed of what their basic beliefs and working theories may be. Whatever one thinks of Tony Crosland's general views or those of Tony

Benn (and I am a very tolerant moderate who can see the intense plausibility of both), there is no doubt that each of them would be more influential if out of government, perhaps even out of the House. The pen is mightier than the mace. We do not lack good administrators, but we lack thinkers with an empathy towards real, ordinary people. We lack sufficient politicians with integrity and almost any with a clear sense of purpose – or if they have it, we can only surmise it by occasional discordant phrases cutting across cautious department briefs, or by knowledge of what they said before they went silent and underground in high office.

The mistake in logic is, however, an even more important factor in explaining why a Labour Government which has had the lion's share of power for the last decade yet lacks any publicly comprehensible sense of direction. 'Pragmatism' is believed to be a thing that wins elections (but only just, it seems). Pragmatism apparently means being practical, or vulgarly that 'truth is what works': the pseudo-philosophy of the careerist or of the manager of a going concern (and if it is not 'going' then not to question if one is in the right trade or working in the best way, but to borrow more and to pray for more oil). The fallacy of pragmatism is that it can only work within a known and accepted context of moral habits, beliefs and principles. It is not self-validating. To be 'purely practical', even, assumes that there are underlying values which are known, shared and understood. If there is no such consensus, then pragmatism is fraudulent – both in the sense of being self-deceiving and of being imposed on others, itself masking an ideology while pretending only to mirror public opinion. The question may indeed be one, as the Archbishop has remarked, of basic values; but whose values and what values? It may not be a problem of the decay of 'good old values' (of competitiveness and individualism?), but of changing values – a search for more fraternity and sociability.

The pragmatist in a changing world is likely to make great mistakes by attempting, for all his hyper-activity, to conserve the unconservable. Pragmatists wasted our national resources by trying, like Alice, to run very fast to stay put in one moving place: the hanging on to 'East of Suez' for so long after there was anything to defend; the defence of the pound in the late 1960s; the belief in a free market for wages amid falling productivity; and the economically crippling belief that houses and jobs should be brought to people and all movements of population, as far as possible, frozen.

The pragmatic politician's contempt for doctrine is almost as misleading as the journalist's habitual attempt to reduce every idea to a personal interest. Journalists often say that the public will only grasp issues if they are personalised, but more often they themselves believe – as the daily quest for novelty amid long-term problems conditions them to believe – that personal factors predominate. So deep is this

contempt for ideas and resulting ignorance about them that it is leading people to call almost any manifestation of real socialist thought
'Marxist' – as if the tradition of the Webbs, Cole, Tawney and Laski had
never existed. Indeed, the genuine Marxists of the book had better
watch out, for the very word is shifting its colloquial meaning to refer to
anyone who believes in Liberty, Equality, Fraternity.

I am not a Marxist. I hold the amiable view that on some things that
very great, if difficult man was profound and right, on others wrong
and that on still more issues he was so over-generalised and abstract as
to be virtually meaningless. If Marxism is a 'growing method', then it
may just become another word for socialism. If Michael Foot is persistently called a Marxist by the Right-wing Press (moderates?), he will
end up by believing that, after all (all those long battles with his friends
Bevan and Orwell against the Communist Marxists), he really is one. I
do not much care. One can be a good man without being a follower of
Christ, and a good democratic Socialist with or without the blessing of
the censorious pedantic priests of Marxism. But I do care intensely for
the theory and spirit of Enlightenment and of the French Revolution:
that mankind will progress by applying reason to the ideals of liberty,
equality and fraternity. Yet revolution is to be seen as a long and
deliberate process of government and popular education and persuasion, not as a dramatic single event. And I am angry when non-Marxist
social democrats refuse to argue with Marxists and take refuge behind
a shallow technological scepticism about the importance of ideas at all
– just as angry as when quests for doctrinal purity disallow any practical political action.

Socialism implies reason and example from both leaders and
followers – not secrecy and perpetual personal exceptions. (That a
Labour Government could prosecute publishers of a book by a
colleague and that a *Labour* Government should flinch at limiting
high incomes!) But a practical socialism means an intelligent appreciation of the different demands of the short-run and the long-run
factors, the pursuit of neither without the other and also a tolerant
recognition that a Socialist party must act on different levels simultan-
eously. Great changes need more planning and time than do immediate responses to short-term problems. If it has been decided to
rehouse the area completely in ten years time, the ancillary services
can be prepared; but in the meantime redecoration and repairs must
continue, especially if the roof is blown off by one of those intercontinental storms really beyond the control of any government.

The Right-wing of the Labour Party is in danger of making a cult of
pragmatism and of realism not as means to ends, but as ends in themselves – an hermaphrodite chasing its own tail. The Left-wing is in
danger of forsaking political means to their ends, which is, in fact,
recurrently destructive of these ends — a Phoenix far too frequent. Too

many Right-wingers have become, indeed, simply careerist smoothies. Too many Left-wingers have simply retreated into sectarian fanaticism rather than face the lapsed, but perpetual and necessary, task of converting the public to socialist principles.

What is the common core of all types of genuine socialism? Basically it is both a theory and a doctrine. The theory is that the rise and fall of societies is best explained not by the experience or cleverness of elites (Conservatism), nor by the initiative and invention of individuals (Liberalism), but by the social relationships of the primary producers of wealth – in an industrial society, the skilled manual worker. The doctrine is that a greater equality will lead to more cooperation rather than competition, and that this will enhance fraternity and thus liberate from inhibition and restriction both individual personality and the productive potential of a society.

In the 1930s the Labour Party had a bad spell when it wanted both to fight fascism and to disarm. We have recently been in a bad spell when we wanted both to maintain free collective bargaining and to obtain social justice for all. This may only have been a temporary aberration. Socialism began and rests on the belief that a free market in wages leads both to intolerable injustice and to a limitation both of productive and of human potential. But the message still has to be got across. A resolute socialist programme would still lose votes.

So if the politics of self-interest is not working and if people are plainly fed up with the ping-pong party electoral battle of 'who's the better manager of the shop?', let us explore (if only for a New Year's Resolution) what a realistic and immediately relevant democratic Socialist argument would be in terms likely to convince the unconvinced, not just the dwindling and thus somewhat touchy party faithful. Let us have a little less on programmes and manifestos and a little more on principles and long-term objectives. So I want to consider what a democratic Socialist (to use again Orwell's careful emphasis, the adjective distinguished from the noun, the means from the end) or a moderate Socialist (that is moderate about means, but not necessarily about ends) should be doing to develop the three basic values of liberty, equality and fraternity. I say 'develop', not work towards 'the goal', because values are not a kind of distant beacon that one day we may reach, thereupon rest, and in the meantime ignore: they are constant companions (if often quarrelsome among themselves and of varying influence upon oneself) on a journey which, while it progresses, yet never ceases. And this journey is governed not by some predetermined selection of an arbitrary point on a dubious map, but simply by agreement about a general sense of direction and how to behave towards each other on the way. Strictly speaking our goals are specifically socialist, but our values are not all specifically socialist – they include such values, good and common values, as truth, freedom, tolerance and fairness, none of which rule out our goals, but all of which may affect the means towards these goals.

Is any sense of direction realistic, however? Before a moderate socialist charges he wants some idea of where he is going, and some hope of being followed. Cromwell once remarked that an army never goeth so far as when it knows not where it is going. And there is an argument against any such politics of purpose at all. Is not the best any government can do simply to keep the ship afloat – as Oakeshott has taught? Wilson is more the Oakeshott figure of a statesman than ever a Heath or a Thatcher. The actual Labour Party is, indeed, to be understood historically as a coalition of interests, primarily the wage-politics of trade unions, and any specifically socialist influence has been at the best marginal. Certainly it is untrue that once-upon-a-time, in the days of the banners and the brass-bands, it was Socialist; and that is has fallen away by treachery, careerism and parliamentary nice-Nellyism. The myth of the Fall is poor history. There is no need to be a bad historian to be a good socialist. Socialism is in the future of the Labour Party, not in its past. For socialism is not a movement; it is a theory which sees the key to social progress in the character of the skilled working man's relations to the factors of production. The Labour Party may not be socialist, but socialism may be more illuminating of its dilemmas and more useful in giving it self-respect and a sense of direction than the non-theory or the 'pragmatism' of the leaders of the moment.

The dilemmas of the Labour Party, loss of membership, loss of support, loss of heart, increasing internal intolerance, may arise not from the lack of realism of its leaders but from their lack of theory and doctrine. Realism and pragmatism must be about something, they cannot feed of themselves; and plainly the customs and habits of the past are failing lamentably. Pragmatism, at the moment, is only concerned with how to keep the party in power. Reducing politics to that level, the electorate will simply judge in terms of immediate management of conventional values, self-interest and prosperity. And since no one can fully control the weather, not even Harold Wilson or Margaret Thatcher, each government will in turn, in these hard times for our country, be judged to have failed: so periods of alternating power may follow, rendering almost impossible any fundamental changes – which is just what opponents of adversary politics seem to want. Doctrine and publicly argued principles must be replenished and revivified if only to break from this truly liberal, capitalist, utilitarian vicious circle. Such doctrines must be realistic as well as heart-felt and clear – and the more heart-felt they are, the more one can compromise in the short run without destroying long-term hopes and integrity.

Socialist ideals are not to be restored, they are yet to be adopted. As one of the founding fathers wrote in 1911 in a once-famous Home

University Library book, *The Socialist Movement*:

> The Labour Party is not Socialist. It is a union of Socialist and trade union bodies for immediate political work.... But it is the only political form which evolutionary Socialism can take in a country with the political traditions and methods of Great Britain. Under British conditions, a Socialist Party is the last, not the first, form of the Socialist movement in politics.

Hardly strengthening my case to quote Ramsay MacDonald. But if he did not last the course himself, back then he happened to be right. Short-run realism and long-run idealism (plus middle-term planning) do not exclude or contradict but complement each other. Even our short-run factors need not be a retreat from Socialism (as cuts in public expenditure are seen) but could be made a prelude to a more socialist system of rewards. A declining economy in crisis may yet produce strident calls for an equality-fraternity of sacrifice. Such a siege-socialism could prove social-fascist, unless we look to our liberties too. But even given the opportunity, the worst of conditions and the best of motives, am I too not falling into the trap of advocating something that would hearten the faithful and lose the elections? What will it benefit a politician if he finds his own soul and loses the whole world? We are indeed fed up with the phariseeism and self-indulgent purity of so much Left-wing sectarian thought. But I am not arguing against their ideals, only against their believing that they must achieve them all at once or not at all. We have all been talking to each other in the Labour movement too long if we cannot see that long before the public will ever want nuances of socialist principle, they are right now very hungry for almost any kind of principles in politics. So great dangers as well as opportunities appear. Some sense of integrity, some sense of move-ment, some sense of common purposes and fraternity, some lessening of injustices in rewards – never mind quite precisely what, is what the public seems hungry for at this very time. The public seem to thirst for something positive, but all they get is people knocking on the doors with questionnaires asking them what policies they want their leaders to lead them with – some leaders! The present leader of the Labour Party seems like an ignorant nurse who believes that constant applica-tion of a thermometer will lower the patient's temperature.

Liberty

Leaders should just try what they believe in and find out if it is popular. But the manner in which socialist leaders try and in which they find out should be distinctively open, participative and subject to correc-tion. The one easily recognisable mark of a democratic Socialist move-ment should be its almost fanatic commitment to more liberty and openness. The means are not the ends but they can make or break the ends. And as even Rosa Luxemburg said of Lenin, a socialism that does not proceed through freedom becomes oppression. All talk of 'socialist liberty', as if it were different in kind from any other, is dangerous nonsense, often deliberate obfuscation. Far-away thoughts? I am no longer sure when one thinks of students howling down Sir Keith Joseph, or of campus bookshop assistants refusing to stock, order, or handle books hostile to what they judge to be 'the student' cause.

More immediately, official talk of 'open government' is rhetorical nonsense when it goes with the maintenance of traditional, conservative controls over publicity, the belief of all autocracies and autocrats that government cannot work well if the reasons why decisions are made can be publicly known. In fact, there is a kind of British half-autocracy: Tony, Alan, Bernard, John, Robin, David, Peter and the statutory woman could have always read – and did – Crossman's *Diaries* without the Attorney-General or a High Court Judge's permission; but not the rest of you. All school kids in the country can be taught that the ombudsman is a 'good thing' – they and their teachers seem captivated by him – but the Government could reply to his criticisms last year of Mr. Benn and Mr. Shore not with honest and beguiling admissions, nor with reasoned rebuttals, but with the ignorant and ignoring contempt that seems to possess modern governments with even the slenderest of mere parliamentary majorities. The Government damps down the Poulson inquiries. And the Labour Party National Executive refused even a Party inquiry into the affairs of the N.E. England Labour Party. Have we come all the way for this?

The Right think that they can pick and choose what liberties to adopt in their own interests – sound on Clay Cross, but hostile to workers' control. Very few are libertarians at heart. But those of the Left who are libertarians at heart often get themselves trapped in bad Marxist logic. Only in the classless society after the revolution can there be true liberty – until then all we have is an instrumental 'bourgeois liberty' or an 'oppressive tolerance'. (Therefore no holds barred in your own strategies, but tactical howls of 'liberty in danger' every time the law comes near you.) But active liberty has a long history, and it was bourgeois in its origins. The fault is not in its paternity but in its prudishness. Liberty is all very well for the likes of us but impossible *en masse*, for all of them.

But we must be promiscuous in liberty if we have any faith in reason and human nature. 'The liberal bourgeois is genuinely liberal', said Orwell, 'up to the point where his own interests stop.' What we must do is constantly to try to persuade people that their idea of self-interest is self-defeatingly narrow; and that ideals widen our horizon into the future, particularly our children's future. 'Do you want *them* to grow up into a world like *this*?' is the strongest practical socialist idealism. It is not so much that the impractical of today can be practical tomorrow, but that in the modern world the practical of today is always the impractical of tomorrow.

Socialist liberty is no different from liberal liberty, except that there is more of it for all: a humanistic faith that ordinary working people have to be drawn into participation and decision-making too, and not just in leisure time but in working life. Of course an incomes policy under Socialism, but ultimately a voluntary one – how else? How else, that is, without ever greater centralised controls and oppression in fewer and fewer hands? If from political democracy we cannot also create economic, industrial and occupational democracy, then we drift towards a '1984' kind of society – though more likely to be one, as Tocqueville imagined, in which the elite dole out welfare rather than privation. So long as they can make the decisions, the masses can have everything possible given to them, except freedom.

If socialist liberty does differ from liberal liberty in one respect, it is in that it goes back, like the men of the French Revolution, to a classical or Roman concept of liberty more than a *laissez-faire* one: not just being left free by the state, which is often to be left high and dry, but that each man and woman should exercise freedom aggressively. A state is neither as strong nor as just as it can be if its inhabitants do not act like citizens – nor is a union, a firm or a school. Citizenship and liberty is enhanced by example and by multiplying participative institutions in all spheres. We could stop short of 'extremist' Socialism and yet make some public stir about that. But what a long way from the practical policies of our great leader's fourth administration.

Equality

Equality is a value basic to any possible kind of socialism. Without a real desire to achieve an egalitarian society, any democratic Socialist movement loses its dynamic and lapses back into the alternating ping-pong politics of the 'I'm a better manager of the shop than Fred' kind (whatever trash the shop is selling, however badly built it is). But the concept has its difficulties. Literal equality, whether of opportunity, treatment or result (or of all three), is almost as undesirable as it is plainly impossible. But an egalitarian society is both possible and desirable. By an egalitarian society I mean a classless society, one in which every man and woman would see everyone else as a brother or sister, a genuinely fraternal society with no conceit or constraint of class to limit fraternity. But it would not be a society in which everyone was exactly equal in power, status, wealth and ability, still less in humane end-products of happiness.

No difficulties about the concept are, however, so great as to warrant abandoning it or treating it as pure ritual of the Labour church – unless one wants to abandon it. One difficulty is that we want, rhetorically, to make something sound positive which is, intellectually, at heart a negative matter. There is no 'complete equality' which can 'finally be realised,' unless genetic engineering was to come to the aid of economic planning (with about equal accuracy and predictability, one would hope). But there are so many unjustifiable inequalities – not just in theory but so flagrantly in practice. The boot should be worn on that foot. If we believe in the moral equality or the fraternity of all mankind, then all inequalities of power, status and wealth need explaining and justifying. They can be justified (here I follow Rawls and Runciman) only if these inequalities can be shown to be of positive advantage to the less advantaged. Some inequalities can be justified, more not – particularly if one adds a vital condition of democracy, actually to ask the disadvantaged. No precise agreement can ever be reached or, if so, for no more than a transitory time and a particular place. Nor can philosophy supply incontrovertible criteria for what is an unjustifiable inequality. But in an egalitarian society *all* inequalities will be called into question, constantly questioned and criticised: they will have to be justified precisely and for themselves; not as an acceptable, general side-product of status or power.

'Less Unjustifiable Inequalities!' may not be a slogan that warms the blood like wine, but that is as well. For there are other values to be preserved, which is always the difficulty. No one value, be it liberty, equality, fraternity, love, reason, even life itself, can at all times override all the others or be sure never to contradict them. Equality could certainly be maximised in a totalitarian society – but only at the expense of liberty, thereby destroying genuine fraternity. The Socialist, having a theory of society, looks at values together, in their social setting and in relation to each other. He no more postpones liberty until the classless society than he reserves egalitarian and fraternal behaviour and example until the classless society. If he does, he will not get there; and when he does, classlessness by itself will not have solved all problems and removed all possibilities of tyranny.

The moderate socialist as egalitarian should not get drawn into the parody argument of exact equality of income and wealth: that is somebody else's nightmare not his dream. Literal-minded distributive socialism is very hard to find – since the time of the Gracchi at least. 'Soak the fat boys and spread it thin', may be good rhetoric, but most people know how thin it would be. Industrial relations are not as bad as they are because the men on the shop floor believe that the cow can make milk without grass or that 'vast profits' are there to be distributed to our direct advantage – about 6p a week more all round, once and for all, on Friday and bust by Monday; but they are bad because men think that it is *unfair* that they should be restrained while their bosses actually write to tell newspapers that in their cases incentives to do better do not begin until about £15,000 a year; and that they have no real incentive to work anyway if their children or the cats' homes cannot freely inherit all their wealth. Workers, oddly, use their eyes and see how much patriotic restraint is practised by those who at least look like ruling classes. They see clearly the gross extravagance of Ascot, of the West End and of the fashionable residential areas. (Photographs of such should be forbidden – they do far more harm to 'our civilisation' than do those pictures of which Lord Longford complains and blames.) And working men do not miss the claim of top civil servants that their salaries should be competitive with industry (as if they, too, shared the Marxist-Capitalist view of the exclusive importance of economic motivation), and should be inflation proof even, on top of a non-contributory pension. What servants of the State! What example! *Quis custodiet ipso custodies,* indeed. Nothing better illustrates the decline of the traditional restraints of the cult of the gentleman and the growth of the moral standards of the speculators and property developers.

Equality is, then, a demand for equal justice not for proportional distribution. But the parody is sometimes accepted, perhaps because some Labour leaders begin to have doubts, from the company they keep, as to the potential popularity of the ideal at all. Most people, they feel, want no more than equality of opportunity; and only then if they are among the disadvantaged in 'the great game', to transfer Kipling's phrase to the happy world of Keith Joseph. This destruction of socialist morals and morale earns newspaper praise as 'realism' or 'pragmatism'. Here the moderate socialist parts company with many Right-wing Labour MPs.

True, ordinary people will commonly get no further than 'equality of opportunity', if you put the question to them in such an abstract and general way. But suppose you ask them if they think it right that the top twenty per cent of incomes (before tax) had seven times greater a share in the total income than the bottom twenty per cent, or (findings of the recent Royal Commission on the Distribution of Income and Wealth) that sixty-seven per cent of the personal wealth in the country is possesed by the top ten per cent? The answer may then differ. And answers will certainly differ in terms of perceptions of the justice or not of particular rewards and relativities.

Here is an incredibly undeveloped area of liberty and openness. We are so full of taboos about disclosing incomes, even though civil servants and teachers are among obvious exceptions. Suppose all incomes were disclosed? Suppose it was a constant topic of debate in the mass media: 'Here's what this man or woman does, here's what they do, here's what they get. Is it fair?' If this happened, justifications for differences would have to be produced and discussed seriously – not as easy, however, as to knock the miners for their muscle tactics, or praise them for their temporary restraint, or to knock MPs for the crass folly of the timing of their own pay award last year.

Amid full openness, many differences and some injustices would remain. Surveys show that many unskilled and poorly paid people seem to believe that almost no salary is too high for the greedy medical consultants – so socialised have we all been about the long and worthy tribulations (investment) of medical education. (Do not let them leave the country, I say, unless they pay it back.) But it is likely that genuine knowledge, publicity and debate would help to raise the floor and bring down the ceiling. By itself it could not create an egalitarian society, but it would be a condition for it. There would emerge, whatever the justifications for particular inequalities and relativities, a public view of a minimum and a maximum income. An incomes policy would be acceptable if it was, thus, a genuinely socialist one; establishing what range of differentiation is tolerable to an informed majority.

Are there still some primitives who think that any income differentials are contrary to socialist principles? If there are, they are less in number, I suspect, than the hypocrites and careerists who can always find some reason for a Labour Government not to enforce some fairly modest, middle middle-class income as a maximum income.

If socialism means anything, the theory is that with greater equality there can be greater fraternity, hence greater co-operation, hence greater productivity – since wealth basically comes from the worker. The record of British management of late hardly impresses one with the claim that only ever-continuing economic incentives lead to efficient management. Power and status count for a lot and so does having a clear and worthwhile job. Real managers like to produce, but the English upper middle class now prefer the City to industry. Their kind of mentality led even a Labour Government to leave 'the white-hot heat of the technological revolution' for the paper battle of saving the pound. (The class of men who would do it better and do it for less are from the foremen, the junior managers, the technical teachers, that border-land between the old skilled workers and the old lower middle class, so many of whose sons and daughters are now, in beliefs and behaviour, so unexpectedly but clearly if precariously classless.)

So much scope for action remains in the direction of greater equality: not to be represented or misrepresented as levelling but rather as a constant, aggressive questioning of the reasons for and the justifications of both existing distribution of incomes and wealth and existing divisions of responsibility between 'workers' and 'management'. Such questioning could prove as popular as it is right. More important for socialism than abstract arguments about formal ownership is progress towards taking all wages and incomes out of the market and determining them by representative arbitration and open comparison of relativities. The media, even now, could give a lead in popularising knowledge of differences between jobs and of different incomes. People are surely fascinated by this. And public policy should work towards complete openness of all incomes. Many differences can be justified. But they must be. We need to develop this as a whole new branch of applied social philosophy rather than of traditional economics. If we had shown one half of the energy in this direction that we have shown in educational policies, an egalitarian society would be appreciably nearer. Indeed, we must beware that, perhaps mainly out of frustration with national economic policies, we do not hope for too much from mere education nor drop out, as it were, from political economy into a fantasy of the comprehensive school as a model of the Socialist commonwealth. Especially in education we should not confuse literal equality of treatment with true egalitarianism. For true egalitarianism is no more – but no less – than the removal of unjustifiable inequalities; and it is a necessary condition, but not a sufficient condition, for fraternity.

Fraternity

To appeal for more fraternity and less fratricide within the Labour movement needs a thick skin as well as a clear head. The Labour movement used to be proud of exhibiting within itself the very fraternity it wished to create in society as a whole, but of late brother seems more eager to revile brother, and sister sister, than to argue with opponents and to seek to persuade the vast majority of the unconvinced.

Any advance towards a Socialist Britain needs, first, more democracy; a greater opening up to popular influence and knowledge of all the institutions that shape our lives. This is real liberty. Secondly, it requires a constant public demand for justification (if any) of each particular inequality of reward, together with gradual but systematic and determined action to reduce those inequalities. This is not equality but 'egalitarianism'. But, thirdly, it requires an attitude of mind, a morality, a psychology, which gives equal respect and care to everyone, irrespective of class, kin, race, religion, office, talent or learning – 'fraternity'. Our preachers should say: 'And now abideth liberty, equality, fraternity, these three; but the greatest of these is fraternity . . .'.

Equality of respect does not, however, imply either – as Runciman puts it – 'equality of praise' or the confusion of sincerity with truth. Is it rational to treat all opinions as equal? And is it brotherly to treat all people as one would ideally have them rather than as they themselves are? Big brotherly, perhaps. But fraternity is treating all men as ends and not means, not just all societies. It does not mean treating everybody the same but according to their different personalities and needs; and it means reconciling conflicts by mutually acceptable, public political institutions.

An enforced equality is the destruction of brotherhood – the dark warning of Orwell's *Nineteen Eighty-Four*. Fraternity can, indeed, exist amid great inequality, but only in times of emergency: the comradeship of the trenches, the Dunkirk spirit, and 'the years of struggle' of both Left-wing and Right-wing political movements. But a fraternity for everyday wear in all seasons is hardly imaginable amid great inequalities which limit common purposes. Doing things together for ourselves in common enhances fraternity – unlike having equal welfare given to us which, if personal involvement is lacking, too often creates jealousies rather than comradeship. Economic controls by themselves can never guarantee a more fraternal society. Simple arithmetical equality could create even fiercer competition. We must not oversociologise. Social conditions can help or hinder but they can neither guarantee the consummation of fraternity – nor even ensure its destruction. Fraternity is an ethic that can and should be chosen and pursued freely. It goes with simplicity, lack of ostentation, friendliness, helpfulness, kindliness, and decent restraint between individuals, not just with the fierce memories of the great occasions, the times of struggle or the Sunday 'socialism' of Saturday afternoon demos.

Fraternity does not mean no leadership; it only means no permanent class of leaders tomorrow and no *noblesse oblige* today – no condescension, no giving favours but rather receiving trust on account of peculiar skills of both empathy and action in helping common and commonly defined purposes. In Beethoven's *Fidelio* the king hails all men as his brothers. But the power and arrogance of a king or a modern leader who thinks that he had such a gift to bestow will of itself negate the brotherhood. Even Edmund Burke said that it was hard to argue on one's knees. Some still try. The boss in a small firm or office who drinks with the men and chats with the girls is only being matey, perhaps even condescending or politic, but not genuinely fraternal unless he seeks for their opinions and takes them seriously about how things should be run.

Nor does fraternity imply the necessity of pseudo-proletarian behaviour. Society is not altered as quickly as a change of costume on a bare stage. The oldest blue jeans will now attempt to hide the newest wealth. But that leaders of working-class parties are commonly bourgeois is neither surprising nor reprehensible. For bourgeois culture stresses individualisic skills of initiative, while working-class culture, in response to exploitation and oppression, stresses solidarity. The culture of the classless society is, indeed, more likely to be bourgeois in the best sense than proletarian. It will encourage and respect individual skills, talents, personality, character; not a new iron mould of conformity, however better than the one that went before. The virtue of class solidarity was an adaptation to class injustice and would become regressive if ever class differentiation vanishes to the point of irrelevance. So the cultural ideals of a democratic socialist movement must be more than the revival of a few folk songs and dialects: amid the new we should sift, refine, adapt, but offer the best of the old to all. And that best includes the moral seriousness of the puritan tradition of individualism as found in Lawrence and in Orwell, neither the purely acquisitive, competitive individualism of capitalism nor the indulgent, permissive, irresponsible individualism of anarchic socialism. Seriousness tempers personality into sociability.

Fraternity must begin at home but be extended to the work-place. It is not simply a luxury for schools or an indulgence for radical teachers. Indeed, we must beware of over-stating the relevance of education to achieving an egalitarian and fraternal society. Far from being the spearhead of Socialist advance, as some hope and others fear, schools may be in danger of becoming the last refuge of noble and frustrated Socialist minds, baffled at the seeming uncontrollability of the national economy or of their national leadership. We must beware of hoping for too much from schools and of overburdening them with the type of concern for 'character education' we all once attacked – not just because it was the wrong kind of character.

As I wrote the original articles on which this essay is based as serial parts in the *New Statesman* , correspondence almost entirely concentrated on the fact that I had admitted openly in a newspaper to sending my sons to a private school. My difficulty was (and still is) that I just do not see the issue as that important compared to gross inequalities of income and housing. State education is not yet a necessary shibboleth of Socialism. As a scholar, I have scholarly values. Some comprehensive schools do, some do not. Amid conflicting values, I make a local choice. I assume that scholarship is among the permitted range of human choices which will be found in a democratic Socialist society. But my generous critics seem to admit only one possible kind of motive in wanting such an education, that of social advance. Their sociology tells them that there is only one real reason for going to private schools; mine tells me that, in any case, the home is more important socially than the school. Fellow socialists seem more worried at individual cash choices involving education than about those involving housing. I am simply not as sure as my critics why, within the higher minimum income and the lower maximum income which I advocate as a socialist wages policy and as our first priority for action, some such choices are thought legitimate, some not; they would matter less if we had such a programme.

I am more worried at the educational fashion for 'mixed ability groups' right down the line in LEA schools. In some subjects the state sector is now almost doomed to inferiority. We may have got the worst of both worlds by leaving the private sector free but seeking to abolish the direct-grant grammar schools. I would hesitate long, however, in the name of liberty before abolishing the private sector in the name of equality until the public sector returns to the original ideal of the comprehensive school: that under one roof pupils would be treated differently according to their different abilities in different subjects or different skills, but never all in the same class for everything, never treated *en masse.* The doctrine of 'mixed ability' classes is either a bad confusion between literal equality and egalitarianism, or more likely a rationalisation of despair at having too few teachers and too many children to make the old ideal of 'to each according to his abilities' work. Knowledge can be used for social status, but limiting access to knowledge will not create equality of status. We must not destroy anything unless there is something better to put in its place, and do not let us destroy education as we destroy privilege. My socialist ideal is a common educational system; but my moderation makes me see this as coming through time and through infinite gradations of different forms of both control and content in education, not through expropriation and proscription. These points are worth labouring because they touch on liberty as well as equality in a way difficult for many Socialists.

The state system has its problems too. Perhaps it is sometimes justifiable to bus children against their will away from their neighbourhood to satisfy intelligence-quotient planning. But we must at least recognise that 'community' suffers, which is also a great Socialist value. We may be making the same mistake as in the new towns policy and the high-rise flats. We must recognise that no one knows if the policy of an initial equal distribution leads to a less discriminatory final result over all, than would positive discrimination in the supply of teachers and resources for the less-favoured schools.

Of course, if all housing were state-owned and equitably distributed and if all environments were made equal . . .

What we do know is that social stratification is still acute inside schools. This is not surprising, for the evidence is strong that schools have little effect on basic values and behaviour patterns compared to the influence of home, the media and society at large. Educational systems work badly, it is good to know, as vehicles for deliberate indoctrination, whether of the Rhodes Boyson and Ronald Butt variety or of the Revolutionary Socialist kind. Most guff is like unto water off a duck's back. Pupils react sceptically against any such abuse or extension of authority. But the schools work better at developing skills to understand the world: they are rather unlikely instruments to change it. If one wants an egalitarian educational system, first we must change society.

Let us get our priorities right. Fraternity is not something to be thrust on kids as a sacred episode before they are pitch-forked into the real industrial word; it is something that has to be applied in the real industrial world. And fraternity is more concerned with individuality than is literal equality: but it is always endangered or frustrated by gross inequalities of power, wealth or status. Certainly education is among these inequalities. But as we are now and will be for some decades at least, once we leave the classroom or the ward meeting, the illusion is over. In the real world, however, there is vast scope for making far more of what is there already – the expertise and experience of the man who knows the job and who cares for the persons and views of his colleagues or workmates. Fraternity is simply taking commonsense and common concern seriously.

The Second Chance

The long summer of national power, prosperity and self-conceit is nearly over and socialists in the Labour Party must face the fact that in times of relative ease we have failed, but that during a winter of crisis we may be given a second chance. (The first chance was squandered from 1945–50.) We have failed not merely through failures of governments to use their power in socialist directions, but more basically through a failure in the days of affluence of the Labour Movement itself to persuade an effective majority of the electorate that we should build a better Britain, not just on occasion manage the shop better. Our declining share of the vote (39.2 per cent in October 1974) is a pitiful basis for radical and freely willed social change. Individual membership of the party, even, continues to decline (probably now no more than a quarter of a million compared to a million in 1953) – despite the help of all those Reds whom Miss Beloff finds under other people's beds. The party now is too small either to reflect public opinion or to be able to influence it.

A genuinely socialist society needs the resolute use of centralised power, but that power is itself powerless, in any modern industrial society, unless it can carry with it popular support. And such support must be found both in the grass roots and in all those groups in which we work or spend our leisure, where both our opinions do count (somewhat) and in which our opinions are influenced (somewhat) by our fellows. Only in war did we achieve a unity of purpose, great productive efficiency and (for a brief and memorable moment) a sense of fraternity. Yes, indeed, a fraternity that largely depended on external threat: nonetheless, it was on the home front between 1940 and 1945 that both the need and the practicality of a welfare state was proved. 'Equality of Sacrifice' and 'Fair Shares For All' became, instead of competitive individualism, both the official ideology of work and popular belief and behaviour.

We could be close to such a situation again. 'Equality of Sacrifice' may be both a national need and a genuinely popular slogan. Perhaps it was always unlikely that the average person would be converted to socialism in relatively affluent times. Socialism does not aim at austerity, but it becomes plausible (particularly its value of fraternity), the idealistic suddenly appears practical, indeed necessary, in times of enforced austerity. Perhaps Socialism is, at heart, a prophecy of what could happen if the capitalist economy breaks down, rather than a safe prediction that it will. But while the free market in wages may not yet be quite beyond repair, its defects have proved so strong both in terms of uncertainty and injustice, that many could now be persuaded that it is not worth repairing. A more planned and egalitarian society, albeit one hungry for and jealous of liberty, will avoid these savage oscillations of prosperity and depression which marked and marred classical capitalism and which now threaten even that minimal certainty of expectations on which the mental health of societies, as well as individuals, depend.

Ordinary working people cannot be expected to practise self-restraint and to suffer or to watch mass unemployment grow while businessmen and top civil servants enjoy huge salaries and the perquisites of office far beyond even middle-class standards; such luxury amid deprivation is not merely indecent and immoral, it grows politically untenable. If governing elites still wish to govern, they must set an example in the patriotism, public spirit and austerity that they preach to others, not themselves get in first in the endless claims for socially useless personal material advantage. The wiser of those new Right-wing intellectuals of free-market liberalism see the difficulty and preach the need for restraint and example to the businessmen. But without sanctions they could save their breath to cool their porridge: they become either naive or hypocritical.

So an egalitarian incomes policy, setting a national maximum and minimum and establishing public machinery to arbitrate relativities between severe limits, should be Labour's policy for the crisis, and the greatest step forward ever towards democratic Socialism. Such arbitration would not be the bureaucratic imposition of 'objective' criteria, but rather publicity for and public discussion of what other people do and get. The object is to establish what people *think* to be fair and will accept as fair, to educate us all in making genuine comparisons, not to pretend that full objective criteria are possible, either of national need or of job specification. Such factors of job evaluation and of statistical evaluations of differentials are highly relevant, but not decisive; a greater sense of fairness is the greatest need. Complete openness about incomes and wealth and constant public debate would create the voluntary basis to emerge for an enforceable consensus on outer limits. And with lower and upper limits there could be a vast simplification of tax and welfare structures. Within such limits, market forces would work; prices can only reflect what people actually want to buy and sell.

A Socialist incomes policy calls for a Left and Centre alliance in the Labour Party. As a moderate Socialist I find *Tribune* both too wild and woolly and the Social Democratic alliance too class-conscious and complacent. The Left at last begins to emerge from the temporary delusion that a free market for wages and the industrial power of a few unions on behalf of their own members can lead towards social justice, or that prices can be controlled when we live by export and import. The Left and the unions will accept incomes policy only if it strikes hard at high incomes, and in this they are both just and sensible. The Right of the party would regard this as impractical. Their version of incomes policy has only been aimed at the unions; and they have for long indeed abandoned any talk of Socialism – except for party workers at weekends – in favour of a kind of John F. Kennedy Democratic Party fantasy complex or complex fantasy.

Some of the Right would actually prefer to do without the party at all and appeal directly to the electorate, rather as some of the Left, for all their rhetoric of 'the people' (remember the Referendum) would prefer to do without the electorate (or elect another one). The Centre of the Labour Party is still warmly but rather vaguely socialist, but has, of late, either been too absorbed in practical work to think very much, living off some very run-down mental capital, or has actually lost hope of the practicality of Socialism in British conditions, but without quite losing their faith. This sleeping giant could be woken by the economic crisis.

Even the Fabian Society shows some glimpses of trying to think about general principles again, rather than the constant administrative war-game of arguing that this or that social service is scandalously under financed and if given more would be the key to a more healthy and salubrious future (the worst legacy – someone had to say it sometime – of the Titmuss school: worthiness, energy, dedication, indeed; but a complete lack of theory, hence of direction: *noblesse oblige* plus B.Sc.(Econ.).

What the Press call 'moderate' is usually the Right of the Labour Party; *i.e.* the centre of the national spectrum. The true moderate in the Labour Party, however, is anyone, whether of the Left or the Centre, who aims at transforming our society to a better one *by political means* and who sees the main priority as themselves persuading the unconvinced, not as enforcing dogmatic purity within the ranks or as threatening freedom of the Press – as if a Press wholly controlled by unions or syndics could convert a pliant public to Socialism, rather than that a more socialist public should be demanding, by how they spend their 10ps, a more socialist Press. Political means are the acceptance of effective representative institutions, including Parliament, above all, but now needing to reach far more people in their own neighbourhoods and work-places than ever Parliament did; and the need to persuade people openly and fairly; not to deceive or coerce them, even for their own good.

Democratic procedures cannot allow, for instance, MPs a property right in their seat; but equally parties must be no more immune than unions, indeed voluntary bodies of all kinds, from reform to ensure a greater and wider democracy (the only answer to infiltration is not less membership and less democracy, but more). But politics and democratic procedures are not ends in themselves. They are ways of pursuing ends. And fairness or social justice is not just the perpetual patchwork fairness of the best possible as we are: it could be something permanently better. All kinds of disputes may always remain; but they can be lifted to a higher level.

The opportunity now presents itself in crisis and in need. The affluent spree is over for ever. Guilt and remorse begin to replace sheer bewilderment, even some fear arises. For even if we can learn to live easily with ourselves again, Europe as a whole still has to come to terms with the Third World. But some hope, too, for there is a mood of seriousness and a thirst for principles. Clear and simple formulations of doctrine are needed as never before. Labour finds its basic principles in trying to create more fraternity and liberty for all, in denying all democratically unjustifiable inequalities, and in acting on the belief that ultimately it is the worker who creates wealth and that his co-operation and mutual aid create fraternity. If the party can show by behaviour and policy that it follows these, then it has a much more compelling and relevant rhetoric than the precarious 'our man is a better manager than yours' into which we have so despicably and foolishly descended.

The pure idealist is useless, but so is the pure pragmatist. We have to work on different levels, to look far ahead as we try to do the best we can right now; to imagine people as they could be, while we deal with them as they are. Political compromises are not sell-outs nor debased pragmatism if the long-term sense of purpose is clear and if we are taking clear steps forward. 'The man who striveth for the mastery', said St. Paul (himself no mean proselytiser), 'is temperate in all things' – if he is really interested in mastery, not just in the negative power of keeping a label saying 'leader' on a private door or 'pure Socialist' on a banner of a purely propagandist weekly. Genuine Socialist leadership is collective. The 'long term' is being quickened by the crisis more than by our own exertions. But can the Labour Party be ready to seize the chance to demonstrate, for the first time since 1945, the relevance of Socialism to the majority not yet convinced? Advance by 'small steps' by all means, as Roy Hattersley argued, echoing Willi Brandt; but steps need to be placed deliberately on top of each other, not scattered surrealistically, one by one, over a landscape as opportunity arises. And we build at a moderate pace towards *Socialism* (not 'radicalism', please). Radicalism is only an attitude of mind, a style, an itch; Socialism is both a theory of society and a moral doctrine. It only needs to be taken seriously.

It needs to be argued. At a time of crisis and national self-doubt, the public are no longer impressed by the shopping-list electoral arguments of 'we did' and 'you didn't', whether based on Left or Right-wing manifestos. It would be a grim irony if the Powells and the Keith-Josephs carried greater weight because of the greater clarity of their principles, than those of the traditional men of doctrine, the socialists of the Labour Party, suddenly turned pragmatic, practical, that is with nothing to offer unless the winds blow fair – which they do not.[2] And so much extreme ideology is the souring of good doctrine by the bland or contemptuous refusal of practical men of politics or administration to think long, to think systematically, to think morally, almost to think at all.

Notes
1. Roy Hattersley, 'The Radical Alternative', *New Statesman*, October 31, 1975. (And in another healthy piece in that journal he wrote about the joys of jogging. I wrote in supporting his claim, only adding that it was difficult to tell in which direction he was jogging. Elephants never forget. This proved to be a good because it was costly joke.
2. Thirteen years later, forgive me for saying 'told you so'. Thatcherism has proved not merely that the traditional doctrine of a great political party can be changed internally but that an elaborate, highly abstract, even (*pace* Hayek and Friedman) 'academic' ideology can be popularised with sufficient force to sustain major legislation and basic changes in society and the economy. Labour's response was confused, belated and then inadequate. (See chapter 16 below, 'Labour's Aims and Values: the Official Version.)

Polemics

Twelve

Mrs. Thatcher Changes the Rules

* From The Scotsman, 29 December 1986.

For many of us life is so comfortable that it takes an almost morbid exercise of imagination to feel that kind of political despair in our own country that is not just fear of a marginally wrong result in a fair and fairly decent contest, but is shock, pain, grief and horror. Normally we reserve these thoughts for the Third World or for aspects of Communist rule. And even then we can always turn the page, close the book, change the channel or switch off. Few of us could bear to have an imagination as acute as that of the philosopher Rousseau who said, in a letter to Mirabeau the elder, that since he despaired of finding a form of government that would set law above the individual, he therefore wanted a perfect individual to be set above the law. He could see no middle way between 'the austerest democracy and the most complete Hobbism'. But when he thought of who had been extolled as god-like: 'Caligula, Nero, Tiberius! Good God! I roll myself in the dust and groan to think that I am a man'.

I groan and want to roll in the dust. And this is not from mad excess of party zeal. Of course it matters who we are governed by. But I must admit that the election of a Conservative Government dominated by people like Walker, Heath, Prior, Gilmore, Baker, Pym, Biffen and Hurd, etc, would not seem like the end of the world. I would groan but not roll in the dust. And compared to a Government headed by – a most unrealistic thought – a Benn or a Heffer, I might not even raise a groan. One can accept many things of which one disapproves, up to a point. I groan to think what has become of our country now that we have a Government with a big lead in the opinion polls and yet which is not merely misgoverning grossly but in a callous and triumphalist manner. Unemployment and disabling poverty have increased greatly during its time in office. But it says only three things: there is not *really* as much as you think; there is nothing that we can do about it that won't destroy the livelihood of the rest of us, and that a good deal of unemployment and poverty is the fault of the unemployed and poor themselves.

How can this have happened? Let me try to face this frightening question. For it flies in the face of all our post-war experience and of what hitherto we had thought of as a kind of national decency, compassion and concern for others. The war first showed us that it was possible to avoid unemployment. After the war it was not merely an object of social policy, shared by all parties, but it was a very sensitive register of election results. Economists generally calculated that about two and a half per cent unemployment was normal and necessary, those between jobs and those seeking better jobs. Anything above that, even one per cent more unemployment, immediately led to measurable election swings of two or three per cent. Was four per cent unemployment even perceptible? Probably not, yet in by-elections, as study after study showed, swings could be correlated with even slightly higher unemployment, even when people were not themselves aware of the figures! It was as if there was some unconscious social mechanism of record in local communities, like bees knowing the need for more honey, or for fewer workers.

And in any case, what really determines how people vote, don't vote or (very rarely) change their vote, when all arguments were said and done about social class of ideology and policy? The best general explanation for significant marginal change is still what Edmund Burke said it was two hundred years ago: 'General Elections are determined by the conduct of the late Administration'. Most people vote as they did before, but enough can be swayed by believing that the Government has done well or badly to settle the matter. How *can* any Government still be ahead in the polls that has seen unemployment rise so spectacularly; poverty and its effects increase to such visible proportions, even to those in work; and the social services, including the schools, above all the Health Service, deteriorate (oh yes, indeed, 'more money spent on them than ever before', but not in real terms when inflation and ageing are considered)? Even the great victory (at a price) over inflation now seems insecure, and the balance of payments again threatens even cynical and tactical increases in public expenditure.

Those are the key issues in the public mind. It also happens that the Government has come under tremendous criticism for politicising the higher Civil Service; for destroying the once famous objectivity of central government's economic statistics; for actually encouraging British capitalists and capital-holding institutions to invest abroad and play the stock market rather than invest in British industry; for favouring American multi-nationals over British companies; for allowing our air-bases to be used for illegal and morally appalling reprisal bombings (probably against the wrong terrorists); to leave Britain isolated in the Commonwealth by our reluctance to move against the brutal and racist South African regime; and has mislead the Press, threatened the impartiality of the BBC and misused MI5 and MI6 for partisan advantage in a manner never seen in this country before except in war-time. And issues of personal autocracy involving the Prime Minister have arisen that can now make us wonder whether we still have cabinet government, collective ministerial responsibility and any separation of powers between the political executive and the Whitehall machine. The charges against the Prime Minister go far beyond 'pig-headedness'. Her destruction of local government for the capital city of the United Kingdom is not seriously believed by anyone to be other than malevolent, autocratic, caprice. She has also lead a frightening shift of power from local to central government. So here is a quite extraordinary record of misgovernment and also of destruction of long established constitutional conventions. She acts as if the other side will never get back, should never get back. And the rules of the game are being changed to that end. She speaks of getting rid of socialism entirely, and the Tebbits and the Lawsons now speculate about a new kind of two-party system: a permanent Conservative majority and a centre party where Tory Wets and Owenites will huff and puff but do no harm.

How has this happened? By every historical and rational test the Tories should be trailing.

Well, of course, it hasn't happened in Scotland; but that is not going to help us here. There is no constitutional remedy. If Thatcher gets back for a third term I don't see any signs in Scotland, as yet, not even in the SNP, of that willingness to go into civil disobedience, even of the kind the old Irish Home Rule Parnellites and Redmondites practised, that might force a Home Rule Bill out of a reluctant Westminster. You may say that it is all the fault of the Labour Party. I don't think so. I believe it has been well led recently. Its revival in popular support since the time of Callaghan and then Foot's leadership is impressive. The criticisms of its leadership and policies that one hears in the quality Press and in the sad little journals of the Left simply don't touch the public mind – like nearly all the failures of the Tory Government I listed. The matters thought important to readers of this paper are simply not those featured in the popular Press.

To realise what it is that keeps Maggie afloat, read from time to time, but then closely, a discarded copy of the *Mail*, the *Express* or the *Sun*. Their readers live in a different conceptual world. To them, for example, the unemployed are unemployed because they don't want to work. It is as if Mrs. Thatcher has been able to persuade, not a majority, but still about forty per cent of the electorate of three things – all of which represent a vast shift from the post-war consensus: that governments have little or no control over 'the fundamental economic forces' that determine the level of employment; that you and I are in jobs not because of luck or initial advantages but because we are virtuous and hardworking (or conversely the others are out of jobs because they are lazy and immoral); and that any attempt by the State from sentimentality to remedy unemployment will be a subsidy to the work-shy and shifty from the pockets of the hard-working and worth.

It is a melodramatic perversion of the Protestant work ethic, It tries to divide the country between the permanent majority of those in work and a new permanent minority of unemployed. If this sombre analysis is correct, it follows that it is absurd for Labour to pretend or fool itself that it can persuade the public that it is, as both Kinnock and Hattersley argue, the party that really believes in industry and productivity. It must reverse the whole conceptual shift. It must fight back from its good old ground of appealing to the decency and compassion in people – while there is some left. Fear creates a terrible selfishness, an unwillingness even to know what is happening to our society. Faith in human decency needs reasserting.

Thirteen

Labour's Principles

* From *The New Statesman*, 19 December, 1986.

A spectre is haunting the Labour Party – to make an unseasonal remark, the spectre of pure thought. We are in the middle of a remarkable revival of democratic socialist thought, this time led by political philosophers and social theorists rather than, as in the 1930s and 1940s, economists – though straight away it must be said that the political philosophers I'll be talking about and stealing from are far more economically literate than a generation ago, just as most economists, no longer wring their hands at political factors spoiling economic calculations but accept that the world is like that, and might be worse without.

There is a practical need to define not merely goals but also principles. 'Goals' define objectives and 'principles' define conduct: where should socialism be going and, quite as important, how should socialists behave in the great here and now, not just in public but in private life? We commonly use the word 'values' to cover both goals and principles. I will. But the distinction is often very important. Some dwell entirely in a world of theory and goals, their private lives carrying no vestige of socialism except the subject matter of dinner table conversation – the trendies, of whom David Edgar provided a Dickensian sketch at a Muswell Hill party in his play, *May Days*.

Such people claim, of course, to be absolutely egalitarian in their love affairs – which may sometimes be true; but they are tactfully silent about that key question of empirical sociology, 'parents class and income'. Others actually practice a life-style socialism, of demos, protests, women's rights, tenants' rights, advice centres, actually helping actual people in trouble. Most of these are aggressively working class and the social traveller has to work harder than ever Orwell did among tramps to be accepted. Many of them, however, are completely innocent of any precise or systematic thinking, simply one shot or two shot crusaders; and the claims made by ecologists, alternative-lifers, Greens and health fanatics to have a *comprehensive* ideology are embarrassing. Consistent and self-contained, yes; comprehensive no.

185

From a rather unlikely centre pure thought has broken out and is beginning, yes, to permeate. The Fabian Society held a large but private meeting after the election defeat of 1983 to discuss what should be done (by, was the unstated major premise, intellectuals). Those invited were all known to be democratic socialists whose discourse was public. Readers of the middle generation will know just what I mean: people who did not limit their thinking to the narcissistic question of the problems that the real world (such as a majority of the skilled working class voting Tory) *posed for Marxist theory*, and people who can write plain, accessible English. The idea arose to set up a philosophy group for democratic socialists.

Thirty years ago political philosophy had almost ceased to be a public discourse, had become an academic discipline, riven by demarcation disputes between Philosophy and Politics, each very internalised and given to such questions as 'does political philosophy exist?' and 'in what sense, if any, are ethical statements meaningful?' Philosophy, in other words, was still trying to escape from a moralistic and metaphysical tradition. But now the atmosphere is different. The debate is still largely internalised but philosophers are ceasing just to say 'meaning is usage' but to examine actual usages, especially of ethical and political – 'essentially contestable' – terms.

They try to examine the conceptual and value assumptions contained in practical activities and social problems. 'Animal Rights', 'The Protection of Privacy', fine; but before you charge off and spend your life on it and demand public resources, spare a moment's thought to define these terms more carefully. They carry no essential meaning, but if you don't adapt your usage to some well known convention, you won't be understood; and if you don't define the terms reasonably precisely any practical application – since concepts may sometimes be born individually but always live together in clusters – will be riven with contradictions. So a younger generation of political philosophers now think in that way, and some sociologists and applied economists have seen the need and caught the style. The huge literature on equality is a good example: philosophical and empirical considerations are separable and must be; but good work knows the other, like the sociologist Julian Legrand and, in politics and social administration, Raymond Plant.

This style of thinking is still too speculative and unsystematic – usually taking one concept at a time, be it rights, liberty, equality, community needs, property etc. etc. – for the many ex-hard or ex-highbrow Marxists who are now coming to terms with democratic socialism. They begin to take seriously Tom Bottomores's old argument that Marxism must be seen as a method of social investigation not as a comprehensive structure of abstract ideas for which 'the correct policy, comrade' can be logically inferred.

Hobsbawm has said much the same, also Edward Thompson, both in an historical mode, whereas Bottomore advocates an eclectic sociology, making use of relevant theories and ideas from wherever they come. Nonetheless, the 'ex-s', liberal, democratic free or young Marxists, what you will, are often reaching the same kind of conclusions as these new Fabians by different routes and from different roots.

Mike Rustin's *Towards a Socialist Pluralism* is good common ground, as was Gavin Kitching's *Rethinking Socialism* with its uncomfortable argument that it is very difficult to create anything but a despotic socialism in a poor and underdeveloped country: equal citizenship is most easily built upon the accumulation of capital of an advanced capitalist society. This so shocked the trendy princes of the *New Left Review* that the book made little impact where it was aimed, though his view of stages was closer to Marx's than theirs and his experience of East Africa profound.

An actual bridge between the democratic Marxists and the Fabian group is Paul Hirst who has moved from being the high priest of British Althusserianism ('daddy, what was that?') into being an actual member of the Fabian Society, centre-Left Labour Party and taking up the cudgels so well in this journal for liberty in the sad Ruskin College (sub-judice) case. He is turning from Marx into a new Sidney Webb – and by god we need one.

What the new revisionist Marxists have in common with the New Fabians (besides freedom of the pages of *Marxism Today*) is pluralism and liberty, as well as equality. And in both philosophical and political senses. To the new Fabians, pluralism arises because any basic values, however well defined, must carry at least different shades of meaning in relation to the other values that a person or group must hold; philosophically these are incorrigible, there are no definitive, single or 'essential' true meanings, but not all are consistent with each other and some are more plausible than others or more practicable in policy.

To the new Marxists pluralism means accepting that not all values are ideologically determined by class or economic formation – even in his late Althusserian stage Hirst was talking about 'the relative autonomy of ideology'; but that nations, regions, ethnic groups, gender groups, say 'communities' (if that catch-all warm but smothering term is well-defined) can be good things in themselves, not all explained as malformations of class interest and economic exploitation. The sociological argument in Hobsbawm's famous *The Forward March of Labour Halted?* (don't forget the question mark) is crucial: that only for a brief period of the late industrial revolution was there *an* English working class. Now we are back in an earlier world of a plurality of working classes with different attitudes, needs and responses conditioned by regional culture and occupation. (Go on, he never said there wasn't such a thing as working class anymore, only *a* work-

ing class. Get it?). Similarly for 'liberty', it is philosophically the negation of determinism. And if there are physical limitations to human life
and activities, within them very important choices can be made:
always choices, even when they are (in the happy lands) torturing you
and escape is quite hopeless. What has all this to do with the Labour
Party in its hour of hope and travail? Let me shelter behind Peter
Kellner. On 28 November, 1986 he gave his whole *New Statesman*
column to a review of a Fabian pamphlet by members of the Socialist
Philosophy Group, *Market Socialism: Whose Choice?* And John Lloyd
wrote a full article about it where interest must be acute (I'm not
joking) in the *Financial Times*.

The pamphlet is important, both for its manner and its content. It is
speculative and analytical, not trying to reach any immediate and
comprehensive policy conclusion. It comes from a group of people
sharing most value assumptions but reasoning and differing among
each other but without that familiar intent to club each other with cries
of 'that's not true socialism'. Of course, as Kellner rightly concluded,
the project must be to modify capitalism by regulation of markets in
the public interest (defined as socialists would define public interest),
not to modify state socialism.

Theirs is a welcome breath of realism. We have to start from where
we are, in a capitalist mixed economy. The models of actual state
socialism are not very appealing and the degree of command and centralisation has a lot to do with the absence of freedom and the suppression of pluralistic elements in such systems. Our own native model of
the nationalised public corporation may be good for the big utilities
and 'natural monopolies', but for little else.

Oh how different it might have been if the Polytechnics of the first
part of this century had produced a generation of socialist engineers
and managers (the mighty vision of Shaw and Wells). Or if
MacDonald had had a working majority and had gone for democratic
educational reform. But to go forward, we start from where we are and
who we are. That is all that 'realism' means. But this new realism has a
sense of direction, otherwise it would be mere time-serving (Wilsonian) pragmatism. The Fabian discussion was stimulated (Sally
Jenkinson's contribution points out, as does David Miller and Saul
Estrin's) by Alex Nove's *The Economics of Feasible Socialism*.

Of course the Labour Party believes in a mixed-economy. But the
term is so ill-defined as often to lead to both scepticism and fudge. It
needs clarifying. The Labour Party's new 'social ownership' policy has
opened up the issues, to almost any interpretation, more than clarifying them. There is still a lot of resistance forthcoming in the party to
facing reality. A quick glance at a bootleg set of proofs of Roy Hattersley's *Choose Freedom: The Future of Democratic Socialism*, shows it to be
a major work that devotes much thought to defining where markets are
appropriate, where not and what kinds of controls are needed.

People have made shibboleths of particular means, but it is the ends that need spelling out and defining. To talk of realism without also talking of principles and of long term goals is, indeed, to invite accusations of time serving. Happily no one is more aware of this than Neil Kinnock. He is a true heir of Nye Bevan. He embodies the old Labour Left's good rhetoric of values. In a series of recent speeches he tried to delineate them – revive them indeed, after Wilson's abandonment – but to point them to modern conditions. There was his Mackintosh Memorial Lecture of June 1983, a shortened version of which appeared in this journal; his Fabian Autumn Lecture of November 1985, 'The Future of Socialism'; and his recent 'Righting the Wrongs of the New Right' to the Gorton Fabian Society on 11 September 1986.

The latter was a passionate attempt to claw back from the Radical Right the reputation of at least being the guardians of liberty. Bryan Gould made a good shot at the same task two years ago, in a book that used some of the Fabian group material. Kinnock deployed not just Tawney's classic argument that liberty for all needs a far greater equality of social condition, but is bold to argue that socialists must accept liberty against themselves. Council tenants don't have to vote Labour to have rights, and exercise individual choices. By implication it is fairly clear what the Leader thinks about boycotts on newspapers. But when Kinnock chose recently to make up a book from speeches and articles, it was from a group of addresses mainly to industry, *Making Our Way: investing in Britains future*. They argue that Labour is the party that can get British industry working again. I suppose this was a tactical choice. It was well-meant. But a lot of it *sounded* (it hurts to say this) like the bombast of Wilson's first term. He still argues that 'the central role in British strategic planning must be performed by a Department of Trade and Industry', but, of course, not a passive one: 'what is needed is an active, entrepreneurial ministry, a ministry of movers, of new ideas, of new initiatives'. I'm frightened that this could just be words, that he hasn't thought it through; that the answers may lie more in the Fabian group's thoughts about controls on markets.

Where he could have given a lead would have been precisely in the area of those other speeches. Let me shelter behind Peter Kellner again. In 1985 he reported having seen on Geoff Bish's desk at Walworth Road a large bundle that was the first draft of a statement on the party's basic beliefs, commissioned by the NEC. What has happened to it? By now it is plainly still-born.

There are three theories: (i) That the leader likes the idea – so much that he can't let go of it himself, but with no time to redo it. (ii) That he fears to reopen old wounds on the NEC. The Benns and the Heffers still view themselves as the priests of the covenant of Labour's values, and that all other versions are merely pragmatic dilutions of their true if esoteric scroll, and to an astonishing extent the Right share this view.

(iii) That the party secretary and the campaign team regard any such statement so close to an election as a hideous hostage to fortune; any reassurance and redirection it would give to party activists is more than offset by opportunities for mischief in the Tory Press.

But if there was such a document (and it is badly needed – win or lose) I think it fairly clear what it would contain. There is an authentic British democratic socialist tradition. Yes, an affirmation of *freedom* and of the social conditions needed for freedom for all, but not just the passive freedom of rights against the state (in the classic liberal tradition), but a positive freedom of active citizenship (in the French republican tradition, or that of 'Scottish democracy'). Yes, an affirmation of *equality* , but egalitarianism rather than literal equality: an application of the now famous argument of John Rawls (I couldn't care less that he is an American liberal) that all inequalities must be exposed and justified to show whether or not they serve the public interest.

Yes, community, 'fraternity' or sociability (each term has some difficulties). We want the warmth, mutual aid and cooperation of true communities, but not, for instance, at the expense of the rights of women (there are communities and communities). Democratic socialists are humanists and heirs to the enlightenment, human rights must override some customs of traditional communities. Just *think*.

Yes *and* no to the State. We need it to further the national welfare and to protect us, but democratic socialism is now, not only in Britain, very sceptical, almost hostile, to putting too much reliance on the state: cultural pluralism is a positive value now, not just a sociological description or the debris of imperfectly articulated class formations, etc. All power does corrupt: some levels are not safe. Or perhaps there is not a party statement of principles and goals because some of these things are still too divisive and need more thinking out, reasoning about and publicising. Policies without solid foundations either collapse or are too easily moveable, dispensable after the meeting or election has been held.

Fourteen

Labour and Electoral Reform

* From *The Guardian*, 4 August 1987.

Of course the Labour Party is going to brush up its image and modernise its policies. But it is still in doubt whether it will be able to do this in any coherent manner, to produce a restatement of doctrine to match Thatcherism's ability to have a popular ideology from which policies appear to flow. Neil Kinnock's instincts are right, but the production of such a document is not easy and will be fought over, and also fought against by pragmatists around him, some of whom forget what happened when Wilson and Callaghan tried to play a purely tactical, non-doctrinal, almost anti-doctrinal politics. Yet image and ideology, however reformed, cannot avoid the great tactical dilemma – so obvious and terrible that it has been made taboo among Labour Party leaders and officials.

Labour's best fought campaign in living memory has still left the Conservatives 146 seats and eleven per cent ahead. Even if the Alliance's challenge of 1983 to be main opposition party has been fought off, anti-Conservative votes are hopelessly split. Yes, fifty-three per cent (ignoring Plaid and the SNP) did not want a Conservative Government; but sixty-five per cent did not want Labour either.

Whatever happens this summer in the 'Alliance,' some third force is here to stay. After the 'to merge or not to merge' trauma it could well have a stronger base. David Steel was wise to get Liberals' blood-letting over quickly; Labour may delay and delay until it is too late.

Anywhere else in Europe, an electoral pact would be the obvious and popular response to the political situation. But, within the Labour Party, there are some who would still rather be in opposition for ever than 'betray socialism'. And even if Labour's leaders negotiated an electoral pact with the Democrats it would be crazy to assume that Democrat voters could simply be delivered by their leaders to Labour, especially Labour as is.

Most Labour strategists seem to agree with the gut instinct of their activists that a continuous attack should be launched on Alliance leaders for the sin of splitting the vote and the general futility of their miserable existence. Labour would then inherit most of the vote.

Some hope! In June 1987 MORI asked voters how they would react if neither the Conservative nor Labour Party won an overall majority in the General Election. Of Alliance votes twenty-five per cent went for another general election quickly, forty-three per cent for a Conservative/Alliance government and only twenty-nine per cent backed a Labour/Alliance government. These figures, together with 'second choice' statistics, suggest that if the Alliance fell apart at this moment, far more refugee voters would go to the Tories than to Labour.

Peter Kellner pointed out recently that Labour's undoubted revival under Kinnock's leadership has now restored its votes to precisely the same proportionate share of each of the five main social class categories as in 1964.

Again, in 1987, a majority of skilled workers voted Labour, removing the shame of 1983! But the absolute numbers of both the skilled and unskilled working class have declined. Working-class consciousness and life-style are still there all right, but not in the numbers. And remember that about thirty per cent of the working classes voted Conservative even in the post-war decades.

To win next time Labour will need to claw back one hundred seats, nearly all of which must be in the South since in the North and in Scotland Labour's cup is already full to overflowing. This would now be a change of historical dimensions.

However much Labour modernises its policies and image, can it now rationally hope for an absolute victory next time starting from a seemingly frozen thirty-two per cent of the vote and needing three million more in Southern England? The cool, honest, and unwanted answer is clear. The leadership must have honesty and courage to face the party with this dilemma now.

The party must grasp that the choice is between its intense conservatism in constitutional thought and an electoral agreement with the Liberal Party or a new Alliance. For, of course, their terms would be electoral reform, probably a Bill of Rights too, a Freedom of Information Act and Scottish devolution... But if Labour aspires to be a United Kingdom, not just a Scottish and a North of England party, with a tincture of Welsh, then PR has positive attractions.

Parts of the country that are completely unrepresented by Labour would at least gain a proportional representation. Mass *de facto* disenfranchisement would be over. The Scottish Labour Party should have made it part of their proposals for a Scottish Assembly. In Northern Ireland all parties, take it for granted.

Under PR Labour might never form a majority government again which the electorate seem unlikely to allow anyway. Yet Labour could be the dominant partner for a very long time. Is the risk worth it that the Conservatives get in again on a minority vote? But electoral arrangements would only work if Labour's policies come closer to what the country wants.

One of the two things most repellent to Liberal activists about the Labour Party is beginning to be tackled by the Labour Party forthrightly: the unrepresentative eccentricity of a few of the English city Labour Parties. But the other is the problem of the power of the unions in the Labour Party, especially when with declining membership and de-industrialisation almost half of union membership are now in the public sector.

So much of Labour's good old altruism can now, as in the defence of the Health Service, be all too easily misrepresented as, in the words of the song, 'we are the job preservation society'. That is the difficult one. But Labour owes it to the country, which would otherwise suffer even longer under Thatcher or her chosen successor, not to shut its ears to negotiations with the Liberals or a new Alliance. If both parties become more clear about their own strength and identities, then they can bargain sensibly.

Fifteen

Two Cheers for Party Loyalty

* From *The Scotsman*, 8 June, 1987

Trotsky said at the Fifth Congress of the Communist International in 1924: 'The English have a saying: "my country, right or wrong". We must say, right or wrong, on separate political issues, it is my party'. No thanks, and look what happened to him. (No democrat he, by the way, just a rival Stalin.) Orwell said 'the writer can never be a loyal member of a party' (he was a member of a party at the time).

I prefer E.M. Forster's 'two cheers for democracy', the title of a wartime essay. 'Three cheers' he said, should alone be given (quoting Swinburne) 'to love, the beloved Republic'. Perhaps, so long as one thinks of love (in *both* senses) in general, like an imaginary country, and not of 'separate issues'. Then it is kindest, to oneself and others, to be a little sceptical as well as greatly loving. That is part of what Montaigne meant by humanism. Poor Morgan Forster can hardly have found, any more than Swinburne, great happiness of fulfilment in his great love – the improbable police constable from Bayswater.

Forster's real love and loyalty was to his craft of writing, and which always called for much rewriting – scepticism and self-criticism. He did not believe that the first thing to fall on paper was the best, authentic and inspired. Would that politicians had such scepticism. Love can be holding off as well as coming on. 'Scepticism', Santayana said, 'is the chastity of the intellect; one does not give oneself to the first set of new ideas that come along.' But, of course, politicians have to take the lead and to go over the top bravely. We cannot all sit at home like Hamlet agonising until an enemy forces action.

But need politicians be quite so self-righteous and quick to blame everything on the others? That's what I've found hard to take in the [election] campaign. I believe that if Kinnock had used his honest image to make a really honest speech about the faults of the Labour Party in the Wilson, Callaghan and Foot eras (not just the bash at Militant), it would have rattled the polls upwards: 'Let us agonisingly admit with wholehearted honesty that in the past the party has made many major mistakes, and we have sometimes claimed to control things that are not essentially subject to control ...' I could have written him one, and just about imagine him delivering it (even if it offended all the old Wilson creeps and courtiers); but Thatcher or Owen? I hope I make you laugh.

Humility is possible in a statesman. That is why the memory of Abraham Lincoln is so important. 'I think the impression was Lincoln was a pretty sad man', Franklin Roosevelt once said, 'because he could not do all he wanted to do at one time, I think you will find examples where Lincoln had to compromise ... to make a few gains. Lincoln was one of those unfortunate people called "a politician" but he was practical enough to get a great many things for his country'. True scepticism (knowing that nothing will be perfect and that 'the best laid schemes o' mice and men ...' etc) and humility and honesty are very close to each other as moral virtues, indeed are publicly impressive virtues. Oddly some of the Tory Wets have touches of it, not just out of dislike of Mrs. Thatcher's arrogance but by temperament: they want to improve things, they have more compassion than her, but they know (a) that limits of manoeuvre are more narrow than most leaders will admit and (b) that nothing turns out quite as good as expected, even when better than before.

And that's what I don't like about the SDP leadership. They seem stuck in a 1960s technological rhetoric, as if constitutional reform and computer reform, in the hands of professional people with Upper Second degrees, will solve most of the heartaches and the thousand natural shocks the flesh is heir to.

I am only saying that like most other people with commonsense some of my attitudes towards Thursday are a wee bit negative. Even in 1974 I put a child-made poster into my Hampstead window: 'Voter, give an honest curse/Defend the bad against far worse. Vote Labour'. Actually I have moved a lot with Kinnock's Labour Party and the scansion wouldn't work to substitute 'imperfect' for 'bad'. But my fears of her in a third term are very great. I'd vote for almost anyone to get rid of her. I did join the Labour Party at 17. So my Labour credentials are good. And I became ward secretary (though a public school boy with a stammer) six months later in a working-class ward of South Croydon, so short even then were some of the parties in solid areas of active members. By 1970 the Hampstead Labour Party tried to throw me out for excessive scepticism, but failed. I had written in the *Observer* that I was 'a banker's order member of the party, it takes away the annual crisis of conscience'. They were horrified to find that bankers' orders were permitted: the old Labour ethos was searching for small sums of money on the doorstep for someone who never had change on a November evening while all the heat – 'No, I won't come in comrade' – escaped from the home.

People were rude enough to be surprised that I didn't join the Great

Secession, when the Wee Frees left the Labour Party in 1981. I wrote that I was 'too old to rat. I'm going down with the ship and the brass band playing'. I thought the situation pretty desperate but knew that the last fight had to be fought inside the party.And, by God, it was won. Poor Shirley. She made the wrong judgement. Had she stayed in with Healey, Hattersley, Radice, John Smith, with whose politics she scarcely differed, she might have been ... But Kinnock's leadership within the party has been superb.

I'd still welcome more frankness about 'residual troubles', and only then the pointing finger at those in glass houses; not just the big and petty City swindlers among Tory MPs, but the many more total cynics and opportunists who see a parliamentary seat as a route to seats on the board, or a ministerial job as a route to a chairmanship.

I was talking to some London teachers the other day, among them old friends and also life-long Labour Party supporters; and several of them lived in boroughs in London where they say they cannot in conscience vote Labour. This is not appreciated in Scotland. I find the Labour Party in Scotland still like 'the good old' London Labour Party I knew before I emigrated. More frankness would have won round more people who recognise and don't like glib evasions. And if anyone believed Kinnock saying 'never' to coalition, they might well have been scared off.

No doubt, however, how I'm voting on Thursday. Labour does show compassion for the other half of the divided nations whom Thatcherites and their Yuppie 'I'm all right Jack' followers simply leave to rot. Labour is aware that the very mortality rates of the poor and the unemployed are horribly higher than those of the middle classes in work. I want to be taxed for them and believe, like Lloyd George in 1906, that graduated income tax is social justice.

And I don't believe that we need a nuclear bomb to be British (and in the circumstances welcome Mr. Powell's support), nor that the Soviets can now ever move West. The state of their economy guarantees that and the West is in danger of losing an historic opportunity for negotiating real peace. Where did this sudden revival of post-war war-scares come from? And why? The answers are obvious and the cynicism involved is appalling.

Sixteen

Labour's Aims and Values: The Official Version

* From *Tribune*, 16 May 1988

I write in sorrow more than anger. Royden Harrison (*Tribune* March 25) has already condemned the Kinnock-Hattersley draft statement of 'Aims and Values' as being 'wordy and vague' and repeating most of the mistakes, by implication, of Hugh Gaitskell's explicit assault on Clause Four. In fairness to him, it now appears that he was reading the Hattersley-Kinnock first draft version before the Kinnock camp struck back (or re-read what they had agreed to). But in candour I don't think that Royden Harrison, or any others of the 'old Left' whom it was meant, in part, if not to please at least to placate, would find the present version much better.

Megnad Desai (*Tribune* March 18 1988) argued that the document, in seeking to answer Thatcherism, has become trapped in many of the assumptions of our opponents, ending up more eager not to offend than likely to please. He also drew attention to the sad banality and flat ordinariness of its language: it does not even read like a historic statement. And Eric Hobsbawm, writing in the April 1988 issue of *Marxism Today*, complained of its excessive 'defensiveness', 'intellectual weakness', 'lack of vision' and parochiality. He also pointed to both the paucity and the emptiness of references to 'democracy', 'decentralisation' and 'technology'. The second and probably the final draft of the statement, before it goes to conference for adoption, reads to me as if some attempts have been made to respond to Hobsbawm's magisterial critique. The changes all improve the document but don't overcome both a fundamental addiction to vagueness and a basic uncertainty as to audience and purpose. I can only add that it is likely to please our opponents because it is an intellectual mess, trying hard with adjectives and abstract nouns to avoid difficult issues, and it will dishearten us because it is neither a classic restatement of the grounds of our beliefs nor a rethinking of them in terms that can be applied to present-day social conditions and policy.

The document has no core: it is a series of surface compromises between democratic socialism and social democracy. It has no sense of history. The party apparently has no paternity or, if so, no pride in it. There is not even an evocative list of the party's great achievements, thinkers and heroes. Perhaps even that was too contentious. Didn't William Morris call himself a communist? Anyway, who has heard of him? And if Aneurin Bevan was to be mentioned then presumably Gaitskell too for balance, so in the result (as committees work) we get neither. Not even R.H. Tawney is mentioned, even though both great men love to quote him – but which passages? Which Tawney do they quote? So the result is neither lively tiger nor dignified lion but a pantomime horse whose head and tail try to sit down together but fall between two stools heavily.

What is really at issue? Why such a statement at all? The demand arose for a statement of *aims* and *values* precisely because, on the one hand, the old Gaitskellite and Wilsonian pragmatism had been seen to have failed and, on the other, many Marxists were beginning to rediscover a sense of values as well as doubts about structural explanations and over generalised theories.

Perhaps the old ethical tradition of British socialism, which had been mocked by Marxists and was good for giggles by managerially and now consumerist minded Fabians, had something to be said for it, if only it could be expressed concisely and with reasons. It would reactivate the party and reassure the country.

Everyone knows that 'Labour cares', but what are its motives for caring? Why is it now easier, asked the leader himself in his Fabian Autumn lecture of 1985, *The Future of Socialism*, to list Margaret Thatcher's beliefs than our own? People used to describe socialism as 'a noble ideal but impractical' and socialists as 'impractical idealists'. But now our old ability to win the moral arguments, or at least to choose to fight on moral high ground, seems lost in the electorally nervous understatements of our Right wing and in the reckless over-statements of the hard Left (such charming and plausible appeals to the electorate as 'Forward the Revolutionary Struggle of the Proletariat', even in its pastoral-Chartist-Methodist-ecumenical-Bennite version).

Searching for agreement on fundamental *theories* socialism seemed a blind alley, or at least one far removed from policy and best left to the difficult pages of the *New Left Review*. But there was a growing, haunting belief that, Left and Right, we all had more in common as regards both values and ultimate aims than might always appear amid controversies over policies and tactics. (Not all differences on tactics are ideological.) And these aims and values were not shared, for instance, by Militants who believed in the cleansing tonic of revolutionary violence, nor by some Social Democrats, within or without the party, who are simply reasonably decent career-minded liberals and not in the least egalitarian or community-minded.

Equality of opportunity is the only equality they know. And the absolute primacy of the economic, which some saw as the foundation-stone of socialist theory, is now only argued by old-fashioned Marxists and neo-Liberal vulgar Hayekians (that is, Thatcherites).

Michael Foot drew attention to the primacy of the ethical in democratic socialism in his essay *My Kind of Socialism* (reprinted from *The Observer* 1982), a fine piece of writing unhappily forgotten in the present debate. And in an essay in his book, *Debts of Honour,* he quoted Ignazio Silone, the great Italian socialist and former Communist, to the same effect:

> I cannot conceive of Socialism tied to any particular theory, only to a faith. The more socialist theories claim to be 'scientific' the more transitory they are. But socialist values are permanent. The distinction between theories and values is still not clearly enough understood by those who ponder these problems, but it is fundamental. A school or a system of propaganda may be founded on a collection of theories, but only a system of values can construct a culture, a civilisation, a new way of living together.

Labour could capitalise on its old woolly moralism: wool is strong when knitted tight. But a distinction should have been drawn between aims and values, the web and the woof.

'Aims' point to future objectives of a general kind, and 'values' are ethical precepts which govern how we behave and how we think it right to pursue aims. An egalitarian society could be the aim, for instance, but if we have libertarian and/or individualistic values as well, these limit some ways in which equality can be pursued. A strong state or a fervid community *could* try to make everyone equal. Similarly if we say, as the astonishing first sentence of the official document does, 'The true purpose of democratic socialism ... is the creation of a genuinely free society', then if we are egalitarian in our values, this will both affect how we pursue that goal and what precisely we meant by it.

I find it very difficult to conceive of a 'free society' as a goal, rather than as a fundamental value: it is only meaningful as a goal if one is attacking a palpably unfree, despotic society. Leaving aside, for a moment, how well or badly the task was done, yet the focus or precise sense of purpose kept on slipping. What Kinnock first seemed to want, to judge by public speeches in the exciting and hopeful early days of his leadership, was precisely a classic restatement of existing aims and values.

He thought that would be good for the party and good for the country – not that marginal or floating voters read pamphlets but they do recognise what parties appear to be animated by. From that, policies could be rethought, and so on in the light of changing circumstances.

Yet, unhappily, others had doubts about the enterprise at all. Better to let sleeping dogs lie and stick to image-making, instant opposition and practical policies. Might not some of our good old values prove electorally embarrassing: the egalitarianism of active party members, or the very mention of 'fraternity' (unmentioned)? Was not all that neo-Bevanite Foot-like moralism precisely what repelled practical people like one's bank manager or one's brother-in-law in advertising who also dislike – 'between ourselves', they'll say if one speaks sensibly to them – Thatcher's holier-than-thou uplift, whether Victorian or Californian.

'Neil can blow his old Bevanism out of his system by giving all those passionate addresses to local meetings, but when it comes to serious drafting in Westminster and the Walworth Road or to the general election ...'

So an unusual event occurred in British politics: a debate among our political leaders and their advisers about a profound theoretical issue: the influence of ideas on action. Had Thatcherism proved so success-ful against the Tory 'Wets' and with socially mobile voters *because* of its doctrinal convictions or *despite* them? Had people welcomed 'a new stress on *values*' – even if the wrong ones (plainly not all values are equal)? Or was Thatcher's conviction politics irrelevant and her electoral success simply a product of (what we never mention in public) the division of the anti-Tory vote and the antique electoral system? If so, ... wasn't this a chance for a sanitised Labour Party to show itself the inheritor of a consensual, practical, non-doctrinal but caring politics (in other words, as Giles Radice and Austin Mitchell at least have the guts to advocate openly, to steal the Liberals' clothes)?

Kinnock temperamentally and originally was of the ideological school. 'You can't beat something with nothing'. 'One should learn from the political success of Thatcher's conviction politics'. But unhappily the pragmatists won. They are usually so much better informed and organised on each particular issue. So far from the project of a statement of basic aims and values being seen as a necessary preliminary to the reviews of policy, both logically and in time; it became itself part of the process of revision, indeed submerged in the process, the values themselves coming up for grabs or drastic redefinition. The horse is now firmly behind the cart. Only Kinnock himself appeared to attach much importance to the orginal enterprise, hoping at first to do it himself with minimal help, but then, defeated by the grim restraints of time in the office of leader and by a badly organised office (coherent and reasoned thought does take time), he could produce only a warm rhetoric and occasional flashes of intellec-tual insight.

One can speculate on one's feet and orate on one's feet, but the one thing one cannot do (contrary to macho political myth) is think on one's feet. What has emerged is a quite lifeless compromise between those who wanted a fundamental statement of aims and values and those who didn't want it at all, only new images and new policies and three-piece suits all round.

It was well said that a camel was a horse designed by a committee. Two sides of a committee, however small, jockeying for position on future policy statements, were always unlikely to produce a classic statement of our aims and values. By a classic statement I simply mean a summary of known and accepted tradition written in language that is memorable and aspires to last. Perhaps if a classic statement had been produced it could then have been argued that Labour's basic values need rethinking. I don't think so, but it is conceivable.

Any statement in politics will have some gaps or fudge. But this one is so riddled with endemic tooth-rotting fudge because it is so intellectually confused between values and policies. Worse, much of the fudge seems to arise not so much from our leader's lasting love of generalities but from a counter-attack against the old Kinnock-Bevanite democratic socialism by social democratic thinkers – people who, to their honour, stayed with the party when the 'Gang of Four' left, but now seem to want, as they see it, the old Gaitskellite policies back as the price of loyalty. Didn't George Orwell once write of 'the back-stairs creeps, the courtiers and the arse-lickers of the Labour Party'?

To see the classic socialist values as a hierarchy headed 'above all else by freedom' is either pure social democracy or sheer intellectual muddle. We do not live in a one-crop moral economy. What is distinctive about democratic socialism, as indeed of any other complex doctrine, is that a small group of characteristic values support but also modify each other, fortify but interrelate, sing in harmony, not unison. To assert the primacy of equality, say over liberty and fraternity is autocratic, just as to assert the primacy of freedom alone, unqualified by other values, is classical liberalism or *laissez-faire* capitalism.

Modern philosophy teaches us (if anyone listens) that there can be no one 'true meaning' of complex concepts like 'socialism', nor a clear and permanent hierarchy of the component values. There is no objection to talking about liberty and freedom first, whether for intellectual, tactical or purely traditional reasons. 'Liberty, Equality, Fraternity!' is a grand old phrase. What is objectionable is to imply that freedom always overrules the others and what is silly is thinking that people will believe us if we say so. As in Roy Hattersley's book *Choose Freedom*, political thought is subsidiary to public relations.

We need to say openly that it follows from our egalitarian values that we believe that a stiffly graduated income tax and high inheritance taxes are elementary principles of social justice. Differential wealth may owe a lot to individual initiative, but wealth itself is a social product.

The Official statement does say clearly that a *more* equal society will mean that more people can make use of otherwise only abstract and potential freedoms. But it does not present egalitarianism as a virtue nor does it clearly say that the freedom of the rich to use their wealth as they like *should* be contained. Social democrats say that taxing the rich as such has very little redistributive effect. Perhaps. But socialists need to say that high taxation is a principle of social justice: none should wallow in it while others want. The opinion polls over Nigel Lawson's tax cuts in general and the starving of the National Health Service show that excessive caution about challenging Thatcher's basic assumptions is unnecessary. Faced by that choice, clear majorities opposed the tax cuts.

The revised version does have more to say than the first draft did about Labour's traditional commitment to local government and it twice invokes 'pluralism', but without saying what it means or even hinting that Labour's tradition once included decentralisation, workers' control and a philosophical pluralist critique of the very idea that the state is sovereign. True, there were always a few Leninists in relation to theory of the state and always far more Webbite-Fabians: 'control the central state and provide uniform welfare for others!'

Indeed judging by nearly everything published in the last ten years by Labour intellectuals and writers, I had thought that we were witnessing not merely a revival but a final victory of the pluralist tradition.

But the draft statement shows that the Fabian centralist mentality is still very strong in – let's be blunt – the Hattersley camp; and that while Kinnock says the right things in a very generalised way, he won't commit himself to structures.

No mention of devolution, nor even good platitudes about us being a multi-national state and society. The Scots will growl, and they are the most radical section of the Labour Party at the moment. And no mention of constitutional reform which was widely debated prior to the delusive 'total victory' of 1945.

The sections on social ownership and the mix of a mixed economy are sensible but so tactical as to mean almost anything to anyone. The 'classless society' has vanished, only 'more equality': even treating everyone as equals as a moral necessity is not clearly stated. The whole thing is not a thoughtful attempt to state what our common values are but is an attempt to pre-empt argument about short-term tactics and immediate policies. It will go through, of course. But it won't stick and will be soon forgotten. It speaks neither to the heart nor to the head. What a pity – what haste and what a wasted chance!

Seventeen

Chequebook History

* From *The New Statesman* 29 April, 1983 about the serialisation of the forged Hitler diaries.

It came a year early. Not until next year will Winston Smith receive his copy of Goldstein's testament from O'Brien – the secret history of how the Party corrupted the ideals of the revolution – only to discover that O'Brien and the Party have forged it. Winston should not have been so gullible, since he works in the Ministry of Truth rewriting back-numbers of *The Times*.

Satires have a way of coming true. Orwell, with grotesque Swiftian imagery, was as much satirising real tendencies in our society as possibilities of a future one. Regimes control and rewrite history. And when we can no longer recover an historical (as distinct from an ideological) past, both truth and freedom are lost.

Foremost among the defenders of truth are historians. Lord Dacre, Master of Peterhouse, director of *The Times*, was once Hugh Trevor-Roper, the historian whose book *The Last Days of Hitler* seemed a classic of good judgement in handling incomplete and disparate contemporary evidence. He has now betrayed his profession in an extraordinary manner. I have no inside knowledge about the affair. I am not expert in German history. But I do know what History as a discipline is supposed to be about and I do care for principles in public life. These two points seem to have been forgotten. A man is not acting as an historian when he spends half a day amid a large archive in a small room in a Swiss Bank and announces in a hastily written article in last Saturday's *Times*, 'I am convinced of its authenticity'.

Lord Dacre added that, after hearing 'the extraordinary story' of the discovery of the diaries and papers (from the interested parties), 'my doubts gradually dissolved'. Not one shred of evidence did he give, only that three leading handwriting experts had confirmed Hitler's handwriting. He simply handed out an endorsement to *The Times's* product like Ashley Courtenay endorsing an hotel; and as if vulgar doctrines of conflict of interest did not apply to a College Master and a Director of *The Times*. Of course, by Monday, faced with waves of scepticism from German historians and anger at how stupidly and unprofessionally the whole business had been handled, he began to admit a 'possibility' of forgery and to argue that more work needed to be done. He said that he 'stood by what he had written on Saturday,' but, 'I admit that the normal method of historical verification has been sacrificed to the perhaps necessary requirements of a journalistic scoop'.

'Perhaps necessary'! I would that Orwell were alive to read that. Not even the *Daily Mail* was so greedily credulous as *The Times* – lacking a guarantee of authenticity, it turned the papers down. *The Times* statement on Monday made clear (friends fall out) that they proceeded on publication plans because 'Lord Dacre expressed his satisfaction that they were authentic'. Lord help us! The great historian had said that the very size and 'volume' of the find made forgery improbable.

Compared to the size of the stakes, Master? If they were forged by German dealers in Nazi memorabilia, the rewards will be vast –thanks to *Stern*, and Rupert Murdoch and the unholy auction for book publishing rights. If they were forged in the East Zone, then the political capital will be vast: to demonstrate the continued ambivalent grip of the Hitler legend on Western opinion and to infiltrate the divisive stuff about Hitler's continual hopes for British support in an anti-Communist crusade. Whoever forged them, they could also possess genuine Hitler remains in which to set their stinking jewel. And this is not to exclude, of course, the possibility that the corrupt German middlemen are 'honest', have had the stuff planted on them.

History is a craft – the Germans would say a *Wissenschaft*, a science. A 'discipline', we would prefer; but if it cannot produce laws, at least its truths come from following accepted objective procedures that can be verified by others, independently, even if judgements will differ. A true historian would not have argued that the material was 'Hitler-like' – indeed, it is – still less have given a seal of approval to a dubious commercial enterprise. He would have told *Stern* (whose chequebook journalism is notorious) and even his friend the editor of *The Times* (whose losses continue) to go to hell, if they did not from the start meet conditions acceptable to professional historians – time, plenty of time; help and other specialists working alongside (but independently); graphologists of their choosing; and money to perform a laborious, boring but conclusive frequency analysis of the use of common words in known Hitler texts compared to these suspect-until-proven texts.

That was an historian's duty. The plausibility of the tale of how the diaries were discovered *is completely irrelevant*. Each of the middlemen, to protect lives or pockets, could be lying; but the product could be genuine. Each of the middlemen could be telling almost nothing but the truth, and yet a false product could have been planted on them. General Hans Baur, who wrote in his memoirs about Hitler lamenting the loss of his diaries (the solitary mention), had spent nine years as a prisoner in the Soviet Union. Could that paragraph of his memoirs have earned him his release; or, alternatively, have given them a long-term idea, a mental mole? When Lord Dacre now centres his worries on the plausibility of Gerd Heidemann's account of their origins, he reveals himself as an old fashioned story-telling historian, exercising English 'good judgement' (oh god!) about people's character and reliability; scorning technique. The authenticity of the texts is the sole issue and, on a matter of such moral, political and scientific importance, there should have been, right from the beginning, before anyone decent would touch it, an international commission of professional historians imposing their own conditions, as Lord Bullock was quick to suggest.

Does the editor of *The Times* think that mortals can believe that an iron curtain separates the Master of Peterhouse's mind as historian from his mindlessness as director of *The Times?* The *Sunday Times* gave it an inside three-page spread, as well as most of the front page: two pages on how they were discovered, written like pastiche Le Carre; one page on their content, simply assuming them to be true; but nothing on tests of authenticity. Even readers of murder trial reports (another good stand-by) demand and tolerate technical discussion of evidence. On 8 May they promised a special 'Hitler chronicle pull-out section in colour'. Nice for the kids, Rabbi. Now, a quarter of a million pounds later, they begin to develop doubts.

Hitler is too big and evil an heritage of the West to be played with for the sake of newspaper promotion. Proving the authenticity of these works is a solemn and a scholarly task and, until it was proved, publication should never have been contemplated. There is a lot to read already for those who are gravely or psychotically fascinated by Nazism. Why should people who have not read standard books want to read Sunday serials of Hitler's diaries? 'Diaries' is probably the clue. The belief that diaries (even if not forgeries) are somehow personal and authentic. Even Lord Dacre warns that these are propaganda and written as propaganda to be read by us, to affect us. Few public men write diaries for their conscience or for objective history: they write them to try to continue to live in posterity. Serialised, we would read them not for the truth, or even be sure that they were true when reading them, but because they had been sensationalised and their owners were hopeful of their pornographic appeal in the great business of a press war. *Nineteen Eighty-Four* has been with us some time, even in Peterhouse and New Printing House Square.

Eighteen

The Curse of Sovereignty and the Falklands War

* From *The New Statesman*, 14 May 1982, written as the British fleet was nearing the Falkland Isles.

Time and again one has heard very practical British politicians quote the very theoretical German, Clausewitz: 'War is a continuation of politics by other means'. One has also heard that 'our sovereignty has been violated and therefore must be restored'. Both these concepts are grossly misleading, actually limiting our scope of action and hence effective political power. But they have been widely invoked, usually after the event, as justifications for our course of action.

Both General Galtieri's initial action and our disproportionate reaction may have had something to do with politics in the narrowest sense. Nonetheless justifications of these actions are important not merely because actors in events themselves want to feel that they are in the right, but because they have to convince others. All power ultimately rests upon opinion and consent: power has to be there, people have to believe it is there, but someone has to carry out the orders. Pseudo-realists of Left or Right may thunder that 'all politics is based on power', but if by power they mean coercion, physical power, weapons, they are simply wrong: someone has to agree to sail the ships and fly the planes. And force by itself can settle nothing. 'Napoleon forgot', said Tallyrand, 'that you can do anything with bayonets except sit on them'. Both Galtieri and Thatcher forgot too.

The Argentinians obviously thought that a swift and relatively bloodless (they knew how heavily we were defending the islands) seizure of the islands was simply a continuation, possibly a culmination, of a long diplomatic dispute. They did not expect our swift and militant response. They knew as little about the state of our politics as we about theirs. We thought that the mere appearance of force would make them withdraw; and withdrawal seemed to be our clearest aim, although there was also a lot said before the sinking of the *Sheffield* about our sovereignty being non-negotiable. I think that sobered many politicians into remembering that politics is inherently about compromise, and that violence is inherently unpredictable. I prefer

Burns to Clausewitz: 'The best laid schemes o' mice an' men gang aft a-gley.'

Hannah Arendt in her book *On Violence* argued that violence is the breakdown of power, not its extension. 'Power', she said, 'is acting in concert'; it always needs people acting together and hence depends upon opinion. Even the peaceable exercise of power can often lead to unexpected results: violence always leads to unexpected results. Violence may not always escalate, but it can always get out of control. The commanders on the spot have to use their judgement, wisely or not.

Now there are many circumstances in which violence is justified. Self-defence is the classic case, personal and national. Machiavelli said (and he was a good republican) that 'when the very safety of the state is threatened, no consideration of right or wrong, of good or evil' should inhibit its defence: *'aux armes, mes citoyens!'* But the Falkland Islands of 1982 are plainly not the defence of the realm in 1940 – our state is not in danger; and attempts to whip up Dunkirk spirit without a Dunkirk plays with lives. The possibilities of justifying violence diminish in proportion to the size, vagueness and futurity of the aims.

The difficulty is that if the precise political aim was 'to get the Argentinians out', a wholly right and proper thing, this was difficult to translate into a war aim without the Islanders getting hurt.

Political control of armed forces is doubly difficult if they themselves are uncertain precisely what they are supposed to be achieving. There has been a confusing multiplicity of aims; and certainly a lack of proportion between the effects intended and the result achieved. Proportion is never easy to judge. If I am attacked by a mugger and resist, while I know that he (or she) *might* fall and crack his skull open, certainly a greater risk of that happening than if I simply hand over my wallet, yet most moralists and, fortunately, the Common Law would not hold me guilty even of manslaughter; but if when the mugger was down I put in a supplementary boot, perhaps from rage, perhaps (godlike) as punishment, perhaps 'to stop him doing it again' (civic spirit), and he died, my action would be criminal.

In the Falklands crisis, from the first dispatch of Mrs. Thatcher's Armada, one cannot get around *the gross lack of proportion between means and ends*. This is not to condone the action of General Galtieri. One must be quite clear on that. It was a breach of international law and it was not even done to rescue an oppressed Argentinian minority. And if one person is treated unjustly, or killed, or sixteen hundred, it is indeed just as heinous as four or six million. Morality is not compound arithmetic. But many things we know to be wrong, we choose to suffer or ignore, while still holding them to be wrong, because we think that positive action to right these wrongs would create, either directly or indirectly, other or greater evils. I charitably suppose that Conservatives think of unemployment in this way. They acknowledge it to be an evil, but they think that any sudden or unusual remedy would be worse.

Morality may not be a question of proportion but political action always is and the military action got out of proportion very quickly. Certainly military action was launched long before all diplomatic and economic means were exhausted. Why so? Wounded national pride or some antique inhibition about sovereignty being non-negotiable? But sovereignty on whose side? Should *we* really worry whose flag flies over the islands rather than how the inhabitants are governed?

Sovereignty has been a greater curse and a source of more conceptual confusion than even Clausewitz's dubious doctrine. For even if one says that something called 'the State' is sovereign, it does not follow that this sovereignty *should* always be used or *can* always be used.

In the great debate on conciliation with America, Edmund Burke took issue with Lord North on the question of sovereignty and cried: 'I care not if we have a right to make them miserable, have we not an interest to make them happy?' Now Burke did, in fact, think that we had that right, but that we should have enough magnanimity not to use it: 'Great empires and little minds go ill together.' Lord North had a little mind and believed in 'sovereignty' as if it were a living thing, and did not conceive how it could ever be 'divided' or alienated. So he sent his Armada across the world.

Yet we have been alienating so much sovereignty. We could once pass out of our system the sub-continent of India, but we strain at the Falkland Islands. Perhaps the last imperial teeth to be drawn hurt the most, or we indulge in one last morbid domino theory, while we still have some dominoes. If the Falklands go, what about Gibraltar, what about Hong Kong and Kowloon? Indeed. Yet, when we withdrew from East of Suez, we made a fundamental decision on which there was no going back, until the Government practised an insular recidivism. Power without responsibility, as with the General, is foul; but the pretence of power when it no longer exists is irresponsible and reckless. Our real power depends upon acting in close concert with our allies and upon political skills, not upon military force. I weep that we have so exposed ourselves as wanting that kind of power again and not having it, as well as for the dead on both sides.

Many Conservatives are still unhappy at heart that we surrendered our sovereignty to Europe: now is the chance to reassert it. Even Michael Foot, while firm on the unpredictability of military violence, seems to believe that if we resumed our sovereignty from Europe, we would therefore have more economic and political powers. And he feels that devolution necessarily means separation: the theory of sovereignty allows for no halfway houses. So, like Burke and the American colonies, Labour may think it unwise to assert our sovereignty to its full on this or some other issue, but they are sure that we must maintain the right if we are to be a proper and prosperous nation. Alas, this is not merely vulgar nationalism, it is also a grievous misreading of history.

The whole doctrine of sovereignty was connected with the rise of nation states. It was held that there could only be internal order (said Bodin amid French wars of religion, said Hobbes amid English civil wars) if there were a single source of power and authority. This sovereign could override all traditional and customary law when the safety of the state was in question. But there was often a deliberate confusion between 'sovereignty' as a legal doctrine, identifying the source of the law, and 'sovereignty' as a political doctrine, asserting that without centralisation of power there would be anarchy. For people then came to believe that the legally sovereign body, for us once 'the Crown', now Parliament, could do anything (that was not, it was usually added, 'naturally impossible').

This confusion was deliberately exploited by the English ruling class. After 1707 they claimed absolute sovereignty over Scotland, the old story being that the lowlanders surrendered their rights to gain security against the highlanders; and over Ireland after 1800, following the failure of the Dublin Parliament to prevent the rebellion of 1798.

What was less often noticed was how much the claim to possess this sovereign power depended upon Parliament realistically choosing not to exercise it! Scotland retained its own ecclesiastical, legal, local government and educational institutions; and Ulster was never governed either as a normal part of Ireland or a normal part of the United Kingdom. For over two centuries, however, our learned books have called our system centralised, unitary, even socially homogeneous (a real piece of nonsense), and knit together by the mystery of the Sovereignty of Parliament. Our constitutional history might be better re-interpreted as a kind of quasi-federalism. This old elite used the myth of sovereignty to contain the Celts and hold down the Empire; but their *parvenu* successors have ended up believing in it.

If, of course, the whole country is threatened, sovereignty becomes meaningful, as in 1914–18 and 1939–45. Indeed, when massive voluntary support animated the formal mechanisms of a sovereign state, a degree of mobilisation and power was achieved greater than that in the autocracies. But sovereignty by itself is not power, power is political not legal, acting in concert, people acting together: the legal framework only gives the opportunity.

Harold Laski in fact once attacked the whole concept of states needing sovereignty: he saw power as essentially 'federal' or 'pluralistic', even between states let alone among powerful groups within them. But he underestimated the demands of times of national emergency. But again, is this a national emergency? The trouble with war and violence – unlike politics – is that too often the only way back seems to be forward, to redouble the stakes – once an Armada is launched.

Many Labour leaders have sounded as if they believed that there could be no compromise with the Argentinians over sovereignty, just as they veer between all or nothing over Northern Ireland: it must either be a normal part of Ireland or a normal part of the United Kingdom. What is much more likely to happen is some kind of compromise will emerge bit by bit, over the years, that simply mirrors the nature of the problem: that Northern Ireland does face both ways, that some people feel themselves Irish, others British, others Northern Irish, while many actually face these two or three ways at once. Some vaguely similar compromise was emerging over the Falklands, if Galtieri had not been impatient or the Foreign Office a little too oblique and dilatory.

And if we conquer the Falkland Islands, even without killing those to be liberated, what would we do with them? Garrison them for ever? As it has been for many years dependent on the Argentine for nearly all supplies, could we or anyone else change that except at a cost that would be wholly disproportionate? If the Argentinians will not compromise over sovereignty, we had better be aware how meaninglesss the concept has become. If they want flags and ceremonies, let it be so; all that is unreasonable is if they want to colonise the islands or to govern the islanders the way they govern themselves. The internal form of government of the inhabitants is the most important factor. Never does it follow in the real world that the claim to own anything means that one has an unrestricted right or ability to do anything one likes with it. We need to exhibit our humanity, tolerance, commonsense and political skill, not to pretend to absolute power and absolute discretion in its use. We have bluffed with peoples' lives, lost political support and – whatever the popular press says – shamed ourselves in the eyes of the civilised world.

Nineteen

Violence: The Warheads and the Terraces

* From *The Scotsman*, 24 June, 1985.

The political philosopher Thomas Hobbes was fond of reminding his readers of the inevitability of death. He argued that the true object of civil society was to minimise the incidence of violent death. For that purpose any society needed a single absolute authority. A man should be happy to die in bed with his boots off – as did Hobbes himself at the age of ninety-one, although several of his closest friends had died violently in the English Civil War because they had quibbled about what was right and just, rather than rationally accepted the rule of whoever at the time could enforce and preserve peace.

Since Sir Keith Joseph wants learning to be of use, I suggest that the Edinburgh University Press prepare a popular bi-lingual summary of Hobbes's *Leviathan* (in Arabic and Hebrew) to sell in the Lebanon. I am working on a version in Basic English for the benefit of the unhappy Mr. Bert Millichip, chairman of the Football Association. We want more from good government than Hobbes would offer us, but we want that at least.

Is this age suffering an exceptional outburst of violence, or is it uniquely violent in itself?

As the newspapers and the TV headlines jumped straight from Bradford and Brussels to Beirut and Belfast, many decent people must have felt, deeply and instinctively, that however totally different these last two events were empirically, yet morally there was something in common – in the callous cruelty of the gunmen and the hooligans, as well as in our own helpless voyeurism. We are moved, but we are convinced that there is nothing we can do about it; so the result is a well-informed indifference. Some just pull down the shutters – an interviewer asked an American tourist 'You're not worried still to use Athens airport?' 'We're on holiday, we are just not going to think about it' was the reply.

But I think that fears that we are in a uniquely violent age are mistaken. We must keep a sense of proportion if we are to act sensibly. If we are to control and limit violence, we must understand its specific forms and not lump everything together from panic or depression. Different diseases need different cures; there are no 'cure-alls'. And there is no real evidence that we do live in a world that is uniquely violent.

In years gone by personal violence was far more common and the incidence of warfare as a normal way of settling disputes was greater. Inner-city riots in hot summers and sporadic vandalism are at least a different response from the poor and the dispossessed than endemic banditry. But saying this can make people very angry.

Two years ago I began a talk to a conference on 'Football and Social Disorder':

> There is a problem of violence in and around football grounds, and football matches do act as a focus for disorder, but the statistics before us do not impress me that it is an especially big problem nor that it is, in any serious sense, symptomatic of, still less corrosive of, modern society in general. Indeed the amount of violence is small compared to crowd statistics as a whole and the disorder is perhaps not suprising in relation to the size of the crowds.

I thought that such plain commonsense would appeal to the assembled police officers and football officials, but I felt them almost coming over the barriers at me. To a man they denounced me as 'academic' and for 'making light of a very serious problem'. I suppose they were after funds, either for more police or ground improvements, so almost instinctively adopted a pseudo-social science rhetoric: that if something wasn't done soon about it the problem would 'escalate' or 'undermine society as we know it'.

Bravely I shouted back that most people don't go to football matches and that societies like ours are hard to collapse: catastropharians and revolutionaries should be locked up together and denied bail; they panic the public and prevent cool thinking.

Of course we live in a world with a unique *potential* for violence. Weapons are more deadly. At the touch of one button, even, it is likely that all higher forms of life would be destroyed. But that does not increase the likelihood of their being used, perhaps the contrary.

Weapons themselves are not violent, human will must activate them. I weep at resources wasted that could be spent on poverty and disease rather than tremble that the Trident and Pershing war-heads are likely to be launched. Much of the fear that violence is getting out of control, whether social or international, is a tribute to our much greater intolerance of violence than in the past. Despite two world wars and the almost as bloody wars in South-East Asia, the average American and European seriously believes that we could rid society of violent and premature death.

We are, of course, really thinking of specific types of violence – not those caused, for instance, by motor cars driven fast by tired or drunk drivers (a far greater killer than football violence) nor of the self-inflicted premature deaths of nicotine addicts.

There is no general cure for violence. And some violence, let us never forget, is justifiable; self-defence, tyrannicide, a 'just war' (all the great Christian moralists agreed); and, unpopular though the thought is, not all revolutions are unjustifiable either. We have to distinguish between types of violence. And we are all so very indiscriminate. Many have called the 'Liverpool' rioters 'murderers'. More accurately they are *criminally irresponsible*: their intent was not to take life, which is crucial in the law of homicide, but merely to have a violent punch-up – as people used to whistle with intent certain tunes on certain Glasgow trams.

Charges of manslaughter rather than mere assault would be just if it can be maintained that it was reasonable to have foreseen that the unpredictability of even limited violence in a football riot was likely to cause death. The risk is disproportionate – especially with a foreign crowd who may not understand the specific rituals, forms and limits of our native violence. And some who cry 'murderers' may actually have praised the clear element of bravery in the deliberate killing of thousands of Argentinian conscripts, a reaction astonishingly disproportionate to the offence and certainly not the result that would have followed by applying even a secular maxim like 'the greatest happiness of the greatest number'.

'Violence,' wrote Hannah Arendt, 'is the breakdown of power, not its extension'. If we had had more power, or looked as if we had, we might not have needed (if we needed at all) to have resorted to violence in the Falklands. If there was a government in power and with power in the Lebanon, the sporadic violence would not occur. And Israel, not having the power it believed it had, failed to enforce the peace by the ill-judged folly of its invasion of the Lebanon, actually increased the very violence it sought to eliminate.

Violence cannot be contained simply by counter-violence. Effective power means getting the political or social conditions right. How long can Israel's friends tolerate her failure to pursue political initiatives more urgently and realistically with the Arabs who will negotiate? How long can we tolerate the social conditions that create the tolerance on the terraces for the deliberate violence of a few? For a very long time it seems. We won't reform British society just to end football violence. We are more likely to close or restrict the grounds and drive it elsewhere.

Twenty

The Politics of Space, and Grief

* From *The Scotsman*, 3 February, 1986

'Failure is Often a Stepping-Stone to Success.' 'If at First You Don't Succeed, Try, Try Again.' I slept under those poker-work mottoes for all the years between primal literacy and premature adolescence; then I was quietly allowed to take them down and incinerate them. I didn't mind the second so much, but the first struck me as fatuous. Surely 'failure' meant an irrecoverable falling off the stepping stones into the whirling current?

Of course, there was never any doubt that they would try again. The President told the nation that he had phoned the families of the Challenger's crew, 'and they all ended by telling me the programme must go on; they would have wanted it that way ... our hopes and our journeys will continue'. Rather movingly in his first speech he 'reminded' the nation that the disaster had occurred on the anniversary of the death of Sir Francis Drake 'who had spent more of his life on water than on land, circling the terrestial globe and pushing back the frontiers of human knowledge on earth as we now do in space'. And, unfortunately, for much of the same mixed motives of economic exploitation and military dominance. The President's extraordinary personal authority does not stem from any premeditated hypocrisy, but from a genuine simplicity that can always put the nicest construction on harsh necessities, or (what Milton called 'ever the tyrant's excuse') 'seeming necessity'. He always appears to mirror popular sentiment. It is the people's will. The American people, indeed the very families of the dead, will that the programme should continue, 'man's conquest of space' as once of the oceans. He forgets, as much as they, that the thing they are willing was thrust on them by himself and his advisers, and behind them that an awful confusion of the Pentagon's global ambitions and the cosmic greed of the civilian defence industry.

The military did not, of course, put all their eggs into this one manned basket. Their satellites can still be launched, and far more cheaply, by rockets. The manned shuttle is important for scientific research, certainly; but far more for military attempts to control space:

214

the manned space station is essential to all 'Star Wars' scenarios. And so is money. Even the research for the Strategic Defense Initiative (SDI) is massively expensive, a quantum leap in defence expenditures at a time when Congress was beginning to grow restive at the palpable nonsense of so much 'overkill,' as mirrored in the rapid growth of the American 'Freeze' movement. This movement is not pacifist, certainly not unilateralist, but is a great commonsense cry that, even granted the truth of the theory of atomic deterrence (bombs in both hands *may* have prevented a re-run of the Second World War between the USSR and the US), *'enough is enough'*.

So the President instinctively sees the need to dramatise NASA's work, to humanise the space programme. First a Congressman in space and then – a brilliant piece of public relations – a schoolteacher in space, a woman teacher in space, a married mother woman teacher with impeccable American virtues in space. I only feel some genuine grief for her. The others were professionals whose job it was and who knew the risk, or if no-one could calculate the degree of risk, at least that it was, even after thirteen flights, deadly risky. I cannot grieve if a boxer is killed in the ring though I did at the Manchester United air disaster long ago, Natural disasters, the town that vanished in volcanic mud, the Mexico City earthquake, the drought that led to the Ethiopian famine, surely these cause deeper, purer grief than small-scale man-made disasters? Sorrow is intense when one knows that there was nothing the poor people could have done. But rage intrudes into grief when men are responsible.

Sometimes rage mingles with grief at the victim: I once dedicated a book on Machiavelli to a man who would, I said, have written something 'truly great' had he 'not got killed in a climbing accident'. Should we not feel some anger at those who create grief and loss in others by deliberately pursuing dangerous pastimes? I am sick of photographs of noble grieving widows and brave children, who should have stopped their foolish, reckless men.

I don't feel anger at Mrs Christa McAuliffe, though I think she was being used in a dreadful way. I feel deep pity for her family, and deep anger at those who used her. I'm sure she believed that hers was a teaching mission and the military mission. But it was in fact a political mission, to ensure through the heartstrings that the purse strings of Middle America will never forsake SDI, 'star wars' as the old actor revealingly called his vision. I may be wrong, of course. She may not have been fooled. She may have patriotically believed with open, starry eyes in both the teaching mission and the military mission. Here would be a case for a scholarly biography of an ordinary person.

By perhaps an even more apt irony of coincidence than Drake's death and Challenger's fall, the issue of the *New York Review of Books* for

January 30 1986 carried a massively long review by Lord Zuckerman of a group of books on the 'Star Wars' controversy, and in it he foot-noted, unusual for a literary magazine, references to a wide range of scientific and political articles and documents on that theme. The *New York Review,* unlike our *Times Literary Supplement,* commonly ranges wider than literature or academic publication. It has the good civic habit of reviewing, from time to time, matters of public controversy whose merits as writing are not always high. Lord Zuckerman is now an old man but with all his fine wits in good working order. He was, remember, strategic planning adviser during the Second World War to General Eisenhower and Air Marshal Tedder, then chief scientific adviser to successive Prime Ministers on defence. He has written extensively on science policy and on science and war. He is, I hasten to add, if it is not obvious, no pacifist. He had few illusions that without power in the West the Eastern block might have shown far greater expansive tendencies post-war.

The books he reviews are not of the kind favoured by British publishers, for or against possession of nuclear weapons. That can be a rather insular preoccupation. As I have said before, I agree with Mr. Enoch Powell on this: there are no conceivable circumstances in which we, or the French, could use a nuclear deterrent independently. It is all in American and Russian hands. It hardly matters. We might just as well spend our money on hospitals if the Pentagon did not want complicity in guilt. No, the books Lord Zuckerman reviews are all con-cerned with *how* to realise the President's vision of an impenetrable 'shield of defence in space' to 'liberate mankind from the prison of mutual terror'. And his slow and dry dissection of their impracticality, not a word about their morality, is devastating. Never has the counter-argument been put so clearly, economically and scientifically, in a manner that the intelligent layman can, if he concentrates for an hour, follow and understand.

> Has anyone other than the American President ever invited scientists to try to render 'nuclear weapons impotent and obsolete', the suggestion would probably have attracted no more attention than had they been asked to square the circle or solve the problem of perpetual motion [began Zuckerman]. But... the President ... spelled out his vision of a future over which the nuclear bomb no longer casts a shadow in such homely terms that it all sounded real. How could the message fail to appeal? There was the promise of vast resources for R & D – a vision, therefore, not merely of peace but ... of work, prosperity and excitement for some.

One expects the word 'all', but 'some' is utterly right. Zuckerman is bitterly angry at fellow scientists who see all this folly simply in terms of money for projects. Zuckerman's arguments are mainly technical:

such systems will not work reliably and are far from foolproof. But his case is also logical: nothing can conceivably be guaranteed, as Challenger's swift fall to earth revealed. Will they call the next one Icarus? An "Impenetrable shield of defence in space" would only stimulate the invention of super-weapons to penetrate it. Can the very survival of *homo sapiens* depend on lack of accidents or on the illusion of a foolproof technology? Do they really believe that technology can answer all human problems? I fear the President does.

Twenty-one

'Reach for the Stars, Cowboy'

* From *The Scotsman*, 20 October, 1986

Do you remember the scene – though it is now, amid the blinkered galloping diurnal myopia of instant news, a whole week ago? Several graphic eye-witness accounts were given and one even heard a snatch of it on the BBC. As the old actor left Iceland, tired and bewildered, he paused in a hangar at the United States air-base and made an impromptu speech to the airmen gathered around. On homely ground again he rallied, cracked a couple of old campaigning jokes and then told them, as if it had been a triumph, that no agreement had been reached because he refused to compromise the safety of 'America and her allies' by negotiating on SDI, 'star wars'. There was a spontaneous yelp of cheering. It was a very ugly sound. It may have done more damage to American diplomacy than all the new tactics of Mr. Gorbachev.

During the week there has been less cheer among America's allies. Even the NATO commanders have made an unprecedented formal protest about not being consulted beforehand or adequately briefed afterwards. A horrible chill must enter the hearts of all sensible political leaders among the allies that the fate of the world is in such frivolous hands.

Of course, 'one can't help admiring him'. So wonderful at his age. Practitioners of geriatric medicine may have cause to be grateful, even if the regime that keeps him going, as for Gladstone, Churchill, Adeneur, de Gaulle and Chairman Mao (to name only a few statesmen who held high office into old age), is not available to most of us: power is good for you. For every man who dies prematurely, ulcerated and worn-out by the crushing burdens of office etc, there is another who finds dominion over others rejuvenating. In many ways Reagan has given the American people what they appear to want: a constitutional monarch. He spends almost as much time disassociating himself for responsibility from economic difficulties and political disasters as he does claiming credit for short-term upswings and for flickering lights at the end of tunnels (Reaganism and Thatcherism

218

have that also in common – humble Chinese are not the only ones to believe that she is Queen). So this old moral militant must typically work his domestic PR magic with non-negotiable demands, like 'no surrender' and 'not an inch' on 'star wars', mainly because negotiation and compromise is too difficult or, even with competent and united back-up (both of which are in question), hard to personalise and present simply. It is all frighteningly hollow. Remember when he was coming out of anaesthesia after the assassination attempt? Even before he trusted himself to speak or could be reasonably sure whether he was going to live or die, he gestured for a writing pad. He scribbled 'I'd almost rather be in Philadelphia'. This was reported by his staff amid widespread laughter and admiration in the States for the old fellow's gamey courage. But I wonder that the clergy of 'the moral majority' didn't declare him heretic and excommunicate *ipso facto*. For the reference, if, you are not up on modern American folklore, was to the alleged dying words of a fellow actor, W.C. Fields. Fields, a notorious libertine and non-believer, was approached by a harsh Catholic hospital chaplain. 'How does it feel to be dying, Mr. Fields?' 'I'd almost rather be in Philadelphia', he replied – a city then justly famed for its attempts to legislate against human nature.

Is it all just public relations with Reagan? Can one's memory stretch back to January and recall who Mrs. Christa McAuliffe was? She was the typically 'American school-teacher,' and mother indeed, who was launched into space and went to her death with NASA's Challenger. If the American people believe after Challenger that 'Star Wars' could work infallibly (and there is no other way in which it could be said to work at all), then this is a triumph of public relations over commonsense. Few leading scientists believe that it is technically possible, although many, some even in this country, alas, are willing to climb on the gravy train for research grants for high-tech bits and pieces. But Reagan is dreaming a national dream that there is a technological answer to every human problem.

I would go further than commonsense. It is also a matter of logic. To say that in the future a hundred per cent safe and certain defensive system could be developed against offensive inter-continental ballistic missiles implies that one can predict unlimited growth in the technologies of defence. This seems to contradict almost everything we know about the history of science and technology: 'challenge and response' and all that. But it is the same logical fallacy that makes so much science fiction implausible (not that that spoils a good read, if that's all that is at stake): that if we can predict the future or travel 'through space and time', then we could prevent the future being as it will be, or even change the past.

The philosopher Karl Popper, in arguing against theories of historical inevitability, mainly Marxist, pointed out that if we think we can predict the future then we must also believe that we can predict future inventions that would change the predicted future!

And not merely Challenger will stick in the memory, but Chernobyl too. There the dog did not bark. The White House publicity machine was remarkably restrained, was indeed, after the first awful, worrying forty-eight hours of Russian silence, deliberately complimentary about the Russian 'openness' and 'frankness' – both remarkably relative terms incidentally, as is the current Russian peace offensive. The mutual interest in playing down the incident was obvious. A civilian disaster anywhere could prejudice American nuclear and SDI appropriations in Congress, just as Chernobyl destroyed the Soviet myth of efficient power.

At the Labour Party conference a sensible motion to call a halt to new nuclear power stations, subject to a wholesale safety review was lost to an unrealistic demand (if industrial society is to survive at all) to set the clock back, based on hope or fantasy that wind and water can replace the planet's declining stocks of oil and coal. The breath was taken away at the scale of the proferred Russian concessions at Reykjavik. God knows the world could still be utterly destroyed even if there had been agreement to the fifty per cent cut in strategic missiles, the ending of testing, inspection, perhaps even to make Western and Eastern Europe nuclear-free, and to 'limit', as there was tentative agreement, intercontinental weapons to 1,600 delivery vehicles with 6,000 warheads. But at least it was a beginning.

Full nuclear disarmament suddenly becomes a possibility not just a dream. At least huge resources could be released for better purposes. The cooler minds in both great powers are now as frightened of the escalating costs as they are of accidental or deliberate nuclear war. And, though a member of CND, I have never believed that any of this armament would ever be used deliberately. The two deterrents do deter. But the cost in fear and misplaced resources (i.e. poverty) is intolerable. Rational recognition of mutual interests is a far better guarantee of peace than science fiction fantasies of national bullet-proof vests.

Now, of course, the Russians were probably playing for world opinion at this stage as much as the President. They can have hardly expected him to deal with such huge and unexpected concessions without warning across the table. There was enough material there for the four-year negotiation at Westphalia that ended the Thirty Years War. But they have changed the climate of expectations radically. It is now reasonably clear what can be done. We should not be disheartened. It is now only a question of time before, in less dramatic circumstances perhaps, an agreement is hammered out, or rather the first of a series of agreements. But nothing is likely to happen while Reagan is still President. His successors will not want their hands tied. Most

Americans are now uncertain more than fervid or polarised. For once the old PR populist seems to have misjudged. It is unlikely that it will be a deeply divisive election issue; Democrats against 'Star Wars' and Republicans declaring it to be real, urgent and unnegotiable. If politics is politics, every candidate will hedge. It is an old man's obsession. The folly will fade with his going.

A week is a long time in politics. The week before last the Press was was full of comment that Labour, otherwise looking so good again, had created a crippling hostage to fortune by declaring that it would both get rid of our nuclear weapons and American nuclear bases. After Reykjavik the boot is on the other foot. Now that the two great powers show that it is possible to move, the possession of nuclear weapons by anyone else is an irrelevance. Can one imagine, as Enoch Powell asked in two extraordinary speeches in 1984, any possible circumstances in which we would use our independent deterrent independently?

He went on to say that our possession of the bomb is not a sign of 'sovereignty' but a 'fig-leaf' for lost sovereignty. And worse than an irrelevance, it could be an obstacle to European disarmament with Thatcher and Mitterrand both playing 'our bomb' as a patriotic card. Few people in this country, moreover, are anti-American; but more and more can distinguish between American society and the absurd machinery of American foreign policy. We will never break with America, but our future must lie *more* with a non-nuclear Europe.

Twenty-two

On Political Courage, or Aunty in her Agony

* From *The Scotsman*, 3 December, 1986 on the occasion of the Director General of the BBC agreeing to an instruction of the Governors to settle a libel action out of Court.

Strange how scraps of old doggerel become impacted in the brain, When I read that the management of the BBC, at the request of the governors, had agreed, contrary to the opinion of their journalists, that Mr. Neil Hamilton M.P.s inimitable comic imitations of old Adolf had not the slightest whiff of empathy about them (unlike John Selwyn Gummer's famous imitations of Enoch Powell), I had a pricking in my thumbs and kept muttering catatonically a quatrain from some American verses, *The Biglow Papers*, written when the Senators from Massachusetts momentarily espoused Henry Clay's attempt at a compromise on slavery:

Massachusetts, God forgive her
Is a-cringing with the rest
When she oughta stayed for ever
In her proud old eagle nest.

One can stop a long way short of saying 'Come back Lord Reith and all your pomposity, hypocrisy, sanctimoniousness and Calvinism are forgiven' and still feel that a pass has been badly sold so that Tebbit's wolf pack, having once tasted blood, now howls for more. Or as the Swan of Avon aptly put it: 'Cowards die many times before their deaths; / The valiant never taste of death but once'. Yet my real text for today is the famous sentence from the Periclean oration, 'the secret of liberty is courage'.

Now Pericles had not been democratically elected by all three sections of the Athenian Labour Party. Scholars call him a 'demagogue'; we would see him as a popular dictator. And the liberty he was really talking about was not individual liberty, the 'Dare to be a Daniel, / Dare to stand alone' stuff, but was a collective and civic liberty from outside interference: Athens maintaining its corporate liberty (however full the prisons were of men like Socrates) against the *barbaroi,* foreigners.

I'm not pushing democracy. I'm not soft. Who ever said that the BBC should be a democratic institution? I don't want the producers (and what about the studio managers, and the secretaries and the porters? voting on the content of programmes on Northern Ireland, the American use of British airbases, or on the Conservative Right. No, I am bewailing a failure in corporate leadership to defend a great national institution against our barbarians. We can hear too much about consumers and the state, or public opinion calling bodies to public accountability (i.e. politicians stopping things they don't like). We should not lapse back to a simplistic old liberal model of the individual and the state. Liberties also pertain to groups and corporations.

Tocqueville once reproved John Stuart Mill for linking liberty solely to the rights of individuals; he offered the opinion that it is a plurality of intermediary groups between the individual and the state who best preserve liberty – anomalies, privileges even, and all; and Mill, unlike Tebbit being a thoughtful and open-minded fellow, was persuaded, agreed, modified his opinions – as he tells us in his *Autobiography*.

Now what actually happened is less clear than some of us first supposed, happy to kill two favourite bird *noires* with one stone: the BBC and Tebbit. It now seems that the BBC management was already talking to the other side about the possibility of a settlement before the governors ordered them to surrender. This is quite normal in big and expensive civil actions, there are often many good reasons for settling out of court even when an action has begun. And among them was a sudden decline in the number of Conservative politicians or officials willing to appear in court for the BBC. That fact is all I need to note. I'm only going on about other people's lack of courage. But there was a world of difference between the BBC management deciding either that they couldn't win or that it would be prudent to reach a compromise, and them being ordered to climb down by the governors; and the Director-General then accepting that direction.

I am not one for conspiracy theories. I don't attach much weight to Mr. Marmaduke Hussey, the new chairman of the governors, being the brother-in-law of a Cabinet Minister. Nearly everyone is nowadays. Anyway, one can balance that by knowing that his deputy, Lord Barnett, when last heard of politically was still enjoying the Labour Whip, and is also chairman of a body even more balanced and eunuch-like than the BBC, the Hansard Society. But one of them should have had the sense to see that if it was known that the governors had intervened, and if they intervened it would be known (imagine trying to keep a secret in a beehive of journalists), it would forever mean that they and not the Director-General would be seen as the judges of the professionalism and integrity of reporters, commentators and producers. And their intervention would make them appear to be wearing Tebbit's half-glasses.

You couldn't reasonably guess who, but you could safely bet that some Labour MP would rise in the House (even before oor Tam) to assert that officials of the Conservative Party had taken more than a speculative interest in the affair. Asquith's classic dictum in the Marconi scandals was forgotten. A Minister of the Crown (or for that matter his appointees) must not merely not act improperly, but not act in any way that could reasonably be interpreted as improper.

The governors also seem to have forgotten the demoralisation caused in the BBC and the egg planted on the face of the Government when the then Home Secretary, Mr. Leon Brittan (remember?), objected to one Ulster thug rather than the other appearing in *Real Lives*, a most unbalanced programme, indeed, about a most unbalanced part of the realm. And we've all forgotten the first fatal selling of the pass when the BBC in 1981 withdrew its invitation to Mr. E.P. Thompson, of CND, to give the Dimbleby Lecture (which I would never now accept) at a time that happened to coincide with the Minister of Defence's (Mr. Heseltine, remember?) campaign against CND.

My view is very old-fashioned and utterly clear. They should not have intervened. But if the BBC had lost the case, with huge costs and damages, they could properly have dismissed the Director-General. It is a hard world at the top. But it is also my view that on the threat of intervention, the Director-General and all of his most senior colleagues who could be found should have threatened to resign; and if the governors had still intervened, he (and as many of them as would still stand up) should have resigned. The suspicion that the BBC can be coerced and bullied is no small matter, and should have made it more difficult for the governors to act. The BBC is, indeed, one of our most important, influential and reasonably impartial (God, it tries so hard – all this obsession with *balance* that now squeezes anyone else out of political discussions except predictable politicians) national institutions. It is far more impartial than the Gas Board, arguably than the Church of England. It conceives its own duty to be impartial while also giving time to all significant differing viewpoints. Which is why it is so hated by Thatchers and Tebbits who think, like the wild Left, that it should only present their views. Tebbit and Thatcher believe, of course, that they want impartiality and that the BBC is persistently and perversely anti-Tory.

Orwell, after he left the Burma police, only ever had one regular office job, in the war-time BBC. He filled his fictional Ministry of Truth with intellectuals all falsifying history or destroying language to command. This was a deadly and unfair satire on his colleagues. He must have believed that intellectuals when faced between loss of principle and loss of job always reason that if they resign some even more time-serving creep from Oxbridge will pinch their shoes.

All this has not helped the morale or the corporate liberty either of the BBC itself or of our poor country, suffering so very much, in so many unlikely ways, from a Government that is willing to take liberties with basic constitutional liberties. If they have no principles or respect for tradition, haven't they any political prudence? What could happen when my lot get in – especially if my lot are as *they* think they are, which happily they are (on the whole) not. But most of all when I think of Aunty in her agony I can't keep out of my head Groucho's cry when caught red-handed: 'I am only fighting to save the honour of this woman, a thing she has seldom done for herself.' But it is now or never, Director-General.

Twenty-three

On Political Silences: The Vanunu Affair

* From *The Scotsman*, 17 November, 1986.

Heinrich Boll has a story about a radio producer who had to edit a repeat of a famous series of talks about the human condition, or something like that, by a great German intellectual. In the post-war atmosphere, the great man had been cautiously Left-wing, mildly agnostic and cautiously optimistic. A generation later, he insists that small adjectives must be dubbed in (and out) to present him as all the time a moderate conservative, a liberal Catholic who was guardedly pessimistic. What he said was so abstract, full of wind and waffle that the task of repointing, while intellectually easy, was technically demanding (and morally disgusting). After a while the producer goes absent. He is found by his colleagues at home endlessly playing silent tapes from his unique pirated collection of silences cut from hundreds of similar, sententious, time-serving utterances.

Of course, it was the Vanunu case that made all this come floating to the surface of my mind. Remember? It is hard to keep track. Vanunu was not the Nigerian discovered in an embassy box at Luton Airport awaiting involuntary transit to Lagos. HMG was upset, for a bit, about that one. No, Vanunu was the Israeli atomic technician, thought to have Palestinian sympathies, who came to this country in September and gave (or possibly sold to) the *Sunday Times* a lot of detail about Israel's 'secret' reactor at Dimona in the Negev. The *Sunday Times* article said that Israel must now have between one and two hundred atomic warheads, making it the world's sixth largest atomic power, non-proliferation treaties notwithstanding. (What a frightening thought. Even if there is American and Russian partial disarmament, these small powers could still destroy all humanity, including the animal liberationists even, whether by accident or chauvinistic zeal.)

Back to the main point. Vanunu vanished five days before the article appeared. Only last week was it admitted by the Israeli Government that he was in Israel under arrest, held incommunicado. The basic Israeli law on State security allows the charge, the trial and the sentence all to be secret. How our Attorney-General must envy them. Censorship has been applied to the Israeli Press to stop all speculation as well as reporting. The presumption is that he was kidnapped and yesterday the *Sunday Times* claimed he had been lured offshore by a woman working for Israeli intelligence. Mossad allegedly were working under instructions not to capture Vanunu on British soil as it would embarrass Mrs. Thatcher's pro-Israeli stance.

Questions in Parliament and direct to our Foreign Office at first only drew the reply that they had noted Israeli denials, and that there was a police inquiry into his disappearance but no evidence that anything illegal had taken place. But someone from the police or the immigration service briefed the Press that there was no record of his leaving by any normal channel. The British Ambassador in Israel tried in a very unusual move to talk to Mordechai Vanunu's lawyer. He is reported to have told the ambassador that he was forbiddeen by law to discuss the case while *sub-judice* (that has a familiar ring). Two Israeli journalists, who I know well, refused to discuss the case with me at all when I phoned them. Considerations of national interest rise high above vague thoughts on human rights. A lesson to me not to waste my money playing the reporter rather than sticking to commentary on high principles. Ten days ago the Israeli Government even issued a statement denying 'that there is any basis to the report that Mr. Peres contacted Mrs. Thatcher in order to inform her about something that never took place'. Then they remained totally silent until last Thursday. Not even disinformation.

Late on Thursday evening (too late for the morning papers, alas) our Foreign Office issued a statement: that following the British Ambassador's inquiry 'the Israeli Government had issued the following statement: "Mr. Vanunu left Britain of his own volition and through normal departure procedures. His departure from Britain involved no violation of British law". In these circumstances', said our statement, 'we have no further comment to make on the present position'. Well did the poet James Thomson write, 'Come then, expressive Silence, muse His praise'. 'Expressive silence' is a good phrase.

'I think that 'present position' is Foreign Officeese for 'we are not letting the matter drop even if No 10 wants it dropped'. It is a pity that Mrs. Thatcher has kept an 'expressive silence' on this case after sounding off so strongly against Syria. She was right to sound off on the Syrian affair and the French Prime Minister was wrong, assuming that the jury was right and that the despicable Hindawi, despicable on any account, was planting a Syrian bomb on to that poor, pregnant Irish girl. He said that he was using her to smuggle drugs and was himself 'fitted up' by Israeli counter-intelligence. The trouble is that when the Israelis so freely adopted the right to kidnap enemies of their State anywhere in the world, whether young Palestinian sympathisers like

Vanunu or octogenarian old Nazis, it is hard to believe that their Mossad agents would stick at anything. The phrase 'of his own volition' presumably means that Mr. Vanunu actually walked out, whether hand-in-hand or supported, rather than being crated up and freighted out. And he could leave 'without any violation of British law' and without a trace if he crossed the Irish border and flew out of Shannon or Dublin. I just find that credulity is stretched too far to think that he left 'of his own volition', as you or I would ordinarily understand the phrase. Why not say 'of his own free will' or 'voluntarily', if that is what they mean? Mr. David Kimsche's English is perfect.

President Reagan was also practising 'expressive silence', of course, about his surreptitious attempts 'to raise the level of diplomatic contact with Iran'. Let us in Christian charity assume that he wasn't so foolishly reckless or hypocritical as to try, after all he said about Libya and Syria and the danger of encouraging hostage-taking, to trade with terrorists or their paymasters for American lives – whether with cake, Gideon Bibles or arms – on the ancient moral assumption (as the late Sir Denis Brogan once put it) that 'only American boys have Mothers'. Let us shed a secret tear for him that that reliable lot broke silence and forced the leader of the moral majority into a humiliating and unconvincing exculpatory speech to the nation. Sorry, not 'arms' but, as he said, 'some replacements and spares for defensive weapons'. What is so morally horrible about both these cases, of course, is not that they exhibit that necessary silence of, say, a government's financial operations that could lead to a speculative gain, or police preparing to trap a villain or even of those few 'secrets of State' that might genuinely endanger the 'safety of the State' as against the more usual convenience or political embarrassment of Ministers, particularly Prime Ministers and Presidents. The full horror is that the silence either masks a total hypocrisy, considering the terms in which the rule of law has been extolled and all violence against the state condemned as terrorism, or else a kind of moral schizophrenia. The aetiology of the disease is complicated but its symptoms are easily described: it is feeling free oneself to behave in a way that one condemns in others.

Both Christian and humanist morality agree on two considerations vital to our civilisation: that actual laws are not always just and that unjust means corrupt any speculative goodness of ends. If a State gets into the habit of acting in what is confusingly called a 'Machiavellian manner', it discredits itself and loses all trust and authority on which political power ultimately depends. He preached not moral schizophrenia but an 'economy of violence' – as hard as necessary but as little as possible at moments of clear and present danger to the State. Otherwise you create your own crises, or reveal what you want to conceal. The Israelis reveal the horror of nuclear proliferation. Bad enough America and Russian having the bombs at all, but now at least they are talking: far, far worse the international irresponsibility of Israel, Syria, India and South Africa. Possessing weapons for pursuit of their own smaller and less calculable national purposes. I have forgotten the case why Britain and France are supposed to be exceptions.

Twenty-four

The Nazi Hunters

* From *The Scotsman*, 10 March, 1987.

The Israelis can be terribly practical and down to earth. The hard working of the reluctant land and universal military service explain this earthy practicality. But they are practical within three obsessive contexts: the defence of the State, the consciousness of religion, and the memory of the past – or rather of that one part of the past, that most terrible of all events of Western history, the Holocaust, that they see as the culmination of all their historic suffering. Each of these factors conditions the other. Back in 1966, when I first visited Israel, it was sobering to look east along any modern street in Tel Aviv and to realise that the hills twenty miles away were a threatening (and a threatened) frontier. But the fierce patriotism of the Israeli goes far beyond pride of achievement and need for defence. It extends to leadership of an overseas Jewish community with its vital political and financial support. This wider community can be conceived only religiously, even by secular Jews, or else in memory of the Holocaust .

It is that memory which stops non-religious Jews from becoming assimilated and sustains support for the State. It is also that memory which inhibits much criticism of Israel by non-Jews in Europe and the United States – and is played on.

It is absence of that memory among the younger generation in Israel that worries the old, especially among children of the Sephardim or oriental Jews to whom European history is remote, almost irrelevant. The older generation are not so much affronted at lack of interest in the terrible extermination camps of the past, as worried that without it the fierce civic patriotism will flag. So there are three motives for the continuing hunting for Nazi war criminals, and the blurring of the distinction between any member of the Nazi Party and a war criminal: justice, vengeance and preservation of the State.

In view of inevitable misunderstanding about what I am about say, let me make gratuitously clear that I am one who fully accepts, in justice and in practice, that the State of Israel does exist and should exist. But, of course, accepting the State does not mean that I accept its

230

present boundaries, its discriminatory constitution, its manufacture of atomic weapons, its failure to negotiate sensibly with the Palestinians, its constant breaches of international law, and its somewhat overly practical and morally relaxed attitudes to selling arms to the South Africans, the Chileans and, it now seems, the Contras. In Britain there is an almost prurient, pornographic interest in Nazi atrocities which has something to do with using wartime memories as a balm for diminished national power and pride. Indeed, I think it could well be time to call a halt, to let the dead bury the dead and to remember that with 'vengeance' the results are usually politically irrational, a danger to the living more than a rectification of the dead or a just punishment for surviving war criminals.

There are purely procedural and legal objections. Think of the unbearably disturbed old man of eighty-six who tried to testify in the Jerusalem court last week. All accounts agree that his memory came and went under the strain, and that for part of the time he talked as if he was back in Poland. The week before a man of seventy-six had confidently and 'without doubt' recognised after forty-three years the American Ukranian Mr. Demjanjuk as 'Ivan the Terrible', himself a mere sixty-seven. Is such evidence in a 'show trial' reliable – a trial broadcast and now televised and eagerly followed by the younger generation to the delight of the old? Is it a court of justice or a stage for a contrived drama of national political education?

Time cannot pardon nor mitigate guilt. But it can make punishment pointless. The unique horror of the systematic and deliberate attempt to destroy an entire people because of their alleged 'race' cannot be lessened by long delayed punishments of functionaries. At least Mr. Demjanjuk was extradited by procedures and with evidence that satisfied an American court. But there is still the nagging thought that no powerful lobby exists against such extraditions, as there is for them and as does exist, for obvious example, against the extradition of certain kinds of Irish criminals from the United States.

Now the Nazi hunters of the Wiesenthal Centre in Jerusalem have passed on a list of seventeen names from Russian sources of alleged Nazi war criminals supposed to be living in Britain, of whom only six have been identified and are still alive. Mr. Greville Janner, MP has threatened to name them in the House of Commons. I hope he has the sense and decency to do no such thing. Some newspapers have named two of the people already, a trial by newspapers has begun. Presumably the names came to them from the Wiesenthal Centre, not from the Home Office. The Home Secretary has made clear that British courts have no jurisdiction over crimes committed elsewhere; that the only case for extradition would be if they had lied in obtaining their original visas; and that in 'no circumstances' would they be extradited to Russia – or, one hopes, to Israel either. The Russians and the Ukrainians have many bitter scores to settle with others. A further thirty-four names have come to Scottish television from Soviet Embassy and other East bloc sources. Incredibly, the head of the Wiesenthal Centre, Mr. Efraim Zuroff, told the Press last Monday that in his organisation's experience 'The Soviet Union had never, fabricated evidence'. Except, presumably, against Russian Jewish dissidents and would-be emigrants.

Such an assertion shows how frighteningly easy it is for the judgement of the hunters to be corrupted by hatred. The dead deserve a better monument than that. They deserve a world that acts justly, even to the unjust, to Jew and gentile and Moslem alike. Should not all this hunting of foul old men have some end?

Twenty-five

Spy Mania: The Twelfth Man Revealed

* From *The Guardian*, 19 December 1986.

Since almost alone my name has not been mentioned in the House of Commons, the press or the Australian courts, the gossip in the clubs and the innuendoes in society have become unbearable. 'What is he trying to hide?' 'Why are they shielding him?' People ignore me and pretend not to recognise me in the street. I have concluded that a full and frank confession of a youthful indiscretion would be best. I have come to love my country in my old age and even to trust in the essential decency and fair-mindedness of most of its inhabitants, with certain exceptions that are not directly germane.

Everyone must know by now who was the fourth man and who is the fifth man, except those who cannot or will not read between the lines of the Sunday newspapers. I will now confess to having been for many years the twelfth man. I was recruited at school by my housemaster. Which of us, if we have to choose, would not put our school before our country? The school shall be nameless but it was in the south of London and not sixty miles from Cambridge, and readily accessible to central London either by train or in those days by tram, a cheap, convenient and anonymous means of transportation.

I was a year behind Reginald Prentice who went on to become a Labour cabinet minister before he 'crossed the floor' or defected to the Tories, a year ahead of Subba-Rowe who went on to become chairman of the so-called 'selection committee' of the MCC, and I was an exact contemporary of I.D.S. Beer who after playing for England at rugby football became headmaster of Harrow, a position of almost unquestionable respectability. The most brilliant of my contemporaries, a man called Tom Espie, vanished unaccountably into Canada and his friend, the chess master Lionel Barden, soon came, of course, to travel extensively in Russia and Eastern Europe. During the war one headmaster committed suicide having fallen into debt gambling on horses, and another was dismissed on being discovered by a governor in the 'West End' in compromising circumstances with women.

When my housemaster recruited me he said that he knew that at first

233

I would hate 'the great game', especially the interminable waiting, but that he wanted me to do it for his sake and the school's. He said I might not ever be called 'to play', but if so he promised me that 'in the field' I would be no more than 'long stop' for a particular exercise, and only if absolutely necessary would I be 'put in' at all and then last. I think I agreed out of love for him. He did not seduce me. It was the Platonic love of the strong for the weak. He was a poet and, in fact, a pacifist, and had said so in his poems. But either nobody read them or if so did not take them seriously, for the powers that be made him commander of the school Officers' Training Corp. Most of the boys bullied him but I sprang to his defence and, being a big boy for my age, bloodied many a nose of those who mocked him. I became his company sergeant-major and woe betide any boy who tried to 'take the mickey out of him'.

I came to hate the school. And, of course, since the school believed in values, standards and patriotism and preached and teached them incessantly, quite naturally, like most other normal boys of good family, I rebelled against them. So the suggestion that I should become twelfth man fell on ready ears into a fertile mind. Even in those days I was sensible enough not to do anything compromising that would have embarrassed him. So not for me street demonstrations, leafleting and slogan writing by which many sought to accelerate the inevitable collapse of the capitalist system. Indeed for cover I joined the Labour Party at the age of seventeen and was conspicuous as a prefect in organising a lunch-time working party to remove the slogan 'Second Front Now' from the wall of the school gym. I also caned a boy for selling Communist Party literature on school premises. It was very old literature in fact for most of it was written by Trotsky.

When I left school I was advised by my housemaster to pursue an academic career and to 'keep my head down and out of trouble'. So I took my role to be that of a long-term mole or a 'deep-sleeper'. This was easy in an academic environment, as was promotion. The sensation that 'normal life' was a 'game' and the habit of deception actually proved advantageous in scholarly endeavour – as possibly with (Sir) Anthony Blunt, whom I never actually met. Also I penetrated the Hansard Society, The Study of Parliament Group, the National Trust and became the confidant of some leading politicians of all parties.

The habit of deception unhappily spread into personal life. But perhaps even my habits of sexual infidelity are not to be explained by biological drive or by sociological conditioning in the sixties but by the inward duality of leading a double-life, so that normal life was in fact, or fancy, a role. It is, indeed, as Le Carre has hinted, Chinese boxes in a hall of mirrors. Perhaps also the actual infidelities were the suppression of a desire to have led a less 'normal' early manhood, sacrificed for the role of twelfth man. Sometimes I think I must have missed something in playing the game 'straight' but sometimes not. But I was never sent for; perhaps my penetrations had not been deep enough.

As the years have passed a recurrent nightmare began to destroy my sleep and sense of self-confident mystery, *could the bastards have forgotten me?* By 1984 this suspicion, that could never have occurred to me in 1944, became a psychological certainty. I threw in my hand and took 'early retirement'. And now I confess. I can hardly be prosecuted for what I have not done, or accused of wanting a large advance for memoirs of a depressingly normal life. Perhaps an unknown controller, after some unknown change of line, gasped out my name to brutal and uncomprehending interrogators. But there is a Russian Jewish name of the same pronunciation, or they may have been thinking of Francis Crick and the breaking of the genetic code. Alas! For the few who rose so high like Philby, Maclean, Hollis, Wright, Lord So-and-so, and a former Leader of the *** Party, there must be hundreds like myself who are either forgotten or who never rose anywhere high or sensitive enough to be brought out to bat or given the ball. Not merely the 'whole establishment' must be riddled with such sad forgotten men.

But in my case the darkest and most self-destructive thought is that my beloved old housemaster, who to tell the truth was always a badly organised man, simply *forgot* to pass on my name. I may never have been what I was.

Index

Act of Union *see* Treaty of Union
Anglo-Irish Agreement *see* British-
    Irish Agreement
anti-Semitism, 44–5, 52
Arendt, Hannah, i, 8, 41–56
    Eichmann in Jerusalem, 51
    On Violence, 5, 76, 207, 213
Aristotle, 5, 6, 33, 130
authoritarianism, 141, 143, 153

Bagehot, Walter, 126, 142
BBC, 135–6, 222–5
Birkbeck College, i, 8, 10, 22
Blunkett, David, MP, iv, 124
Boyle, Kevin B., 83, 86-7
Britain *see* United Kingdom
British-Irish Agreement, 71, 77, 81, 124
Burke, Edmund, 68, 100, 182, 208

Camus, Albert, 58, 76, 128
Canovan, Margaret, 41
centralisation, 143–4, 183
citizenship, 4, 16, 113–16, 150, 153–5
    167, 190
    and civic culture, 12–13
confederalism, 73–4, 75, 83 *see also*
    federalism
consensus, 68, 159, 161
consent
    American (1775), 78
    and Ireland, 87–8
    in Locke, 79, 91
    and majority will, 82, 83, 87, 104
    and power, 78
    and violence, 77, 83
constitution, 82, 104–5, 121
    Antony Wright on, 124
constitutional law, 65
    reform, 116, 118–23, 124
    in Northern Ireland, 81
    and Labour Party, 62, 105–6
    thinking, 60–5, 72, 81–2
constitutionalism, 107
Cox, W. Harvey, 124
culture, English, 66, 103

de Valera, Eamon, 88, 93
decentralisation, 107-9, 116
democracy, 5, 6
despair, political, 181
devolution, 70, 89–90, 104–25,
    and Northern Ireland, 119–20
    and Scotland, 118–19
    and Wales, 119–20

Dicey, A.V., 65
discrimination, 129–32
    in education, 131, 133
    Eileen Fry on, 130–2, 134
    in employment, 131, 132, 134, 135–6
    and legislation, 126–45 esp. 134–5,
    137–8
    positive, 132–3, 135–7, 140, 155
    racial, 131–2, 135–6, 137, 141–2
    religious, 134, 135
    sexual, 132, 135–7, 142

education
    core curriculum, 13–14
    and egalitarianism, 173–5
    extramural, 25, 28
    and industry, 13, 14, 19, 27
    for mature students, 9–10, 21, 26–7
    political, 116
    and positive discrimination, 133
    and practicalities, 15–16
    self-government in, 7
    and social mobility, 11–12
    timing of, 8–12, 28–9
Edwards, Owen Dudley, 125
egalitarianism, 167–71, 173–4, 176, 190,
    200
electoral reform, 191–3
    shifts, 182–4

Fabianism, 117, 186, 187, 188, 189, 198,
    202
Falklands crisis, 206–10
federalism, 62, 69–70, 112, 122
    and Ireland, 73–4, 92, 108
    Nordic Council, 75
Fitzgerald, Garett, 84, 91
Forum *see* New Irish Forum
fraternity, 170, 171–5, 190
freedom *see* liberty
Friedrich, Carl J., 33, 54

gentleman, cult of the English, 102, 106
    115–16, 169
government
    forms of, 5, 8
    power, 107
    Tory, 181–3
Great Britain *see* United Kingdom

Hadden, Tom, 83, 86, 87
Haughey, Charles, 73–4, 80, 92
historical verification, 203–5
Hitler diaries, 203–5